SELF-THEORIES

ESSAYS IN SOCIAL PSYCHOLOGY
MILES HEWSTONE, UNIVERSITY OF CARDIFF, GENERAL EDITOR

Essays in Social Psychology is designed to meet the need for rapid publication of brief volumes in social psychology. Primary topics will include social cognition, interpersonal relationships, group processes, and intergroup relations, as well as applied issues. Furthermore, the series seeks to define social psychology in its broadest sense, encompassing all topics either informed by, or informing, the study of individual behavior and thought in social situations. Each volume in the series will make a conceptual contribution to the topic by reviewing and synthesizing the exisiting research literature, by advancing theory in the area, or by some combination of these missions. The principal aim is that authors will provide an overview of their own highly successful research program in an area. It is also expected that volumes will, to some extent, include an assessment of current knowledge and identification of possible future trends in research. Each book will be a self-contained unit supplying the advanced reader with a well-structured review of the work described and evaluated.

Published titles
Sorrentino and Roney—*The Uncertain Mind*
Van der Vliert—*Complex Interpersonal Conflict Behaviour*

Titles in preparation
Bodenhausen and Macrae—*Stereotype Use*
Carnevale—*The Psychology of Agreement*
Gaertner and Dovidio—*Reducing Intergroup Bias*
Kruglanski—*The Psychology of Closed-Mindedness*
Mackie—*Emotional Aspects of Intergroup Perception*
Semin and Fiedler—*The Linguistic Category Model*
Turner—*Social Identity and Self-Categorization Theory*
Tyler and Blader—*Cooperation in Groups*

SELF-THEORIES: THEIR ROLE IN MOTIVATION, PERSONALITY, AND DEVELOPMENT

CAROL S. DWECK
Columbia University

Essays In Social Psychology

Psychology Press
Taylor & Francis Group

New York   London

Psychology Press
Taylor & Francis Group
711 Third Avenue
8th Floor
New York, NY 10017
www.psypress.com

Published in Great Britain by
Psychology Press
Taylor & Francis Group
27 Church Road
Hove, East Sussex BN3 2FA

© 2000 by Taylor & Francis Group, LLC
Psychology Press is an imprint of Taylor & Francis Group

Printed and bound by Edwards Brothers, Inc. Lillington, NC   27546

International Standard Book Number-13: 978-1-84169-024-7 (Softcover)
Cover design by Fielding Rowinski

Library of Congress Cataloging-in-Publication Data

Catalog record is available from the Library of Congress

Visit the Taylor & Francis Web site at
http://www.taylorandfrancis.com

and the Psychology Press Web site at
http://www.psypress.com

CONTENTS

About the Author

Carol S. Dweck is Professor of Psychology at Columbia University. She is a leader in the fields of motivation, personality, and developmental psychology, and her research contributions have been widely recognized. Her previous books include *Personal Politics* (with Ellen Langer) and *Motivation and Self-Regulation Across the Life-Span* (co-edited with Jutta Heckhausen).

PREFACE

I have always been deeply moved by outstanding achievement, especially in the face of adversity, and saddened by wasted potential. I have devoted my career to understanding both. For almost 30 years, I have done research on motivation and achievement. This book presents the findings from my research, and, as you will see, many of these findings challenge conventional wisdom.

Because I am first and foremost a researcher, I have tried to convey to the reader my love of the research process—how research can address deep and real questions in a precise way, how exciting it is to learn something important you didn't know before, and how each study raises pressing new questions for the next study to explore. Research lures you down uncharted paths, with each turn revealing something new.

Research is also extremely difficult. The experiments must set up lifelike situations. Each one requires a host of new measures, all of which have to be refined and tested. There are countless details of experimental design that have to be observed for the results to be valid. Our experiments often involve over 100 students, yielding masses of data for analysis. The reader is spared these details, but the research buff can find them by consulting the research papers that are cited in each chapter.

A few details, however, are in order. The reader should know that all of the results cited in this book are statistically significant ones, that is, ones shown by statistical tests to be reliable findings. But keep in mind that almost no findings in psychological research are all or nothing. Not every student in an experimental group did the same thing. The results describe what the group as a whole, on average, did.

Many thousands of students have participated in our studies. Who are these students? They range from preschool through college. They come from all over the country—from rural towns as well as from large cities—and they represent many different ethnic groups. So the findings are not limited to a narrow segment of our society but have broad applicability.

It is also important to know that all of the students in our studies are there on a voluntary basis and are encouraged to discontinue their participation at any point along the way if they wish to. Each session, in addition, ends with a highly positive experience, in which the students master difficult material.

When I talk about the research I will typically use "we." This is because almost all of the research was carried out in collaboration with my graduate students and postdoctoral fellows. One of the joys of a research career is working closely with extraordinary young scholars, and I have been particularly fortunate in this regard. This work would not have been possible without them.

Much of this book is about how people make and sustain commitments to things they value. I would like to dedicate the book to my husband, David, who taught me a great deal about this process.

Carol S. Dweck
New York, January, 1999

INTRODUCTION

At this point in a book, the author usually places his or her work in a theoretical context: What are the past theories in the area—in this case, theories of motivation, personality, and their development? What were they trying to explain? What is my theoretical approach? What are its advantages?

However, these are questions that are hard to address in an interesting or enlightening way before we have a common ground. Once we share a body of knowledge, the same questions become much more interesting.

This opening section therefore will be short. I will very briefly present my approach and explain the purpose and the contents of the book. Then, in the next-to-last chapter, I will return to the broad theoretical questions.

☐ The "Meaning System" Approach

My work is built around the idea that people develop beliefs that organize their world and give meaning to their experiences. These beliefs may be called "meaning systems," and different people create different meaning systems. In this book I spell out how people's beliefs about themselves (their *self-theories*) can create different psychological worlds, leading them to think, feel, and act differently in identical situations.

The idea that people's beliefs or theories form a meaning system has a venerable history in philosophy and psychology (e.g., Kelly, 1955; Langer, 1967; Pepper, 1942; Whitehead, 1929, 1938) and forms the basis of much exciting work in many fields of psychology, including

Social-personality psychology (Epstein, 1990; Janoff-Bulman, 1992; Hamilton & Sherman, 1996; Kruglanski, 1989; Lerner, 1980; Semin & Gergen, 1990; Wegner & Vallacher, 1977)

Clinical psychology (Beck, 1996; Greenberg & Pascuale-Leone, 1997)

Cross-cultural psychology and psychological anthropology (Hirschfeld & Gelman, 1994; Shweder, 1993; Shweder & LeVine, 1984)

Cognitive psychology (Murphy & Medin, 1985)

Developmental psychology—both social development (Goodnow & Collins, 1990; Lewis, 1997; Saarni, 1993) and cognitive-language development (Carey, 1996; Nelson, 1996; Wellman & Gelman, 1992).

In fact, Piaget, the titan of cognitive developmental psychology, realized near the end of his life that simply focusing on logical thinking and its development was not enough. He came to believe that the meaning systems that people adopted were as important or even more important in shaping their thinking (Piaget, Garcia, & Feider, 1989; Piaget, Garcia, Davison, & Easley, 1991; see Overton, 1990).

I heartily endorse this belief, and I further suggest that the meaning-system approach, with its emphasis on how people organize and understand their world, can bring these different areas of psychology closer together.

☐ The Goal of the Book

The goal of this book is to shed light on how people work. On the basis of extensive research with children and young adults, I address the question of why sometimes people function well and sometimes they function not so well, behaving in ways that are self-defeating or destructive. In the course of examining this issue, we will come to understand better why some people exceed expectations, while others fail to fulfill their potential.

Toward this end, I present research that spells out adaptive and maladaptive motivational patterns:

- How they are fostered by people's self-theories
- Their consequences for the person—for achievement, social relationships, and mental health
- Their consequences for society, from issues of human potential to stereotyping and intergroup relations
- The experiences that create them

Throughout I show how examining children's and adults' self-theories illuminates basic issues of human motivation, personality, the self, and development.

☐ Overview of the Book

In the first six chapters, I lay out our model of achievement motivation. I show how students' theories about their intelligence set up the goals they pursue, and how the theories and goals set up adaptive and maladaptive achievement patterns. I also demonstrate effects on real-world achievement. I go on to show how each self-theory forms the core of a whole meaning system, a personal framework for understanding achievement.

In the next chapters, I explore more general issues about intelligence and achievement, and I present research that takes the model into new domains beyond intelligence and achievement. This research shows how the model can shed light on other important personal and interpersonal phenomena, such as

- Why some people fall prey to depression and loss of self-esteem when setbacks occur

- Why, contrary to popular opinion, confidence, self-esteem, and past success are not the keys to adaptive functioning
- Why some people display self-defeating behavior in social relationships
- Why some people judge and label others rapidly
- Why some people hold stereotypes more strongly than others and why they form them more readily

I then tackle the question of where these implicit theories and goals come from—what kinds of experiences can foster them. Here, for example, I present some surprising new findings that praising intelligence (or other basic traits) rather than raising self-esteem sets up maladaptive self-theories, goals, and coping patterns.

In the final chapters, I explore the implications of our findings for the concept of self-esteem, suggesting a rethinking of self-esteem, its role in motivation, and the conditions that foster it. I then place my theoretical approach in the context of several past and present theories of personality, motivation, development, and mental health, drawing out what I think are the advantages—for theory, research, and application—of an approach that focuses on people's belief systems and goals. I conclude by confronting a series of difficult questions about the issues I raise and the positions I take throughout the book.

This book contains both findings from 30 years of research and opinions I have developed based on these findings. I hope that both will stimulate thinking, debate, and, most of all, more research.

1

CHAPTER

What Promotes Adaptive Motivation? Four Beliefs and Four Truths About Ability, Success, Praise, and Confidence

The hallmark of successful individuals is that they love learning, they seek challenges, they value effort, and they persist in the face of obstacles (see Sorich & Dweck, in press). In this book, I present research that explains why some students display these "mastery-oriented" qualities and others do not. This research challenges several beliefs that are common in our society:

1. **The belief that students with high ability are more likely to display mastery-oriented qualities.** You might think that students who were highly skilled would be the ones who relish a challenge and persevere in the face of setbacks. Instead, many of these students are the most worried about failure, and the most likely to question their ability and to wilt when they hit obstacles (Leggett, 1985; Licht & Dweck, 1984a,b; Licht & Shapiro, 1982; see also Stipek & Hoffman, 1980).
2. **The belief that success in school directly fosters mastery-oriented qualities.** You might also think that when students succeed, they are emboldened and energized to seek out more challenging tasks. The truth is that success in itself does little to boost students' desire for challenge or their ability to cope with setbacks. In fact, we will see that it can have quite the opposite effect (Diener & Dweck, 1978, 1980; Dweck, 1975; Kamins & Dweck, in press; Leggett, 1985; Licht & Dweck, 1984a; Mueller & Dweck, 1998).
3. **The belief that praise, particularly praising a students' intelligence, encourages mastery-oriented qualities.** This is a most cherished belief in our society. One can hardly walk down the street without hearing parents telling their chil-

1

dren how smart they are. The hope is that such praise will instill confidence and thereby promote a host of desirable qualities. I will show that far from promoting the hoped-for qualities, this type of praise can lead students to fear failure, avoid risks, doubt themselves when they fail, and cope poorly with setbacks (Kamins & Dweck, in press; Mueller & Dweck, 1998).

4. **The belief that students' confidence in their intelligence is the key to mastery-oriented qualities.** In a way, it seems only logical to assume that students who have confidence in their intelligence—who clearly believe they are smart—would have nothing to fear from challenge and would be somehow inoculated against the ravages of failure. It may seem logical, but it is not the whole story, or even most of it. Many of the most confident individuals do not want their intelligence too stringently tested, and their high confidence is all too quickly shaken when they are confronted with difficulty (Henderson & Dweck, 1990; Hong, Chiu, Dweck, & Lin, 1998; Zhao, Dweck, & Mueller, 1998; see Hong, Chiu, & Dweck, 1995).

There is no question that our society's ideas about success, praise, and confidence are intuitively appealing. They grow out of the reasonable conviction that if students believe in their abilities, they will thrive. How can that *not* be true?

I am not suggesting that failure and criticism are more beneficial than success and praise. Nor am I arguing that a feeling of confidence isn't a good thing to have, but I will argue that it is not the heart of motivation or the key to achievement.

As I describe my program of research on these issues, you will understand why each of the beliefs just presented is erroneous. You will understand why ability, success, intelligence praise, and confidence do not make students value effort, or seek challenges, or persist effectively in the face of obstacles. And why they may often have quite the opposite effect.

What, then, *are* the beliefs that foster the mastery-oriented qualities we wish for?

☐ Two Frameworks for Understanding Intelligence and Achievement

Mastery-oriented qualities grow out of the way people understand intelligence, and there are two entirely different ways that people understand intelligence. Let's look first at the view that does *not* promote mastery-oriented qualities as successfully.

The Theory of Fixed Intelligence

Some people believe that their intelligence is a fixed trait. They have a certain amount of it and that's that. We call this an "entity theory" of intelligence because intelligence is portrayed as an entity that dwells within us and that we can't change (Bandura & Dweck, 1985; Dweck & Leggett, 1988).

This view has many repercussions for students. It can make students worry about how much of this fixed intelligence they have, and it can make them interested first and foremost in looking and feeling like they have enough. They must look smart and, at all costs, not look dumb (Bandura & Dweck, 1985; Dweck & Leggett, 1988; Sorich & Dweck, in press).

What makes students with an entity theory feel smart? Easy, low-effort successes, and outperforming other students. Effort, difficulty, setbacks, or higher-performing peers call their intelligence into question—even for those who have high confidence in their intelligence (see Dweck & Bempechat, 1983).

The entity theory, then, is a system that requires a diet of easy successes. Challenges are a threat to self-esteem. In fact, students with an entity theory will readily pass up valuable learning opportunities if these opportunities might reveal inadequacies or entail errors—and they readily disengage from tasks that pose obstacles, even if they were pursuing them successfully shortly before (Bandura & Dweck, 1985; Hong, Chiu, Dweck, & Lin, 1998; Leggett, 1985; Mueller & Dweck, 1998; Sorich & Dweck, in press; Stone, 1998; cf. Diener & Dweck, 1978; Elliott & Dweck, 1988).

I will show how we encourage vulnerabilities in our students when we try to boost their self-esteem within this system. The well-meant successes we hand out and the praise for intelligence we lavish on them does not encourage a hardy, can-do mentality. What it does is foster an entity theory, an overconcern with looking smart, a distaste for challenge, and a decreased ability to cope with setbacks (Dweck, 1975; Kamins & Dweck, in press; Mueller & Dweck, 1998). What's the alternative?

The Theory of Malleable Intelligence

Other people have a very different definition of intelligence. For them intelligence is not a fixed trait that they simply possess, but something they can cultivate through learning. We call this an "incremental theory" of intelligence because intelligence is portrayed as something that can be increased through one's efforts (Bandura & Dweck, 1985; Dweck & Leggett, 1988).

It's not that people holding this theory deny that there are differences among people in how much they know or in how quickly they master certain things at present. It's just that they focus on the idea that everyone, with effort and guidance, can increase their intellectual abilities (Mueller & Dweck, 1997; see Binet, 1909/1973).

This view, too, has many repercussions for students. It makes them want to learn. After all, if your intelligence can be increased why not do that? Why waste time worrying about looking smart or dumb, when you could be becoming smarter? And in fact students with this view will readily sacrifice opportunities to look smart in favor of opportunities to learn something new (Bandura & Dweck, 1985; Leggett, 1985; Mueller & Dweck, 1998; Sorich & Dweck, in press; Stone, 1998; cf. Elliott & Dweck, 1988). Even students with an incremental theory and *low* confidence in their intelligence thrive on challenge, throwing themselves wholeheartedly into difficult tasks—and sticking with them (Henderson & Dweck, 1990; Stone, 1998; cf. Elliott & Dweck, 1988).

What makes students with an incremental view feel smart? Engaging fully with new tasks, exerting effort to master something, stretching their skills, and putting their knowledge to good use, for example to help other students learn (see Bempechat & Dweck, 1983).

These are the kinds of things—effort and learning—that make incremental students feel good about their intelligence. Easy tasks waste their time rather than raise their self-esteem.

☐ A Different View of Self-Esteem

Self-esteem, we will see, is something completely different in the incremental system. It is not an internal quantity that is fed by easy successes and diminished by failures. It is a positive way of experiencing yourself when you are fully engaged and are using your abilities to the utmost in pursuit of something you value.

It is not something we *give* to people by telling them about their high intelligence. It is something we equip them to get for themselves—by teaching them to value learning over the appearance of smartness, to relish challenge and effort, and to use errors as routes to mastery.

In the following chapters I describe the consequences of the two theories of intelligence for motivation and achievement. But to understand the impact of the theories better, let us first take a closer look at what the theories create: the patterns of vulnerability and hardiness that students display as they confront difficulty.

CHAPTER

When Failure Undermines and When Failure Motivates: Helpless and Mastery-Oriented Responses

Of all the things that intrigued me when I began this work, none intrigued me more than this: Many of the most accomplished students shied away from challenge and fell apart in the face of setbacks. Many of the less skilled students seized challenges with relish and were energized by setbacks. How could this be?

But the story got even stranger. Many very skilled students questioned or condemned their intelligence when they failed at a task. Many of the less skilled students never even remotely entertained such thoughts.

You'd think that vulnerability would be based on the "reality" of students' skills. But it isn't. Vulnerability is not about the actual ability students bring to a task. If it's not about the reality of their skill, what *is* it about? What could cause bright students to think of themselves as dumb and fall apart just because they are having some trouble with a task? These questions led us to search for the processes that are at the heart of students' motivational problems.

☐ The Helpless and Mastery-Oriented Patterns

We started by identifying two distinct reactions to failure, which we called the *helpless* and *mastery-oriented* patterns (Diener & Dweck, 1978, 1980; Dweck, 1975; Dweck & Reppucci, 1973). Martin Seligman and Steven Maier (Seligman & Maier, 1967) first identified helpless responses in animals. In their research, some animals failed to leave a painful situation because they believed, erroneously, that the circumstances were beyond their control.

We used the term "helpless" to describe some students' view of failure—the view that once failure occurs, the situation is out of their control and nothing can be done (Dweck, 1975; Dweck & Reppucci, 1973).[1] We later extended the helpless response to include all the reactions these students show when they meet failure: denigration of their intelligence, plunging expectations, negative emotions, lower persistence, and deteriorating performance (Diener & Dweck, 1978).

We used the term *mastery-oriented* to refer to the hardy response to failure because here students remain focused on achieving mastery in spite of their present difficulties (Diener & Dweck, 1978, 1980).

Let us examine these patterns in action by taking a close look at the research that revealed them. In this research, by Carol Diener and me (Diener & Dweck, 1978, 1980), we gave fifth- and sixth-grade students a series of conceptual problems to solve. All children could solve the first eight problems, with hints or training if they needed it. But they could not solve the next four problems. These problems were too difficult for children their age, and so we could see how they reacted to this sudden obstacle. That is, we could see what happened to their thoughts, feelings, and actions as they confronted difficulty.

How did we do this? First, we could track changes in students' problem-solving strategies because the task we chose allowed us to pinpoint the exact strategy they used on each problem. So, we could look at the problem-solving strategies they used before the difficulty, compare them to the strategies they used after the difficulty began, and see if they showed improvement or impairment.

Second, we tracked changes in the thoughts and feelings they expressed while they worked on the task. We did this by asking them to talk out loud as they worked on the problems. We told them, "We're really interested in what students think about when they work on the problems. Some students think about lunch, some think about recess, some think about what they're going to do after school, and others think about how they're going to solve the problems." In other words, we gave them license to divulge any thoughts and feelings no matter how seemingly inappropriate. And they did. As with the strategies, we could see the changes in what they talked about before and after the difficult problems began.

We also asked students a number of questions after the difficult problems—for example, how well they thought they would now do if they went back to the original success problems, and how many problems they remembered getting right and wrong.

When we examined the students' strategies, along with the thoughts and feelings they expressed, we could see two dramatically different reactions.

But first I should explain a few things. One is that before the experiments we divided the students into two groups: those who were likely to show the helpless response and those who were likely to show the mastery-oriented response. We did this by asking them to fill out a questionnaire (Crandall, Katkovsky, & Crandall, 1965); we knew from our past research that this questionnaire could predict who would show persistence versus nonpersistence in the face of failure (Dweck, 1975; Dweck & Reppucci, 1973; see also Weiner & Kukla, 1970). But now we wanted to see whether it would predict a whole array of mastery-oriented and helpless responses.

Second, in all of our studies that involve any difficulty, we take elaborate steps to make sure that all students leave our experiment feeling proud of their performance. We have worked out detailed procedures for giving students feelings of mastery on the difficult tasks. To begin with, we explain to them that the failure problems were in fact too difficult for them because they were actually designed for older children: Because they had done so well on the earlier problems, we wanted to see how they would do on these. We then carefully take them through to mastery of the difficult problems, praising their effort and strategies—which, we will see, is what fosters master-oriented responses. This procedure, of course, varies somewhat from study to study, but in all cases we go to great lengths to ensure that students interpret their experience as one of mastery.

Finally, you may be curious about what percentage of students tend to show a helpless response and what percentage tend to show a mastery-oriented response. The answer is that it's about half and half. There are some students in the middle (maybe 15%) who don't really fit into either group, but aside from that the remaining students divide pretty equally between the helpless and mastery-oriented groups. This is true for all of the studies I discuss throughout the book. I am never talking about a few extreme students. I am talking about almost everyone.

☐ The Helpless Pattern

When we monitored students' problem-solving strategies and their statements as they went from success to failure, two very distinct patterns emerged. Let's look first at the group showing the helpless response and examine their thoughts, their feelings, and their performance.

Maybe the most striking thing about this group was how quickly they began to denigrate their abilities and blame their intelligence for the failures, saying things like "I guess I'm not very smart," "I never did have a good memory," and "I'm no good at things like this." More than a third of the students in this group spontaneously denigrated their intellectual ability; none of the students in the mastery-oriented group did so.

What was so striking about this was that only moments before, these students had had an unbroken string of successes. Their intelligence and their memory were working just fine. What's more, during these successes their performance was every bit as good as that of the mastery-oriented group. Still, only a short while after the difficult problems began, they lost faith in their intellect.

And they did so to such a degree that over a third of the children in this group, when asked whether they thought they could now solve the *same* problems they solved before, did not think they could. The students in the mastery-oriented group *all* were certain they could redo the original problems, and many of them thought the question itself was a ridiculous one.

Not only did the children in the helpless group lose faith in their ability to succeed at the task in the future, but they also lost perspective on the successes they had achieved in the past. We asked the students to try to remember how many problems they had solved successfully (there were eight) and how many problems they had not (there were four). Thus the correct answer was that there were twice as many solved problems as unsolved ones.

But students showing the helpless response were so discouraged by the difficulty that they actually thought they had more failures than successes. They remembered only five successes, but they remembered six failures. That is, they shrank their successes and inflated their failures, maybe because the failures were so meaningful to them. The mastery-oriented group recalled the numbers quite accurately.

Thus, the students showing the helpless response quickly began to doubt their intelligence in the face of failure and to lose faith in their ability to perform the task. To make matters worse, even the successes they had achieved were, in their minds, swamped by their failures.

How did they *feel* about the whole situation? When we looked at the emotions they expressed during the task, we again saw a rapid change with the onset of failure. These students had been quite pleased with themselves, the task, and the situation during the successful trials, but they began to express a variety of negative feelings once they began having trouble with the task. Many claimed they were now bored, even though they had been happily involved only moments before. Two thirds of the students in the helpless group expressed notable negative affect; only one student in the mastery-oriented group did so.

We also began to note some very interesting ways these students had of dealing with their anxiety and self-doubt. For example, one child, in the middle of the failure problems, stopped to inform us that she was soon to be an heiress, and another reported that she had been cast as Shirley Temple in the school play. In other words, they tried to call attention to their successes in other realms.

Other children in this group tried to distract attention from their failures in an equally novel way: They tried to change the rules of the task. Since they did not seem to be succeeding on the task as we defined it, they would make it into a different game and succeed on their own terms. One boy, for example, kept picking the same wrong answer (a brown object) because, he kept telling us, he liked chocolate cake.

In other words, these students were no longer applying themselves to the problem at hand.

Not surprisingly, we saw big drops in the performance of this group. On the success problems, all of them had been using sophisticated and effective problem-solving strategies for children their age. In fact, they were every bit as good at the task as the mastery-oriented students. But during the difficult problems, two thirds of them showed a clear deterioration in their strategies, and more than half of the children in the helpless group lapsed into completely ineffective strategies. For example, they would just keep making wild guesses at the answer instead of using the information they were given. Or they might just keep choosing the answer on the right hand side. Or, like the boy described above, they kept picking answers for personal reasons that had nothing to do with the real task. These are strategies that preschool children might use, not fifth graders. And they are not strategies that would have allowed them to solve even the easier problems they had solved earlier. In short, the majority of students in this group abandoned or became incapable of deploying the effective strategies in their repertoire.

But wasn't this in some ways a realistic and even adaptive reaction to the failure problems? Weren't they in fact too difficult to be solved by these students? The trouble with this "helpless" response was, first, that these children gave up trying far too quickly, before they had a real idea of what they were capable of doing. The second, even more important, thing was that they did not simply decide in an objective manner that the task was too hard: They condemned their abilities and fell into a depressed or anxious mood. These ways of dealing with obstacles make the helpless response a clearly less adaptive one.

What's more, in other studies we gave students readily solvable problems after the difficult ones (e.g., Dweck, 1975; Dweck & Reppucci, 1973). In fact, we gave them problems that were almost identical to problems they had solved earlier in the session. Yet, students in the helpless group were less likely to solve these problems than the students in the mastery-oriented group. This was true even though everyone was highly motivated to solve the problems. In some of these studies (Dweck, 1975; Dweck & Reppucci, 1973) we made absolutely sure that students were eager to solve the problems by having them work toward very attractive toys that they had personally selected.

These findings show that the helpless response is not just an accurate appraisal of the situation. It is a reaction to failure that carries negative implications for the self and that impairs students' ability to use their minds effectively.

☐ The Mastery-Oriented Pattern

The mastery-oriented response stands in stark contrast. Let's begin by looking at how these students understood the difficult problems. We saw that students in the helpless group blamed their intelligence when they hit failure. What did the students in the mastery-oriented group blame? The answer, which surprised us, was that they did not blame anything. They didn't focus on reasons for the failures. In fact, they didn't even seem to consider themselves to be failing.

Certainly, they had bumped up against difficulty, but nothing in their words or actions indicated that they thought this was anything more than a problem to be tackled. So, while the students in the helpless group had quickly begun questioning their ability (and had quickly lost hope of future success), students in the mastery-oriented group began issuing instructions to themselves on how they could improve their performance.

Some of these were self-motivating instructions: "The harder it gets, the harder I need to try," or "I should slow down and try to figure this out." Some of these were more oriented toward the cognitive aspects of the task, such as reminding themselves of what they had learned so far about the problem they were working on.

Almost all of the students in the mastery-oriented group engaged in some form of self-instruction or self-monitoring designed to aid their performance; almost none of the students in the helpless group did this. So, in response to obstacles the mastery-oriented group just dug in more vigorously.

They also remained very confident that they would succeed, saying things like "I've almost got it now" or asking for a few more chances on a problem because they felt sure they were on the verge of getting it. About two thirds of the students in the mastery-oriented group—but virtually none of the students in the helpless group—issued some sort of optimistic prediction.

How did they feel? This group tended to maintain the positive mood they had displayed during the success problems, but some of them became even happier about the task. We will never forget one young man, who, when the difficult problems started, pulled up his chair, rubbed his hands together, smacked his lips, and said, "I *love* a challenge." Or another, who as the difficulty began, told us in a matter-of-fact voice "You know, I was *hoping* this would be informative." Or another child who asserted cheerfully, "Mistakes are our friend."

For us, it was as though a lightbulb went on. We had thought that you coped with failure or you didn't cope with failure. We didn't think of failure as a thing to embrace with relish. These students were teaching us what true mastery-oriented reactions were.

So, far from lamenting their predicament, the mastery-oriented students welcomed the chance to confront and overcome obstacles.

How did they perform? In line with their optimism and their efforts, most of the students in this group (more than 80%) maintained or improved the quality of their strategies during the difficult problems. A full quarter of the group actually improved. They taught themselves new and more sophisticated strategies for addressing the new and more difficult problems. A few of them even solved the problems that were supposedly beyond them.

This response stands in clear opposition to the helpless response, where students took the difficulty as a sign of inadequacy, fell into a sort of despair, and remained mired in it. The mastery-oriented students, recognizing that more would be required of them, simply summoned their resources and applied themselves to the task at hand. Thus, even though they were no better than the helpless children on the original success problems, they ended up showing a much higher level of performance.

Were they fooling themselves by remaining optimistic on a task that was essentially beyond them? As I mentioned, some of them actually mastered the task through their efforts. But that aside, what did they have to lose by trying? What did the effort cost them? Not much, because—and this is crucial—*they were not seeing failure as an indictment of themselves*, and so the risk for them was not great.

For the students in the helpless group, however, their whole intelligence, and perhaps their self-worth, seemed to be on the line, with each unsuccessful effort undermining it further (see Covington, 1992). There, the risk could hardly be greater.

☐ Helpless and Mastery-Oriented Responses in the Classroom

After spelling out the helpless and mastery-oriented patterns, we wanted to make sure that these patterns actually affected students' learning in school. We wanted to be completely sure that we were not just creating and studying a laboratory phenomenon, and so we devised a new unit of material for students to learn in their classrooms: "Psychology, Why We Do the Things We Do."

In this study by Barbara Licht and me (Licht & Dweck, 1984a), we identified fifth-grade students who were likely to show the helpless response and those who were likely to show a mastery-oriented one, again by means of a question-naire. Then, some time later, in their classes, we gave these students instructional booklets that guided them through the new material.

How did we check for a helpless response? Half of the booklets had confusing patches near the beginning. The question was whether students who were prone to the helpless response would be hampered in their learning after they experi-enced the confusion.

We looked for a subject to teach the students that would be different from any-thing they had learned in school. We didn't want them to come to the task with preconceived notions about how good they were in that subject. We also wanted to teach them something that they could later use to solve problems we gave them, so that we could test their mastery of the material.

What we taught them were some of the principles of learning. They learned, with amusing examples and illustrations, that if they did something (like going dancing) and a good thing resulted (like having a good time), then they were likely to do that same thing again. Similarly, they learned that if they did some-thing (like eating some food) and a bad thing resulted (they got sick), then they'd be less likely to repeat the behavior. Finally, they learned that a big good thing outweighed a small bad thing (and a big bad thing outweighed a small good thing) in determining whether they were likely to repeat the behavior.

At the end of the booklet was a seven-question mastery test. We considered stu-dents to have mastered the material if they got all seven questions correct, since the questions were fairly direct ones that stuck close to the material we had pre-sented. If students did not demonstrate mastery on the first booklet, they were given a review booklet and another mastery test.

We took steps to prevent students from perceiving the review booklets as mean-ing they had failed. When a review booklet was necessary, the experimenter said to the child in a friendly, nonevaluative tone: "You didn't *quite* get it all yet, so I'd like you to review this. I put an 'X' back here by the kind of question(s) that you missed. So pay special attention to that (those) question(s). But I'd like you to review it all again." Altogether, students had four opportunities to master the material.

To see how the helpless response would affect learning we made two different versions of the initial instruction booklet—one that contained difficulty and one that did not. In both versions, near the beginning, we inserted a short section of irrelevant material, namely, a passage on imitation. In one version, the passage was written in a clear, straightforward way, but in the other it was written in a muddy and tortuous style, a style that looked comprehensible on the surface but was quite confusing. Here is a sample of the confusing passage:

> How can one best describe the nature of the people who will most of all be that way which will make the imitating of others happen most often? Is it that these are the people we want to be like because they are fine or is it that these are the people we want to be liked by?

Now, this passage had nothing to do with the real material the students had to learn, and so the confusing passage did not rob them of any information they needed to solve the mastery problems later. But it allowed us to see how confusion at the beginning of a new unit would affect learning for students who were prone to a helpless response.

The results were striking. When students received booklets that had no confusion, those who were prone to a helpless response and those who were prone to a mastery-oriented response looked pretty much the same. Over two-thirds of the students in both groups mastered the material during the session: 76.6% of the helpless group and 68.4% of the mastery-oriented group got the seven mastery questions correct—not a significant difference. This is right in line with our previous findings that before failure occurs the two groups of students seem to have equal ability at the tasks we give them. In this study we also had the IQ and achievement-test scores of the students, which again showed the two groups to be equivalent in their current academic skills.

However, when students got the booklet with the confusing passage, the two groups looked very different from each other. The mastery-oriented students still looked good, with 71.9% of them mastering the material. However, the students in the helpless group clearly suffered from their confrontation with confusion: Only 34.6% of them were able to master the task. This means that many students who had the necessary skills failed to learn the material because they couldn't cope with the initial confusion, the same confusion that didn't disrupt the mastery-oriented group one bit.

One reason we chose a confusing passage as the way to present an obstacle was that new units may pose just this kind of obstacle, especially as students go on in school. For example, as students move on from arithmetic to algebra, geometry, or trigonometry, new concepts and new conceptual frameworks are being introduced. Students may have no idea how these new concepts relate to what they learned before, and they may find themselves in the dark for a while.

Students prone to the helpless pattern may easily react with self-doubt and disruption, deciding prematurely that they aren't any good in the subject. This would put them at a real disadvantage as school progresses, especially in areas of math and science that really ask the student to enter a new conceptual world.

This study showed that a helpless response could hamper learning of new material in a classroom setting, and made it even more important for us to understand the underlying causes of the helpless and mastery-oriented responses.

☐ Some Thoughts About the Two Patterns

I have been stressing the fact that the helpless and mastery-oriented groups are equivalent in the cognitive skills they bring to a task. The reason they may end up displaying such different levels of performance is that one group essentially retires its skills in the face of failure, while the other continues to use them vigorously.

Why is it difficult for us—and often for teachers—to realize that very bright students may display this pattern? Perhaps because much of the work bright students receive is relatively easy for them and they are usually able to avoid really confronting difficulty. Then why should we be concerned? The reason is that sooner or later everyone confronts highly challenging work, if not in grade school, then certainly at some point later on. Rather than meeting these challenges head on, helpless students may suffer unnecessary self-doubt and impairment.

Equally important, students are confronted with more and more choices as they go on in school (Eccles, 1984). The choices that ensure ready success and avoidance of failure are likely to be limiting ones.

It is also important to realize that the helpless response, if it is a habitual response to challenge, will not just limit students' achievement of tasks that others give them. It will limit their achievement of their own goals. All valued, long-term goals involve obstacles. If obstacles are seen as posing a real threat and if they prompt grave self-doubts and withdrawal, then pursuit of these goals will surely be compromised.

If, on the other hand, difficulty is treated as a natural part of things and challenge is welcomed, how can this help but foster the achievement of goals?

The effectiveness of a mastery-oriented approach was dramatically illustrated in the following conversation I overheard between two undergraduates I'll call Charles and Bob. They were talking about a very challenging computer-science course, one that was meant to weed out the fainthearted. Charles had taken it twice, receiving a D the first time and a B+ the second. Bob was currently taking it and was expecting at most a C but was thinking that he too might take it over. They then went on to discuss whether they would major in computer science. Never once did either of them consider whether he might not be good in this subject. They simply saw computer science as a subject in which you had to work really hard and maybe retake some of the most challenging courses. Their decision about whether to major in it would rest, they decided, on how interested they were in it and how hard they were willing to work.

I had little doubt that if these young men did decide to pursue computer science they would succeed admirably. Yet I was amazed by this conversation. It was so different from how I was in college. If I had received a grade that was less than I had hoped for, I would never have dreamt of discussing it in public. Moreover, if I had ever received a C or D in a course, I would never in a million years have considered majoring in that subject. I'm sure that my interests would have immediately shifted elsewhere. I admired Charles and Bob greatly for keeping their options open and for recognizing that with continued effort they could master skills they valued.

Are we saying that dogged persistence is always the best strategy? Not really. While recognizing the importance of confronting obstacles, we can also recognize the importance of knowing when to opt out of a task—say, when it is truly beyond someone's current capabilities or when the cost of persisting is too great (see Janoff-Bulman & Brickman, 1981, for a cogent discussion of these issues).

The mastery-oriented response is one that allows persistence, but it does not force anyone to persist when a rational analysis suggests doing otherwise. In fact, overpersistence can in some ways be more like the helpless response. Some may refuse to give up because an admission of defeat is too great a blow to their ego.

Richard Nixon, in the wake of the Watergate hearings, was facing almost certain impeachment and conviction. Yet for a long time he refused to give up his presidency, saying, "You're never a failure until you give up." He was equating giving up not simply with failure but with *being* a failure.

In both cases—either getting out too quickly or staying in too long—the maladaptive response is based on the concern that failure spells serious personal inadequacy.

After we pinpointed the helpless and mastery-oriented patterns, a very important question remained: *Why* do students of equal ability have such dramatically different reactions to failure? As we will see in the next chapter, the belief that failure measures you is a key factor.

☐ Note

1. See also Heckhausen & Dweck, 1998; Heckhausen & Schulz, 1995; Rothbaum, Weisz, & Snyder, 1982; Rotter, 1966; Skinner, 1995; Skinner & Wellborn, 1994; Weiner & Kukla, 1970; Weiner, Heckhausen, & Meyer, 1972, for discussions of beliefs about control and their implications for coping.

Achievement Goals: Looking Smart Versus Learning

Why do some students react to an obstacle as though it's a painful condemnation, when others see the same obstacle as a welcome challenge? Maybe, we thought, achievement situations are about totally different things for different students. For some students, they are tests of their intelligence, and when they hit problems they're failing the intelligence test. For the others, the same situations are opportunities to learn new things.

So Elaine Elliott and I proposed that helpless and mastery-oriented students have different *goals* in achievement situations, and that these goals help create the helpless and master-oriented responses (Dweck & Elliott, 1983; Elliott & Dweck, 1988; see also Dweck, 1986, 1990, 1991).

We identified two different goals. The first is a "performance goal." This goal is about winning positive judgments of your competence and avoiding negative ones. In other words, when students pursue performance goals they're concerned with their level of intelligence: They want to look smart (to themselves or others) and avoid looking dumb.

Sometimes students do this by playing it safe and completely avoiding mistakes. Other times they do it by taking on a harder task, but one they think they're pretty sure to do well at. Actually, the best tasks for purposes of looking smart are ones that are hard for others but not for you.

The other goal is a "learning goal:" the goal of increasing your competence. It reflects a desire to learn new skills, master new tasks, or understand new things—a desire to get smarter.[1]

Both goals are entirely normal and pretty much universal, and both can fuel achievement (Ames & Archer, 1988; Elliot & Church, 1997; Harackiewicz, Barron, Carter, Lehto, & Elliot, 1997; Stone, 1998). All students want to be validated for their skills and their accomplishments. They also want to develop their skills and knowledge. So it's not that there is anything wrong with either kind of goal.

In fact, in the best of all possible worlds, students could achieve both goals at the same time. That is, they could pursue tasks with the aim of developing their abilities, and these tasks could also earn them the positive appraisals they seek. And this is sometimes possible.

Unfortunately, in the real world, learning and performance goals are often in conflict, and the question becomes: Which is more important? The tasks that are best for learning are often challenging ones that involve displaying ignorance and risking periods of confusion and errors. The tasks that are best for looking smart are often ones that students are already good at and won't really learn much from doing.

What do students do when the two goals are pitted against each other and they must pursue one or the other? They must choose a task that would allow them to look smart, but at the sacrifice of learning something useful and important. Or they must choose a task that would allow them to learn something new and useful, but at the sacrifice of looking smart.

Different students, when asked to choose, opt for different goals. About half of them select performance goals as their preferred goal and half select learning goals (Dweck & Leggett, 1988; Farrell, 1986; Mueller & Dweck, 1997; Sorich & Dweck, in press; Stone, 1998). Although I have argued that both types of goals are natural, we have found that an overemphasis on performance goals is a danger signal.

 First, an overemphasis on performance goals can drive out learning goals, leading students to pass up valuable learning opportunities if they involve any risk of errors. Second, an overemphasis on performance goals can foster a helpless response. How would this happen?

☐ Goals Create Helpless Versus Mastery-Oriented Responses

A performance goal is about measuring ability. It focuses students on measuring themselves from their performance, and so when they do poorly they may condemn their intelligence and fall into a helpless response.

A learning goal is about mastering new things. The attention here is on finding strategies for learning. When things don't go well, this has nothing to do with the student's intellect. It simply means that the right strategies have not yet been found. Keep looking.

In a study by Elaine Elliott and me (Elliott & Dweck, 1988), we showed how performance and learning goals can directly create helpless and mastery-oriented responses.

In this study, with fifth-grade students, we *gave* students a performance goal or a learning goal. The students who were given a performance goal were told that their ability would be evaluated from their performance on the upcoming task. In contrast, the students who were given a learning goal were told that the task would offer them an opportunity to learn some valuable things.

This sort of thing happens all the time in classrooms. Some classrooms emphasize evaluation and ability and foster performance goals in students. Others emphasize progress and mastery on valued tasks and foster learning goals (Ames, 1992; Maehr & Midgley, 1996; Midgley, Anderman, & Hicks, 1995; Stipek, 1996).

In fact, in our study, all students got the same task to work on. But some approached it with performance goals and some with learning goals.

The task began with a series of successes, and the two goal groups performed equally well on them. These were followed by several difficult problems. As in earlier studies, we charted what happened to students' thoughts, feelings, and performance as they went from success to difficulty.

What happened was very interesting. Many of the students with performance goals showed a clear helpless pattern in response to difficulty. A number of them condemned their ability, and their problem-solving deteriorated.

In sharp contrast, most of the students with learning goals showed a clear mastery-oriented pattern. In the face of failure, they did not worry about their intellect, they remained focused on the task, and they maintained their effective problem-solving strategies (see Ames, 1984; Ames & Archer, 1988; Stipek & Kowalski, 1989; cf. Butler, 1992).

This study showed the power of goals. We did not start out by identifying children who were prone to a helpless or mastery-oriented pattern. We simply gave children different goals and showed how these goals could *produce* the helpless and mastery-oriented responses. When children are focused on measuring themselves from their performance, failure is more likely to provoke a helpless response. When children are instead focused on learning, failure is likely to provoke continued effort.

This study also had another facet. Some children were told at the start of the study that they had the ability to do really well at the task. Others were told (temporarily) that their level of ability at the task was not so high. For students with performance goals, this message made a real difference: Students who were certain of their high ability were more likely to hold on in the face of failure and remain mastery-oriented. But students who thought their ability was lower fell right into a helpless response.

For students with learning goals, this message made no difference: Students who thought they had lower ability were *just as* mastery-oriented as those who thought their ability was high. They were just as challenge-seeking and just as effective in the face of difficulty. This means that with a learning goal, students don't have to feel that they're already good at something in order to hang in and keep trying. After all, their goal is to learn, not to prove they're smart. I think this is one of our most interesting findings, and I will return to it throughout the book.[2]

What about students who naturally favor performance versus learning goals? Are they more prone to a helpless pattern, and would this show up in a classroom setting?

☐ Goals and Classroom Learning

The next study, by Edwin Farrell and me (Farrell & Dweck, 1985), was designed to see how students with different goals would do in a real-world setting that presented them with a clear challenge.

In this study, we gave junior high school students new material to learn as a week-long unit in their science classrooms. Over the week, students received instructional booklets that taught them how to solve new kinds of problems. They learned, for example, how to balance weights on a balance beam that had arms of different length. The booklets contained many illustrative examples and gave students many opportunities to solve problems using what they had learned.

After the learning phase, students were given a test that asked them to use what they had learned to solve new kinds of problems. These new problems had not directly been taught but were based on the very same principle that they had just learned. Would the students use their existing knowledge to figure out the new problems that they now confronted?

At the very beginning of the study, we assessed students' goals for this upcoming science unit. We classified the students into those who had performance goals (those who wanted a task that they could be sure to do well on or look smart on) and those who had learning goals (those who hoped to learn something new even if they didn't perform well).

Everyone, of course, wanted to learn the material, but only students who were willing to undergo difficulty for the sake of learning were classified as having predominantly learning goals. Those who cared most about looking smart or not looking dumb were considered to have predominantly performance goals.

We also gave all the students pretests to make sure that one group was not higher in mathematical skills or numerical reasoning. The two groups (those with performance goals and those with learning goals) were entirely equivalent in these areas. What's more, they were entirely equivalent in how well they learned the unit they had been taught. Yet, when we looked at how the students with the different goals fared on the test with the novel problems, there were very clear differences.

First, the students who had learning goals for the unit scored significantly higher on the novel problems than the students with performance goals.

Second, when we looked at the amount of work students produced as they attempted to solve the novel problems, the students with learning goals produced 50% more written work. This means that the students with learning goals were working much harder in their attempt to confront the challenge.

And third, from their written work on the test we saw that the students with learning goals far more often tried to apply the rule they had learned as they worked on test problems. This was true even for learning-goal students who did not end up solving the test problems.

In fact, several other researchers have found that students who take a learning-goal stance toward a task or toward their schoolwork tend to use deeper, more effective learning strategies and to apply what they've learned more effectively (Ames & Archer, 1988; Graham & Golon, 1991; Pintrich & Garcia, 1991).[3]

In short, the students with learning goals were much more mastery-oriented in their approach to the challenging new problems. The students with performance goals, although just as able, were thrown off by the novelty of the test problems. They probably spent too much time worrying about their ability to solve the problems and not enough time solving them (see Roeser, Midgley, & Urdan, 1996).

When are students with performance goals most vulnerable? Recent research suggests that it is when they are focused on the negative—when they are focused on the possibility of failure and their need to avoid it (Elliot & Church, 1997; Elliot & Harackiewicz, 1996; Middleton & Midgley, 1997). In the next chapter, we explore why some students, even very successful ones, might focus on the negative: Why failure looms large in their thoughts and why the possibility of failure is so undermining.

In summary, overconcern with ability and worrying about its adequacy leaves students vulnerable. But another important question remained: *Why* are some students, many of them very bright, so worried about their level of ability?

☐ Notes

1. Researchers now use a variety of terms for the two types of goals. Performance goals are sometimes called *ability goals, ego-involved goals,* or *normative goals* (because the student wants to compare favorably to others). Learning goals are also called *mastery goals* or *task goals.*
2. Learning goals also seem to foster and sustain greater instrinic motivation—personal interest in a task (Butler, 1987, 1988; Mueller & Dweck, 1998; see also Csikszentmihalyi, 1988; Deci & Ryan, 1985; Heyman & Dweck, 1992).
3. It is also important to mention that researchers have successfully applied this goal analysis to other areas, examining, for example, the goal orientations of athletes (Duda, 1992) or workers in organizations (Button & Mathieu, 1996). In Chapter 10, I show how we have applied the goal analysis to social interactions.

Is Intelligence Fixed or Changeable? Students' Theories About Their Intelligence Foster Their Achievement Goals

We began to think, Mary Bandura and I, that what made students obsess about their level of intelligence was the particular way they thought about their intelligence (Bandura & Dweck, 1981). The whole idea of worrying about intelligence and trying to document it all the time implies that you think of it as a fixed, concrete thing. You only have a certain amount of it, so you'd better show that it's enough and you'd better hide it if it isn't.

We also thought that what made some students so oriented toward learning was a different way of thinking about their intelligence. If you are focused on developing your intelligence, it implies that you think of your intelligence as a dynamic and malleable quality, something that can be cultivated through your efforts.

So we identified two different "theories" that students can have about their intelligence—a fixed, entity, theory and a malleable, incremental, theory. In the entity theory, intelligence is a fixed, concrete, internal entity, whereas in the incremental theory, intelligence is a more dynamic quality that can be increased.[1,2]

Then we set about testing the idea that these different theories lead students to value and pursue different goals. An entity theory, with its idea of fixed intelligence, should make students concerned with showing they're smart and so should foster performance goals. An incremental theory, with its idea of malleable intelligence, should make students concerned with getting smarter and so should promote learning goals.

If we could find the beliefs behind the two kinds of goals, we would understand much more about the mindset that created the continual need to validate versus the desire to learn. We could then begin to think about enhancing students' motivation to learn by changing their beliefs about their intelligence.

In two studies—one by Mary Bandura and me with fifth and sixth graders (Bandura & Dweck, 1981) and one by Ellen Leggett and me with eighth graders (Leggett, 1985; see Dweck & Leggett, 1988)—students' theories of intelligence were measured. We generally do this by having students agree or disagree with statements such as

"Your intelligence is something about you that you can't change very much."

"You can learn new things but you can't really change your basic intelligence."

"You have a certain amount of intelligence and you can't really do much to change it."[3]

Then, some time later, students were given an array of tasks to choose from and asked to pick the one they would like to work on. The first two tasks offered performance goals. Sometimes performance goals involve playing it safe and completely avoiding mistakes, as in the first task, which was described as "easy enough so you won't make mistakes." Other times, as in the second task, performance goals involve taking on a harder job, but one you think you're pretty sure to do well at. This task was described as being "like something you're good at but hard enough to show you're smart."

The third task offered a learning goal. It reflected a desire to learn something new even at the risk of looking dumb right now. This task was described as being "hard, new and different—you might get confused and make mistakes, but you might learn something new and useful."[4]

Students in these studies were given the chance to choose any task they wanted to. We made it clear that all the choices were equally acceptable, and that students in the past had preferred different ones. We were interested in whether students with different theories of intelligence would pick different goals to pursue.

Would students holding an entity theory of intelligence try to look smart by pursuing a performance goal? Would students holding an incremental theory try to increase their abilities by choosing the learning goal?

We found a clear and significant relation between the students' theories of intelligence and their goal choices: The more students held an entity theory of intelligence, the more likely they were to choose a performance goal, whereas the more they held an incremental theory, the more likely they were to choose the learning goal.

In the study with eighth graders, for example, over 80% of students with an entity theory chose a performance-goal task—with a full 50% choosing the very easy task, the one that ensured flawless performance. This means that fewer than 20% of these students were willing to try to learn something new when it involved the risk of errors.

In sharp contrast, the majority of the incremental theorists (over 60%) chose the learning-goal task despite its challenge and risk, or perhaps because of it. Of the rest, most chose the challenging performance task. Only a very small minority avoided challenge entirely. So again, the belief in fixed intelligence seems to orient students toward performance goals, and the belief in malleable intelligence seems to orient them toward learning goals.

College students reacted in very much the same way. Recently, Claudia Mueller and I, as part of a larger study, identified college students with different theories of intelligence and then looked at their goals (Mueller & Dweck, 1997). We asked them to read a number of statements and tell us how much they agreed or disagreed with each one. Included among the statements were four that pitted a preference for learning goals against a preference for performance goals.

Students who held an entity theory of their intelligence differed strongly and significantly from students who held an incremental theory on every one of the four statements.

Entity theorists agreed significantly more with the following statements:

"Although I hate to admit it, I sometimes would rather do well in a class than learn a lot."

"If I knew I wasn't going to do well at a task, I probably wouldn't do it even if I might learn a lot from it."

In contrast, incremental theorists agreed significantly more with

"It's much more important for me to learn things in my classes than it is to get the best grades."

The fourth statement had a slightly different format. It said:

"If I *had* to choose between getting a good grade and being challenged in class, I would choose . . ."

Students then circled either "good grade" or "being challenged." Most of the incremental theorists (68%) opted for being challenged. Only 35% of the entity theorists wanted a challenge; the rest chose the good grade.

So, with this group, too, students' theories of intelligence told us whether they'd be more oriented toward learning and challenge, or toward grades and performance.

But sometimes we have to admit ignorance and show our deficiencies in order to learn and do well in the future. What would happen then? Would entity theorists still hide their deficiencies and avoid a learning goal, even if it would harm their future performance?

Ying-Yi Hong, C.Y. Chiu, and Derek Lin found the ideal situation to answer this question. At the University of Hong Kong all classes are conducted in English, all reading is in English, and all exams are taken in English. Yet not all students who enter are proficient in English. Some, in fact, have done rather poorly on their English proficiency exam. Obviously, these students are at a real disadvantage when it comes to doing well in their courses.

In this study (Hong, Chiu, Dweck, & Lin, 1998, study 3), with entering freshmen, students' English proficiency scores were obtained and their theories of intelligence were assessed. They were then given a survey asking their opinion about the course offerings for the upcoming semester. Embedded in this survey was a question about their interest in a remedial English course.

Students were first reminded that in virtually every course offered, the effective use of English is important for learning and doing well. Then they were asked whether they would take a remedial English course if the faculty offered it. They marked their answer on a scale ranging from "absolutely no" to "absolutely yes."

As you would expect, those students who were already proficient in English did not register a high degree of interest in the remedial course. What about those with low proficiency? Among these students, the incremental theorists said that they were very likely to take such a course—but the entity theorists were not very interested. In fact, they were no more interested in the course than were the students with high proficiency, who didn't need it.

In this study, then, students expressed their interest in a learning opportunity that could remove a major obstacle to doing well. How could it be that entity theorists were not eager to pursue this opportunity? After all, their chief goal is to do well.

Maybe they did not wish to fully admit and confront their deficiency or maybe they did not think they were good enough at English to do well in the remedial course. Either way, the choice is highly self-defeating.

In summary, we have seen that holding a fixed theory of intelligence appears to turn students toward concerns about performing and looking smart. Holding a malleable theory appears to turn students toward concerns about learning new things and getting smarter. We have also seen that the entity theorists' concerns about looking smart can prevent them from seeking learning opportunities, even ones that could be critical to performing well in the future.

☐ Do Theories of Intelligence Cause Students' Goals?

We saw that students' theories of intelligence predict their goal choices, but do the theories directly cause the goal choices? To find this out we decided to change students' theories of intelligence (temporarily) and see if we also changed their goals.

How did we change students' theories? To do this, Yvette Tenney, Naomi Dinces, and I wrote two vivid passages for fifth-grade students to read (as reported in Dweck & Leggett, 1988). The passages proposed in colorful and convincing terms either the entity or the incremental theory. They both talked about historical figures and current personalities of notable achievement, such as Helen Keller, Albert Einstein, and the young Rubik's cube champion. But one passage, the entity passage, chalked up their achievements to their fixed, innate intelligence. The other, incremental, passage credited their acquired intelligence.

The incremental passage told, for example, of how Helen Keller as a young girl didn't even know any words and how Albert Einstein as a young man didn't always do too well in school. However, it stressed that they developed the intelligence that led to their accomplishments. The passage did not mention hard work, diligence, or anything else (aside from the theory of intelligence) that could influence the students' goal choices.

Half of the students read the entity passage and half of them read the incremental passage. Everyone read two other passages that were also included—one on dreams and one on animal communication. This was done so that students wouldn't think there was a connection between the theory of intelligence passage and the goal choice they were then asked to make.

Later, in a different phase of the session, all students were asked to choose the kind of task they'd like to work on. Two of the choices were performance-goal tasks because they reflected concerns about looking smart and not looking dumb. One task was easy enough to avoid mistakes and one task was difficult but was like something they were good at.

One task was a learning goal task because it reflected a desire for challenging learning even at the risk of mistakes. This task was described as something that was hard and maybe confusing but would allow the students to learn something new.

Students who read the different theory-of-intelligence passages chose different tasks. Students who read the entity-theory passage were significantly more likely than the others to select a performance-goal task to pursue—they wanted to look smart. This also means that those who read the incremental theory passage were more likely to select the learning goal task to pursue—they wanted to become smarter.

These findings show that the idea of fixed intelligence made students concerned about their own level of intelligence and led them toward tasks that promised favorable judgments. The findings also show that the idea of acquirable intelligence made students value tasks that would develop their abilities, without concern for how smart they might look in the short run.

There are a few interesting things about these findings. One is that they show that students' theories of intelligence can have a direct effect on their goals and concerns. Theories of intelligence *cause* students to focus on performance goals or learning goals.

Another is that they show we can influence students' theories. Although the students came to our study with their own theories, what we told them had a clear impact. This means that people's theories of intelligence are malleable. As we will see throughout, students may arrive in our experiments with strong and long-standing beliefs, but we can, at least temporarily, tune them into a different one.

We don't really know how long the influence would have lasted, because after our experiments we tell the students what we were doing and what we hoped to learn. In this case, we showed them the two passages and discussed with them the two different views of intelligence.

☐ Manipulating College Students' Theories of Intelligence

We've succeeded in influencing students' theories of intelligence in other studies as well. One such study, with college students, was conducted by Randall Bergen (Bergen, 1992). For the study, Bergen wrote two *Psychology Today*–type articles, complete with graphics. Through the use of vivid case studies and what was said to be the latest scientific research, each article made an extremely compelling case for one of the theories. In fact, even other graduate students in our lab, not knowing the origins of the articles, believed they were real. Here is a sampling that gives the flavor of the articles. Both began in the following way:

Adam Steagal is gifted. Although he is just eighteen months old, he can understand over 2000 words, has a speaking vocabulary of 500 words, and is even able to identify five different species of birds . . . At the age of 8 months he was . . . investigating everything in the Steagal household. All babies are curious, but Adam's curiosity led him to new heights of baby creativity. He was not simply banging on pots and pans; Adam had learned to dismantle a toy camera and put it back together again. He had the coordination to handle small objects, the ability to remember how parts fit together, and could concentrate on the camera for almost an hour. Most children can't do what Adam was doing until they are at least three or four.

The entity-theory article went on to explain Adam's exceptional abilities in terms of fixed, innate intelligence, concluding that the brilliance of Mozart and Einstein was mostly built into them at birth:

Their genius was probably a result of their DNA, not their schooling, not the amount of attention their parents gave them, not their own efforts to advance themselves. These great men were probably born, not made.

The incremental-theory article began the same way but went on to explain baby Adam's unusual abilities in terms of his challenging environment. It concluded that the brilliance of people such as Leonardo da Vinci and Albert Einstein was a result of their actions and their environments, not their genes.

Bergen found that the articles had a clear impact on students' theories of intelligence and on their persistence in the face of failure, a topic we take up in the next section.

Ying Yi Hong, C. Y. Chiu, Derrick Lin, and I (Hong, et al., 1998, study 4) also used these articles to influence college students' theories of intelligence. This study was designed as a follow-up to the study we just described, in which entering freshmen were asked about their interest in a remedial English course that could aid their scholastic performance.

The aim of this next study was to see if students who were *given* an entity theory of intelligence would pass up a chance to enhance their deficient skills, just as the students with entity theories had done in the original study. In this study, college students were first given Bergen's *Psychology Today*–type articles as part of a reading comprehension test. Half of them read the vivid and convincing version that espoused the entity theory and the other half read the vivid and convincing version that espoused the incremental theory. After answering some questions about the passage they had read, students went on to the second part of the study, a nonverbal ability test.

Here they worked on a set of problems and received feedback that they had done relatively well (better than 65% of the other students) or relatively poorly (worse than 65% of the other students). However, before moving to the next set of problems, students were offered a tutorial "that was found to be effective in improving performance on the test for most people." All of the students had room for improvement. The question was: Who would take advantage of this tutorial?

Interestingly, most of the students who had done fairly well elected to take the tutorial. Of the students who had done relatively well, 73.3% of those given an incremental theory and 60.0% of those given an entity theory said they wanted to take the tutorial. These numbers were not significantly different. This means that when entity theorists have done fairly well and aren't afraid that they will expose an alarming degree of ignorance, they are willing to take remedial steps.

Among those who had done poorly, a different story emerged. The students who were exposed to the incremental theory still wanted the tutorial (73.3% elected to take it). However, those who were exposed to the entity theory rejected the opportunity to improve their skills. Only 13.3% of the students in this group said they wanted to take the tutorial. Once again, when students have a fixed view of intelligence, those who most need remedial work are the ones who most clearly avoid it.

In short, we have shown that it is possible to influence students' theories about their intelligence, and that when we do so we influence their goals and concerns. Those who are led to believe their intelligence is fixed begin to have overriding concerns about looking smart and begin to sacrifice learning opportunities when there is a threat of exposing their deficiencies. Those who are led to believe their intelligence is a malleable quality begin to take on challenging learning tasks and begin to take advantage of the skill-improvement opportunities that come their way.

As a grade-school student I was shown firsthand how theories of intelligence could affect students' desire to learn. My sixth-grade teacher, Mrs. Wilson, was an extreme entity theorist. She believed fervently that intelligence (as reflected in an IQ score) was a deep-seated trait that affected all endeavors, and she conveyed this to us at every turn. She seated us around the room in IQ order. She handed out every coveted responsibility, from clapping the blackboard erasers to carrying the flag in the assembly, on the basis of IQ. Next to our names in her roll book were our IQ scores written in large black numbers.

It didn't seem to matter to her that this class was already selected for IQ—it was the top-track class of a large school with a very achievement-oriented student body.

The cost for the students with the lower IQ scores is clear. Here they were, after achieving well all through grade school, being told that they were inferior. If they took on any challenging learning tasks and made mistakes, this would only confirm Mrs. Wilson's negative view of them. But the costs for the higher-IQ students were also great. They had to keep proving themselves. Every standardized test held the threat of dethroning them. If they did poorly on the next IQ test they would lose their seat, their responsibilities, and the respect of their teacher. As you can imagine, it was not an environment in which students focused on seeking challenges and on their love of learning, but an environment in which validating intelligence—and trying not to invalidate it—was paramount.

☐ Implicit Theories and the Meaning of Performance Goals

This brings us back to a question I posed in the previous chapter: What would make some students, even successful ones, so concerned with their intelligence and its adequacy or inadequacy? What would make some students chronically worried about failure? I suggest that an entity theory of intelligence may lie at the heart of this. Within an incremental theory, a failure just means that your present strategy or your present skills are inadequate, but within an entity theory, a failure can cast doubt on your global permanent intelligence—definitely something to avoid. Let us look at a study by Stone (1998) that examined this issue directly.

In his study, he measured fifth graders' theories of intelligence and assessed their goal choices. This was the first step, and he found, as we had found before, a strong difference between entity and incremental theorists in their goal preferences. Only one of the entity theorists opted for the challenging learning task, while over half of the incremental theorists did so.

As an aside, it is interesting that when Stone later questioned the students about the value they placed on the learning- and the performance-goal tasks, entity and incremental theorists looked similar. Both said they highly valued both types of tasks. Only when the two types of tasks were pitted against each other, and choosing the learning task meant really risking errors and confusion, did the entity theorists opt out of the learning-goal task. This means that if you give entity and incremental theorists questionnaires that ask them about learning goals and performance goals separately (not pitted against each other), the difference between the two groups may not emerge. In the abstract, entity theorists may believe learning goals are just great, but in the concrete, when confronted with the choice, they would rather validate their intelligence than risk invalidating it by trying to learn something difficult.

Next, regardless of which task they picked, Stone told the students that he'd like to ask them some questions about both types of tasks. One thing he asked them was to rate the extent to which they thought the performance-goal task measured (1) their present skill level on this type of task, (2) how smart they are in general, and (3) how smart they will be when they grow up.

Both entity and incremental theorists agreed that the task measured their present skill level. That was what they had been told about the task. In fact, for some reason, incremental theorists agreed even more than entity theorists that the task could assess their current skills. (Perhaps they did not need to "defend" against having their skills measured, because as we will see in a moment, that's all they thought was being measured.)

However, when it came to the next two questions, the entity theorists agreed significantly more than the incremental theorists that the task measured not only how smart they were in general but also how smart they would be when they grew up. In no way had the task been presented to them as a measure of their global intelligence, and certainly not as a measure of their permanent intelligence. Yet the entity theorists read this into it. Wouldn't you be afraid of failure if each intellectual task you confronted could tell you how smart you were now and would be forever?

Another very striking thing that emerged in this study was the flexibility of the incremental theorists. They seemed to be able to plunge wholeheartedly into either performance goals or learning goals depending on what the situation called for. When they were presented with the performance-goal task and questioned about it, they said that of course they would want to look smart if they were given that task. They had been told that this task was one where they could look smart but not learn anything much, so why *not* try to test their skills? That's what the task was good for.

When they were questioned about the learning goal—where they were told they could learn something important but not look very smart—they dropped the performance goal and focused on the learning aspect of the task. I stated earlier that both learning and performance goals are essential to success. This means that the ability to adopt them appropriately and pursue them flexibly would be a great asset (see Dodge, Asher, & Parkhurst, 1989; Dweck, 1996; Erdley, 1996, and Rabiner & Gordon, 1992, for discussions of the importance of coordinating goals).

In summary, we have shown that students' theories of intelligence set up an emphasis on performance versus learning goals. We've also shown that performance goals may mean different things to entity and incremental theorists. For incremental theorists, a performance-goal task tests a specific skill at a specific point in time. For an entity theorist, the same task tests their global intelligence now and into adulthood. I have suggested that this difference may create a focus on and fear of failure among entity theorists. But it may allow incremental theorists to flexibly adopt and coordinate both kinds of goals.

☐ Notes

1. For other work on lay theories of intelligence, see Carugati, 1990; Goodnow, 1980; Heyman & Gelman, 1997; Sternberg, Conway, Ketron, & Bernstein, 1981; Yussen & Kane, 1985.
2. As many of you know, psychologists have fiercely debated the issue of fixed versus malleable intelligence (see, e.g., Herrnstein & Murray, 1994, vs. Binet, 1909/1973; see Sternberg & Jensen, 1992).
3. See Appendix for the complete theory of intelligence measure.
4. See Appendix for our current goal choice measure.

CHAPTER

Theories of Intelligence Predict (and Create) Differences in Achievement

It was now time to put our ideas to the test: Would students' theories of intelligence predict their actual school achievement? Would incremental theorists pull ahead of entity theorists as they went on in school and faced more and more challenging work?

☐ Achievement Across a Challenging Transition

To answer this question, in two separate studies (one with Valanne Henderson-MacGyvers and one with Lisa Sorich), we followed students over the transition to junior high school (Henderson & Dweck, 1990; Sorich & Dweck, in press). We chose this transition for a particular reason. I've stressed all along that children showing the helpless and the mastery-oriented responses are equal in performance and ability until failure occurs. They also tend to be equal in their school achievement in grade school. Why is this? Why aren't the vulnerable children already lagging behind their challenge-seeking, persistent, mastery-oriented peers?

Grade school typically provides a low-key environment in which the work tends to be carefully paced and teachers try to keep failure to a minimum. If vulnerable children do not encounter difficulty they will not be hampered in their achievement. (As you will see, I am by no means advocating challenge-free academic environments.)

However, with junior high school the situation often changes dramatically. For many students, the work suddenly becomes quite a bit harder, the workload becomes greater, the grading becomes more stringent, grades become more important, and the instruction often becomes far less personalized (see Eccles & Midgely, 1989; Farrell, 1990; Midgley et al., 1995). This is exactly when we would expect vulnerable students to start showing drops in achievement relative to their more mastery-oriented peers.

If it's true that holding an entity theory of intelligence raises concerns about how smart you are and makes intellectual challenge and failure threatening, then this transition should pose a real threat to entity theorists. Their intelligence is certainly on the line in a setting where they are being evaluated on a host of new intellectual tasks. What's more, these tasks may seem to them to be an even better index of their intelligence than the tasks they faced in grade school. In short, the new environment may provide a poor match for these students, who tend to prefer safe tasks and certain success. In fact, I have met many people who have told me that junior high was exactly the time that they stopped thinking they were smart and that their academic achievement went into decline.

On the other hand, if an incremental theory orients students toward challenging learning opportunities and encourages them to see setbacks as a natural part of learning something new, then this new environment provides a better match for incremental theorists. Incremental theorists should give themselves the time and leeway to master the new, more difficult tasks.

Specifically, we predicted that students who entered junior high with an entity theory of intelligence would be more likely to show a helpless response in their new environment: a tendency to doubt their intellectual ability in the face of failure, greater apprehension or anxiety about their schoolwork, and a decline in achievement relative to their peers. In contrast, we predicted that students who entered with an incremental theory would be more likely to look mastery-oriented over this transition: focusing on strategy and effort in the face of difficulty, showing lower levels of anxiety, and maintaining or improving their academic standing.

To test these predictions, Henderson and Dweck (1990) studied students as they entered the seventh grade and grappled with their first months of junior high school. At the beginning of the school year, before they had received any formal feedback, we measured students' theories of intelligence and also their confidence in their intelligence (to find out what role confidence might play in their adjustment).

On the confidence measure, students chose between two statements, one expressing low confidence in their intelligence and one expressing high confidence:

"I usually think I'm intelligent" versus "I wonder if I'm intelligent"
"When I get new work in school, I'm usually sure I'll be good at it" versus "When I get new work in school, I often think I may not be good at it"
"I feel pretty confident about my intellectual ability" versus "I'm not very confident about my intellectual ability"

Then, to see whether students doubted their ability in the face of obstacles or instead focused on effort and strategy, we asked them questions about their reactions to the failures or difficulties they might encounter in their schoolwork. We also asked them about the emotions they were experiencing toward school and their schoolwork.

Finally, to evaluate how they were actually doing academically, we first went back to their sixth grade records for their past grades and achievement test scores. We then waited and looked at the grades they earned on their seventh-grade report cards. The question here was: How well did the students do compared to how well we would expect them to do on the basis of their past achievement? Did their achievement rise or fall relative to their peers? Our predictions were borne out. Students who came to junior high school believing in fixed intelligence were at a disadvantage.

Let's look first at their grades. The students with an entity theory showed a marked decline in their class standing. On the whole, those who had done poorly in sixth grade continued to do poorly in seventh grade. But many who had been *high* achievers in sixth grade were now among the lower achievers.

What surprised us most was that many students who showed this decline from high to low academic standing were entity theorists who had *high* confidence in their intelligence. Why? How could it be the students with faith in their intellectual ability who did so poorly? I'll return to this question and give it a good deal of attention because in psychology and in our society at large confidence is seen as extremely important and "empowering." Yet in our research we have seen that within an entity theory, confidence in intelligence does not always prevent helpless responses to difficulty.

Students holding an incremental theory provided a real contrast. They showed a clear improvement in their class standing. In general, those who had done well in sixth grade continued to do well. But many of those who had been among the lower achievers in sixth grade were now doing much better, often entering the ranks of the high achievers.

What fascinated us here was the fact that many of the incremental theorists who showed the most impressive gains in class standing were those with *low* confidence in their intelligence. These were students who did not believe they were particularly high in intellectual ability, but they believed that this ability could be developed—and they appeared to be working on just that.

I've suggested this before, but it bears emphasizing here: When students have an incremental theory of intelligence, they don't have to feel they're already high in ability in order to take on challenging learning tasks in a vigorous way. Our findings thus show that students' level of confidence was not nearly as important as their theory of intelligence in helping them meet and conquer this difficult transition.

The findings also revealed the predicted differences in students' thoughts and feelings. Students were asked what explanations they would give themselves if they were to receive poor grades in school. They were given a series of possible thoughts or explanations to choose from, some blaming their intellectual ability ("Maybe I'm not smart enough") and others focusing on strategy ("Maybe I'm not studying the right way") or effort ("I should work harder next time"). We compared the answers of students with the two theories of intelligence. Those who held an entity theory were significantly more likely to say that they would doubt their intelligence if they received poor grades. In contrast, the students with an incremental theory were significantly more likely to think that maybe their strategies should be revised or their effort should be stepped up.

Also in line with our predictions, when we asked students their feelings about school, the groups differed. Entity theorists were significantly more apprehensive about their schoolwork and tended to be more anxious about school in general.

Thus, students' theories of intelligence did in fact predict real-world achievement. Entering a challenging scholastic setting with a belief in fixed intelligence seems to set students up for self-doubt, anxiety, and drops in achievement. The entity theory puts a premium on immediate demonstrations of intellectual ability rather than on mastery over time. By not giving students the leeway to acclimate to the new challenges, by not letting them put their self-judgments of intelligence on hold, it may have led them to premature conclusions about their chances of doing well in this new environment.

The incremental theory, instead, aids students by setting up a desire for challenge and the expectation that mastery is a process that takes place over time and with prolonged effort. It is a theory that allows students a grace period while they struggle with the escalated demands that confront them.

Why did the entity theorists with high confidence in their intelligence show such a decline in achievement? After all, many of them were stars in grade school and apparently knew it. We will talk a good deal more about confidence and its role in these patterns, but for now I suggest that maybe these were the students who were able to demonstrate their intelligence in grade school over and over. Perhaps they were the ones who were in the ideal performance-goal situation in grade school: They could dispatch their assigned tasks with speed and accuracy and little effort compared to their peers. Maybe these were the students who were then the most thrown by the heightened demands of their new school, demands that could not be dispatched with the same ease. But instead of getting into the fracas with vigor and risking indictments of their intelligence, they behaved in ways that caused their academic studies to suffer. Perhaps they were stinting on their effort, an issue to which we will also return (cf. Berglas & Jones, 1978; Covington & Omelich 1979; Juvonen, 1995; Midgley, Arunkumar, & Urdan, 1996; Rhodewalt, 1994).

How permanent was the decline in achievement for these students? Were they just temporarily knocked off balance by the difficulties they encountered, but regained their footing as time passed? Or did they remain at a lower rung of achievement? To answer this question, we looked in on the same students again a year later, when they were in eighth grade. We found that this group showed some recovery in their class standing, but, on the whole, they were still clearly below where they had been in grade school.

This means that many of these students were still "underachieving" compared with what their sixth-grade grades and achievement-test scores told us they could be doing. Maybe they were still reluctant to exert the effort necessary to succeed. Maybe they had lost too much faith in their ability to succeed, or maybe they never mastered the study strategies for approaching the new, more difficult work. It may also be that once students fall behind as challenging tasks are being taught, it's very difficult to catch up. They've missed learning the skills that are now assumed and are being built on. At any rate, it is ironic that those students who are most concerned with looking smart may be at a disadvantage for this very reason.

☐ More About Theories of Intelligence and Achievement in Junior High

Our next study (Sorich & Dweck, in press) fleshed out these findings even further and provided more insight into the ways students confront achievement challenges. Here, once again, we studied students who were beginning their first year in junior high. In contrast to the students in the previous study, who were mostly Caucasian and lived in semirural Midwestern towns, the students in this study were largely minority students who lived in a major Northeastern city.

Once again, we had the achievement-test scores that the students had earned the previous year (in sixth grade) and again we measured students' theories about their intelligence and their confidence in their intelligence as they embarked on seventh grade. We also assessed their achievement goals, their beliefs about effort, and their reactions to hypothetical failures. We then waited to see what grades they earned at the end of the semester.

When we classified students into entity and incremental theorists, we saw that they had had virtually identical achievement-test scores (both in English and Math) the previous year. They both valued academic achievement equally. Entity and incremental theorists also had identical degrees of confidence in their ability as they confronted the seventh grade. Yet once again, confidence was not enough, for when we examined the grades they earned at the end of their first semester of junior high, we saw very large differences: Incremental theorists earned significantly higher grades than entity theorists in English and in math, almost a full grade higher in both subjects. (Incidentally, when we looked at students' grades and achievment test scores the next year, in eighth grade, the differences were still there.)

Entity and incremental theorists also differed on most of our other measures as well. They differed, as we might expect, on their achievement (learning versus performance) goals. For example, incremental theorists agreed far more than entity theorists that

"I like schoolwork that I'll learn from even if I make a lot of mistakes."
"It's much more important to me to learn new things in my classes than it is to get the best grades."
"I like schoolwork best when it makes me think hard."

In contrast, entity theorists agreed far more than incremental theorists that

"The main thing I want when I do my schoolwork is to show how good I am at it."
"I mostly like schoolwork that I can do perfectly without any mistakes."
"I have to admit that sometimes I would rather do well in a class than learn a lot."

You can see that incremental theorists, as in our previous work, were much more interested in challenging learning goals and less interested in performance goals than were the entity theorists. They wanted to meet challenges and acquire new skills rather than have easy work that would make them look smart.

We also saw, in a related vein, that entity and incremental theorists differed in when they felt most successful. Entity theorists felt most successful when they out-shone other students, even if they weren't learning much. Incremental students felt most successful when they made progress, even if others still outperformed them: "I feel successful when I improve in school even if other students are getting higher scores than me." "If your scores are going up, you are a success, no matter how well anyone else is doing."

So, we again found a strong connection between students' theories of intelligence and their achievement goals—this time in a study where these factors predicted actual achievement.

Previously, I suggested that maybe entity theorists' attitudes toward effort played a role in their declining performance. Maybe some entity theorists were used to being smart and doing well with little effort, and the more difficult work in junior high came as a big shock. I have a lot more to say about effort beliefs in the next chapter, but I will say here that when we looked at students' attitudes toward effort, we saw important differences.

Although they wanted very much to do well, entity theorists had a strong desire to minimize the effort they put into their schoolwork (see Maehr & Midgely, 1996). They agreed significantly more strongly than incremental theorists with statements such as:

> "Schoolwork is like chores—it has to be done, but you don't want to take much time doing it if you can help it."
> "I try to spend as little time on my schoolwork as I can get by with."

Entity theorists also agreed, more than incremental theorists, that working hard made them feel dumb and that effort won't do much for you if your ability level isn't high (see Stipek & Gralinski, 1996).

It is easy to see how these differences in effort beliefs can contribute to differences in academic attainment. If entity theorists feel that effort is undesirable and ineffective, then they may simply not do what it takes when they hit schoolwork that demands energy and persistence. Incremental theorists, viewing effort as a more trustworthy ally, may have clearer paths to achievement.

In fact, students' responses to our hypothetical failure scenarios supported this idea. We told the students to pretend that the following really happened to them:

> You start a new class at the beginning of the year and you really like the subject and the teacher. You think you know the subject pretty well so you study a medium amount for the first quiz. When you take the quiz, you think you did okay, even though there were some questions you didn't know the answer for. Then the class gets their quizzes back and you find out your score: You only got a 54, and that's an F.

Among other things, we asked students, "What do you think you would do next?" and we gave them a series of options to rate. The options included the following:

> "I would spend more time studying for tests."

"I would try not to take this subject ever again."
"I would try to cheat on the next test."

Incremental theorists tended to give higher ratings than entity theorists to the first option. In other words, students with an incremental theory would readily apply the additional effort they believe is required to do well in the future.

The other two options can be seen as low-persistence or low-effort choices. They don't suggest that the failure can be overcome through effort and instead suggest that the student avoid further toil in this subject area. Entity theorists gave higher ratings to these options. They were somewhat more likely than incremental theorists to say that they would try not to take the subject ever again, and they were significantly more likely to say that they would try to cheat on the next test! These are hardly plans that would promote mastery of the difficult material that was facing them. So although we were delighted that the students could be so honest about their plans and feelings, we were disconcerted that this was a way that entity theorists considered coping with a challenge.

These two studies (Henderson & Dweck, 1990; Sorich & Dweck, in press) examined real-world coping with academic challenges, and found that students holding an incremental theory fared significantly better—emotionally and intellectually—than those holding an entity theory. Students holding an incremental theory were less prone to doubt their abilities in the face of difficulty, and were more prepared to respond to difficulty with high, sustained effort. This may well be the reason that they ended up with higher grades.[1]

☐ Theories of Intelligence Across the College Years

A large-scale study done at the University of California at Berkeley by Richard Robins and Jennifer Pals recently tested our model in college students (Robins & Pals, 1998). They examined whether students' theories of intelligence predict their achievement goals, their helpless versus mastery-oriented responses, and their grades over the college years. Robins and Pals were also very interested in whether students' theories predict changes in their self-esteem as they go through college.

First, they found that theories of intelligence did indeed predict the goals students valued in college. Entity theorists emphasized performance goals, while incremental theorists emphasized learning goals (e.g., "The knowledge I gain in school is more important than the grades I receive").

Next they found that entity theorists were more likely than incremental theorists to blame their failures on low ability, feel distressed and ashamed about their academic performance (their college GPAs), and report that they tend to give up in challenging situations ("When I fail to understand something, I become discouraged to the point of wanting to give up"). Incremental theorists, on the other hand, when asked to describe how they felt about their college GPA, reported that they tended to feel more determined and inspired. They also reported that they tended to persist more in challenging situations ("When something I am studying is difficult, I try harder"). Thus, entity theorists displayed the cognitive, affective, and behavioral components of a helpless response, whereas the incremental theorists displayed the more mastery-oriented reactions.

In this study, entity theorists had entered Berkeley with higher SAT (Scholastic Aptitude Test) scores; however, this did not translate into higher achievement. Thus, entity theorists appear to have underachieved relative to their test scores. What happened to the self-esteem of the two groups? On average, entity theorists had lower levels of self-esteem than incremental theorists during college, and the gap widened significantly over the 4 years. This suggests that the college experience served to erode the self-esteem of the entity theorists relative to that of the incremental theorists. Specifically, a path analysis indicated that the performance-goal focus of the entity theorists, along with their negative affective responses to their academic work (e.g., shame, distress) and their helpless behavioral responses all contributed significantly to their loss in self-esteem.

Finally, Robins and Pals (1998) traced the stability of students' theories of intelligence over their years of college and found the theories to be quite stable $r = .70$ from one year to the next and $r = .64$ over three years, corrected for any unreliability in the measure). This shows that although implicit theories can be influenced when we manipulate them directly in our experiments, they tend to be rather stable individual differences, with widespread ramifications.

What if students' implicit theories were manipulated in real life? Would this make a difference for how students fare in college?

☐ Narrowing the Achievement Gap by Teaching an Incremental Theory: Reducing Stereotype Threat

Joshua Aronson of the University of Texas has launched an important series of studies to address the achievement gap between African American students and their Caucasian counterparts during college. This gap is evident even for African American students who have a high degree of college preparation, for example, very high college board scores; they tend to perform much below what would have been predicted for them on the basis of their past performance (see Steele, 1997a, b; Steele & Aronson, 1995). Is it perhaps a question of motivation rather than one of ability?

To understand this phenomenon, Claude Steele, Joshua Aronson, and Steven Spencer (see Aronson, Quinn, & Spenser, 1998; Steele & Aronson, 1995; Steele, 1997b) proposed the idea of "stereotype threat." This is the threat that members of a stigmatized group can experience when they think they're in danger of confirming a negative stereotype of their group—for example, a stereotype of lower ability. In an elegant set of studies, Steele & Aronson (1995) showed that this concern, when evoked in a testing situation, can indeed undermine performance on intellectual tasks.

Aronson (1998) and Aronson and Fried (1998) have now gone on to show that the harmful effects of stereotype threat can be reduced when the ability in question is presented as malleable, or when students can be trained to think like incremental theorists. This has been shown both in lab experiments (cf. Wood & Bandura, 1989) and in real-life interventions.

The transition to college, like the transition to junior high school, can be a very challenging one. Aronson reasoned that the climate of a predominantly white college adds an extra burden for African American students. Coming up against the intellectual elite of the country (as at Stanford University, where the research was conducted) may evoke for them the stereotype of their group as having a lesser amount of fixed intelligence. This in turn may interfere with their achievement efforts. (For example, it could lead them to make low-ability attributions for any difficulty they may be having, create distracting doubts when they are trying to perform intellectually, or foster a defensive withdrawal of effort.)

To test this idea, Aronson and Fried (1998) decided to see whether teaching undergraduate students an incremental theory would reduce the stereotype threat and improve their college performance. For this purpose they used a short film presenting scientific explanations, researchers' testimonies, neurological graphics, and research findings to the effect that every time people meet a challenge, exert mental effort, and learn something new, their brain grows neurons and they become smarter.

This film was shown to groups of African American and White undergraduates and was accompanied by a lecture that also stressed that intelligence can be cultivated. Next, to reinforce the incremental message, the students wrote letters to grade-school children teaching them their new view of intelligence and how it expands with work.

Aronson and Fried then compared the end-of-term (and end-of-year) grades earned by the students who had seen the incremental film to the grades of the students who had not. They found that for students who had not received the incremental message, the gap between the minority and majority of students was the same as before: The GPAs of the majority students were significantly higher than those of the Black students. However, for the students who *had* received the incremental message, the gap was appreciably reduced. In other words, Black students who learned the incremental theory of intelligence and the incremental approach to challenge and achievement, showed a marked improvement in college achievement. What's more, they reported enjoying school more and seeing themselves as more academically oriented than their peers in the control group.

☐ How Do the Theories of Intelligence Produce Their Effects?

We have seen that students' theories of intelligence affect their achievement and their ability to cope effectively. How does this happen? The two theories seem to create entirely different frameworks for students. Once students adopt a theory of intelligence, it affects what they value, how they approach intellectual tasks, and how they interpret and respond to what happens to them.

A belief in fixed intelligence raises students' concerns about how smart they are, it creates anxiety about challenges, and it makes failures into a measure of their fixed intelligence. It can therefore create disorganized, defensive, and helpless behavior.

A belief in malleable intelligence creates a desire for challenge and learning. In fact, some incremental theorists tell us that they worry a task will be too easy for them and, essentially, not worth their while. Setbacks in this framework become an expected part of long-term learning and mastery and are therefore not really failures. Instead they are cues for renewed effort and new strategies.

☐ Note

1. See Stipek & Gralinski, 1991, and Faria, 1996, for studies showing a relation between theories of intelligence and school performance in grade-school and high-school students, respectively; see Faria, 1996, and Hong, Chiu, Dweck, & Lin, 1998, for studies showing that theories of intelligence affect achievement choices and outcomes in other cultures as well.

CHAPTER

Theories of Intelligence
Create High and Low Effort

Imagine two college students. One works really hard. He attends his classes diligently, studies hard, and puts lots of work into papers and assignments. In general, he gets B's in his courses. The other has spotty class attendance, studies right before an exam, and tends to write his papers at the last minute. He also gets B's. Who has more ability?

You see a puzzle in a science magazine and it's labeled "Test your IQ!" You work on it for very long time, get confused, start again over and over, and finally make progress, but very slowly, until you solve it. How do you feel? Do you feel sort of dumb because it required so much effort? Or do you feel smart because you worked hard and mastered it?

In the previous chapters, we saw that *failure* has different meanings in the entity- and incremental-theory frameworks. In the entity-theory framework, it means low intelligence; in the incremental-theory framework, it is a cue to try something new. *Effort* also has different meanings in the entity and incremental frameworks. In the entity-theory framework effort measures intelligence, and it (like failure) signifies low intelligence. In the incremental-theory framework, effort is what turns on people's intelligence and allows them to use it to full advantage (cf. Covington & Omelich, 1979; Surber, 1984).

☐ The Meaning of Effort

To find out how different students view effort, Ellen Leggett and I (Leggett & Dweck, 1986) first measured eighth-graders' theories of intelligence and their goals. We then probed their beliefs about effort by asking them to agree or disagree with a series of statements. Some statements portrayed effort as a negative thing, where exerting effort means you have low ability. For example:

"If you have to work hard on some problems, you're probably not very good at them."

"You only know you're good at something when it comes easily to you."

"Things come easily to people who are true geniuses."

Other statements portrayed effort as a positive thing, where exerting effort activates your ability and allows you to use it to the fullest. These statements, for example, read:

"When you're good at something, working hard allows you to really understand it."

"When something comes easily to you, you don't know how good you are at it."

"Even geniuses have to work hard for their discoveries."

Students who embraced the entity theory–performance goal framework endorsed the first view. If you have to work hard at something, it means you're not good at it. If you're good at something, you shouldn't need effort.

Notice that these students were agreeing with statements that didn't say anything about how hard the task in question is. This means they believe that even on very hard tasks you shouldn't have to try hard if you have real ability. If you do have to try—even on very hard tasks—then you don't have the ability.

In the example I gave at the beginning of this chapter I portrayed two college students, one working hard for his B's and the other breezing along and getting the same grades. But I didn't mention what kind of courses they were taking. Maybe the one who was working harder took a much heavier courseload and much more difficult and demanding courses. In this case, it would be inappropriate to try to judge the two students' relative ability from the effort they expended.

Students operating in the incremental theory–learning goal framework had precisely the opposite belief. They viewed effort as something that, far from undermining your ability, allows you to fully use your ability and realize your potential. Even geniuses, the most able of people, need effort.

College students seem to feel the same way. In a study conducted by Claudia Mueller and me (Mueller & Dweck, 1997), entity theorists agreed significantly more than incremental theorists with statements such as:

"If you're really good at something, you shouldn't have to work very hard to do well in that area."

"I sometimes feel that the more effort you have to put into your school assignments, the less intelligent you probably are."

Students with the incremental theory squarely disagreed with these assertions.

Finally, in a recent study, Hong, et al. (1998) induced an entity or incremental theory in college students by giving them the *Psychology Today*–type articles I described earlier. We found that students who were taught the entity theory now thought high effort indicated low intelligence significantly more often than the students who were taught the incremental theory did.

What does this mean for students confronting a difficult task? This is exactly when high effort is needed. Yet what a conflict this poses for students with an entity theory pursuing a performance goal and eager to show high ability. High effort may be necessary for success on the task, but high effort will automatically spell low ability.

This means that when students are operating in this framework, their sense of their ability is continually challenged. It would be hard to maintain confidence in your ability if every time a task requires effort, your intelligence is called into question.

It also means that precisely when your greatest focus and strategizing is called for, you will be ruminating about the dangers of expending effort (and even worse, about the dangers of expending effort and still failing).

It is in this framework that you would expect to see defensive behavior, and you do. Frederick Rhodewalt (1994) predicted that entity theorists would be the ones who intentionally withhold their effort when they must confront a difficult task—by not studying enough before a test or by leaving things until the last moment—and that is exactly what he found (see also Midgley, Arunkumar, & Urdan, 1996). This strategy is termed *self-handicapping* (Berglas & Jones, 1978; Jones and Berglas, 1978) and the reasoning behind it goes like this: If you withhold effort and do poorly, you can still think highly of your ability, and you can preserve the belief that you *could* have done well had you applied yourself. If you somehow happen to do well anyway, then this is the supreme verification of your intelligence.

But by withholding effort, especially on important tasks, entity theorists may be sabotaging long-term goals for the sake of short-term judgments (Zuckerman, Kieffer, & Knee, 1998).

Perhaps the saddest result of this belief is that students may never come to *value* effort. Effort is one of the things that gives meaning to life. Effort means that you care about something, that something is important to you and you are willing to work for it. It would be an impoverished existence if you were not willing to value things and commit yourself to working toward them. Yet, as you may remember, Sorich and Dweck (in press) found that students holding an entity theory strongly held the goal of minimizing the effort they put into their schoolwork, even though they wanted to perform well.

Students holding these effort beliefs may also never come to understand the results that effort can produce. If the ideal is to coast along and do well, they may seek tasks, courses, majors, or careers that can be performed without much effort, rather than ones that allow them to stretch their abilities in unforeseen ways. One of the great pleasures in life is surprising yourself by attaining skills that you've admired and maybe even thought were beyond your reach. Yet, both Stipek and Gralinski (1996) and Sorich and Dweck (in press) found that students holding an entity theory had little faith in the effectiveness of effort.

So for entity theorists, compared with incremental theorists, effort is a sign of low ability, it is aversive, and it is believed to be ineffective.

When students are working within an incremental framework, there is no conflict about exerting the effort that a challenging task requires. Effort is entirely in harmony with the short-term and long-term goal of these students—learning.

These are the students who continually impress us in our studies by solving problems they're not supposed to solve and by attaining skills that are "beyond" them.

☐ When Do You Feel Smart?

We have seen that for students working in the entity-theory framework, all kinds of things call their intelligence into question. Unfortunately, many of these things, such as errors or effort, are necessary and inevitable in many learning situations. So, when will these students feel smart? And how does that differ from when students holding an incremental theory would feel smart? We decided to ask them.

As part of larger studies with grade school and college students, Elaine Elliott, Valanne Henderson-MacGyvers, and I said to students: "Sometimes students feel smart in school and sometimes they don't. When do you feel smart?" Entity theorists gave answers that were quite different from those of incremental theorists.

The grade-school children with an entity theory of their intelligence said they felt smart:

"When I don't do mistakes"
"When I turn in my papers first"
"When I get easy work"

In other words, these students felt smartest when they performed tasks easily, without errors, and more quickly than their peers. The entity theorists in our college sample gave us the same kinds of answers. They said things like "When I ace an exam" or "When the others are struggling, but it's easy for me."

This is just what we would expect given what we've learned about the beliefs and goals of students working in this framework. These findings give us even more support for the idea that challenge is often undermining to students with a fixed view of their intelligence and that their ideal situation is one in which they can coast past their fellow students.

The answers of students with an incremental theory provided an interesting contrast. The incremental grade schoolers said they felt smart:

"When I don't know how to do it and its pretty hard and I figure it out without anybody telling me"
"When I'm doing schoolwork because I want to learn how to get smart"
"When I'm reading a hard book"

The college students said similar things: "When I'm working on something I don't understand yet." They also said things like "When I'm using what I know to teach someone else." So here, we find that *using* their intelligence to confront the challenge of difficulty and confusion is what makes these students feel smart. What's more, instead of feeling smart when they see their peers failing or struggling, these students feel good about their abilities when they can use them to help their peers learn.

Thus, another feature of the incremental framework is that it can foster a more cooperative atmosphere among students because everyone can feel smart by applying their intellectual abilities to the problems they face. In the entity-theory framework, it is only the winners who can feel smart, and only if they did not have to work too hard to win.

It has become a common practice in much of our society to praise students for their performance on easy tasks, to tell them they are smart when they do something quickly and perfectly (see Damon, 1995; see also Berglas, 1990; Meyer, 1982). When we do this we are not teaching them to welcome challenge and learn from errors. We are teaching them that easy success means they are intelligent and, by implication, that errors and effort mean they are not.

What should we do if students have had an easy success and come to us expecting praise? We can apologize for wasting their time and direct them to something more challenging. In this way, we may begin to teach them that a meaningful success requires effort.

CHAPTER

Implicit Theories and Goals Predict Self-Esteem Loss and Depressive Reactions to Negative Events

As we have seen, holding an entity theory makes students vulnerable. But how vulnerable? Are they as vulnerable as people who have genuine psychological problems? For example, are they as vulnerable as people who are depressed? We were deeply curious about this because when people are depressed, they often respond to failure with self-indictment and helpless responses—just like entity theorists.

So in a study with college students by Wenjie Zhao, Claudia Mueller, and me (Zhao et al., 1998), we set out to compare the failure responses of entity theorists to those of students who were in a period of depression. How similar would they actually be?

To do this, we first gave students the Beck Depression Inventory (Beck, Ward, Mendelson, Mock, & Erbaugh, 1961), a questionnaire that asks 21 questions about symptoms of depression. For each symptom there's a list of statements, and the students picked out the one statement that best described how they'd been feeling in the past week.

There are mood symptoms, such as feelings of sadness or dissatisfaction. Here, for example, students had to choose one of four statements that ranged from "I do not feel sad" to "I am so sad or unhappy that I can't stand it," and from "I get as much satisfaction from things as I used to" to "I am dissatisfied or bored with everything."

There are bodily symptoms, such as changes in sleeping or eating patterns. Here, for example, students chose one of four statements that ranged from "My appetite is no worse than usual" to "I have no appetite at all anymore."

There are self-related symptoms, such as feelings of low self-worth. Here the statements ranged from things like "I do not feel like a failure" to "I feel that I am a complete failure as a person." Or "I don't feel disappointed in myself" to "I hate

44

myself." Finally, there are symptoms that relate to indecisiveness or lessened ability to focus.

On the basis of their answers, we identified students who were moderately depressed or worse, and they formed our depressed group. Although most of these students were not clinically depressed or unable to function, they were definitely experiencing a period of depressive symptoms.

We also measured students' theories of intelligence, and the students who were *not* depressed were divided into the two theory groups. In all, we had three groups of students: the depressed group, the nondepressed entity theorists, and the nondepressed incremental theorists. We could then see how these three groups responded to failure.

Over two experimental sessions, the groups reacted to a difficult intellectual task and to several hypothetical failures. Here, I focus on their responses to the hypothetical failures.

Students were given three vignettes that vividly described important failures. In one, they were asked to imagine that they ardently wished to go to graduate school in a certain discipline. However, despite considerable effort, their performance on the Graduate Record Examination (a critical factor in graduate school admission) was extremely disappointing.

In another vignette, they imagined that they had finally found a major that suited them, but again, despite notable effort, they did poorly on the midterm and final of a key course.

In the third, they imagined that they were taking a class that was critical to their future aspirations, but that they made a poor showing in a major class presentation, in sharp contrast to their classmates who had preceded them. Here is the third vignette:

> During your second semester at school, you took a very important course in which each student would have to present their essays to the class. Within a couple of months, some students presented their essays and all of them did very good jobs; their essays got good evaluations from both the professor and the classmates. Now it is your turn! You spent the whole night preparing for this presentation and chose your favorite essay. But after your presentation the next morning, it turned out that the professor and your classmates didn't seem to like it very much.

After each vignette students were asked: What would this make you think? How would you feel? What would you do?

We compiled and scored students' responses to see how students holding an entity theory compared with those holding an incremental theory and with those in the depressed group. Who would use the failures to measure and judge the self? Who would report strongly negative emotional reactions? Who would give up, and who would devise new plans for future success?

For almost all of the measures, entity theorists looked just like the depressed students, and both were significantly different from incremental theorists.

First let us look at judging the self on the basis of the failures. Students with an entity theory, like the depressed students, were more likely to judge their entire intelligence on the basis of the failure experience. When asked following each vignette "What would you think?" they said things like "I would think I was dumb" or "I would think I wasn't smart enough to make it." This response was quite rare among students with an incremental theory.

What was even more striking was the fact that students in the entity and depressed groups did not stop at simply judging and derogating their intelligence. Many of them went on to indict the whole self, saying that they would feel worthless, they would feel like losers, or they would feel like total failures (cf. Janoff-Bulman, 1979). Again, this response was rare among incremental theorists. Thus, entity theorists, like depressed students, were more likely to see failure as a measure of the self (cf. Abramson, Metalsky, & Alloy, 1989; Nolen-Hoeksema, Girgus, & Seligman, 1992; Peterson & Selgiman, 1984; Seligman & Nolen-Hoeksema, 1987).

What about emotional reactions? None of the students thought they'd be pleased by the turns of events we depicted, and almost everyone thought they would be at least disappointed or dejected. However, the entity theorists and the depressed students, significantly more often than the incremental students, said they would react to the failure with extreme negative emotions. They said, for example, that they would be devastated or that they would feel hopeless or totally depressed.

What would they do? Once again, the entity theorists looked very much like the depressed students in their desire to simply quit or escape from the arena in which the failure took place. They said they would drop the class, change their major, or forget about graduate school. In this they differed from the incremental students. The incremental students were significantly more likely than the other groups to lay out their plan for turning the failures into successes. They reported the new strategies or the heightened effort that they would apply in the future.

It's important to realize that the entity and incremental theorists came into the situation with a number of strong similarities. They had equivalent performance on an analytical-ability test we gave them, so it was probably not the case that their different reactions were based on differences in their intellectual skills. They placed equal value on doing well academically, so this was not a factor.

They also had equal confidence in their intelligence before the experiment, so the differences were not based on differing opinions of their intellect prior to the setback. This shows once again that confidence is not the key to helpless responses.

And there was no difference between them in their scores on the depression inventory, so the differences were not due to entity theorists being more depressed. Yet, when they confronted failure, entity theorists looked just like the depressed group.

The interesting thing was it did not even have to be a real failure to evoke the depression-like thoughts, feelings, and plans. For the entity theorists, just the idea of a major failure brought forth spontaneous reports of harsh self-judgments, extreme negative feelings, and a desire to escape rather than persist.

In a second study (Zhao et al., 1998, study 2) we again found that entity theorists reacted to failure scenarios in a way that was very similar to depressed students. Here, we assessed students' entity theories across several domains and found that the more entity theories students held, the more they looked like the depressed students as they reacted to the failures.[1]

In these studies we focused on nondepressed entity and incremental theorists and compared them with depressed people. We have not yet looked in detail at how implicit theories might affect people who are already depressed, but we are very interested in this question. In Zhao et al. (1998, study 2) we did look in a preliminary way within the depressed group. We found that those holding more entity theories were more depressed. Specifically, they had higher scores on the questions from the depression inventory that asked about self-worth and about negative affect—exactly the kinds of questions that reflect helpless reactions (as opposed to the questions that tap bodily symptoms or indecisiveness).

But we are also interested in the questions of whether an entity theorist who is depressed looks different in his or her coping from an incremental theorist who is depressed. In my teaching, I have noticed large differences among students in the extent to which they let things go when they are depressed. Some stop functioning, falling behind in school and letting their relationships suffer. Others struggle to keep things under control, so that when they "return" from the depression, they have a full life to go back to.

It might be the case that incremental theorists, even when depressed, maintain much more active coping in their lives than do entity theorists. Although they may not be functioning at the level of nondepressed incremental theorists, they may retain a belief in the importance and efficacy of effort. Entity theorists, even when they are *not* depressed, have less faith in what effort can do and derive less enjoyment from challenge and effort, so that when they *are* depressed, dealing with the demands of their lives may be more than they can manage. If these predictions are correct, it may mean that incremental theorists tend to have less serious and shorter depressions than entity theorists.

☐ How Goals Can Contribute to Depression

We saw in a previous chapter how performance versus learning goals could set up helpless versus mastery-oriented responses to setbacks. Since then I have focused mainly on how students' theories of intelligence can themselves foster these different goals and responses. But we now return, for the moment, to goals, for Benjamin Dykman of Washington State University has shown dramatically how people's goals can contribute to self-esteem loss and depression when they encounter negative events (Dykman, 1998).

As a first step in this impressive research program, Dykman took the performance versus learning goal distinction and expanded it beyond achievement into two broader classes of goals that people could pursue in all phases of their daily lives. He called the goal that was analogous to the performance goal a "validation-seeking goal," and the one that was analogous to the learning goal a "growth-seeking goal." He then developed a narrative portrait of the validation-seeking individual and the growth-seeking individual, and, guided by these narratives, created and validated a 36-item Goal Orientation Inventory to assess people's tendency to pursue validation and growth goals. Below are the narratives that describe the valid.tion-seeking and the growth-seeking individuals, each followed by sample items from the allied scales.

> Validation-seeking individuals are those having a strong motivational need to establish or prove their basic worth, competence, or likability. Stemming from this need to prove their basic worth, competence, or likability, validation-seeking individuals show an accompanying tendency to appraise difficult or challenging situations as major tests or measures of their basic worth, competence, or likability. In other words, validation-seeking individuals see their basic worth, competence, or likability as being "on the line" when faced with challenging or difficult situations. (Dykman, 1998, p. 143)

Items from the 16-item validation-seeking scale included: "Whether it be in sports, social interactions, or job/school activities, I feel like I'm still trying to prove that I'm a worthwhile, competent or likable person"; "I feel like I'm constantly trying to prove that I'm as competent as the people around me"; "I feel as though my basic worth competence, and likability are 'on the line' in many situations I find myself in"; "I feel like I'm always testing whether or not I really 'measure up.'"

> Growth-seeking individuals are those who have a strong motivational need to improve or grow as people, develop their capacities, and realize their potential. In line with Maslow's view of the self-actualized person, growth needs supersede such safety needs as concern about failure and self-esteem protection (growth-seekers make "growth choices" over "fear choices"). Thus, growth-seeking individuals are willing to confront challenge or adversity in order to grow, improve, and reach their fullest potential. Stemming from these growth needs, growth-seeking individuals show an accompanying tendency to appraise difficult or stressful situations as opportunities for learning, growth, and self-improvement. (Dykman, 1998, p. 143)

Examples of growth-seeking items are: "When I approach new or difficult situations, I'm less concerned with the possibility of failure than with how I can grow from the experience"; "My attitude toward possible failure or rejection is that such experiences will turn out to be opportunities for growth and self-improvement"; "Personal growth is more important for me than protecting myself from my fears"; "Realizing my fullest potential in life is more important to me than protecting myself from the possibility of failure."

What did endorsement of these two types of items predict? To find this out, Dykman conducted five studies in which he examined how well goal orientation predicted depression, anxiety, loss of self-esteem, and coping in the face of negative events.

In the first study, Dykman administered the Goal Orientation Inventory to a large number of college students, along with a variety of other questionnaires. In addition, he obtained their scores from the Scholastic Aptitude Tests (math and verbal). Consistent with our findings in the study by Zhao, Dweck, & Mueller (1998), there were no differences in Scholastic Aptitude Test scores as a function of goal orientation. Thus it was not the case that some students were continually seeking validation because they were less intellectually able than others.

However, there were strong relationships between students' goal orientations and other measures. First, validation seeking was a highly significant predictor of current depression, depression in the recent past, and general proneness to depression. Growth seeking was a highly significant *negative* predictor of the measures of depression: Those who scored high on growth seeking were less likely to be depressed, to have been depressed in the recent past, or to be generally prone to depression.

Validation seeking and growth seeking were also strong predictors of anxiety. Validation seeking predicted high levels of social anxiety, fear of failure, and anxiety about unfamiliar situations, whereas growth seeking predicted low levels.

In his next studies, Dykman (1998) looked at anxiety, coping, and depressive reactions in actual situations. The results he obtained on the earlier questionnaires were again obtained in these more real-life situations. Validation seekers were significantly more anxious about an upcoming midterm exam than growth seekers. In coping with very stressful life events, validation seeking predicted self-blame and disengagement, whereas growth seeking predicted more active, constructive coping. Finally, as their real-life levels of stress increased, validation seekers reacted with escalating depression far more than growth seekers did.

To study self-esteem loss in the face of setbacks, Dykman also asked students to respond to hypothetical scenarios. These were detailed narratives of life events, such as failing or doing well on an examination or being on a date that is going poorly or well. As expected, goal orientation did not predict reactions to the positive scenarios, but it did predict reaction to the negative ones. Students who were high on validation seeking were the ones who responded to the negative events with reports of greatest self-esteem loss.

In summary, these studies provide strong evidence that goal orientation can be an important factor in adaptive and maladaptive functioning, predicting depression, anxiety, self-esteem loss, and coping in the face of setbacks. It is now important to integrate these findings with our own findings on the relation between implicit theories and depressive responses to setbacks. As we have shown in our work, implicit theories and goal orientations are closely related, and it is highly possible that people with entity versus incremental theories of the self have strong validation-seeking versus growth-seeking goals.

☐ A Word About Self-Esteem and Self-Worth

Unlike our implicit theory measures and our goal measures, Dykman's goal-orientation measures are highly related to people's self-esteem. In our work, people's self-theories are typically not related to their self-esteem, their confidence in themselves, or their optimism that things will work out for them.

It is possible that Dykman's goal-orientation measures are somewhat more extreme than our theory or goal measures, and indeed that was his intention since he sought to identify goal-orientation styles that created high and low vulnerability to depression. Validation-seeking individuals are ones who are constantly riddled with the need to prove themselves and are worried that they will not succeed in doing so. Growth-seeking individuals seem much more upbeat and unafraid. Moreover, these tendencies are general. Validation-seeking individuals seek out validation for their competence, their likability, and their basic worth.

However, it would be interesting to see if validation seeking and growth seeking are still highly predictive of depression and anxiety when the effects of self-esteem are removed. In other words, does people's goal orientation make them more or less vulnerable to depression over and above their level of self-esteem? Our own findings suggest that it would.

Dykman also discusses the concept of "contingent self-worth" and proposes that people who are high in validation seeking have a sense of contingent self-worth: They feel worthy when they succeed and unworthy when they fail (see Baldwin & Sinclair, 1996; Burhans & Dweck, 1995; Covington, 1992; Harter, 1990). His proposal makes perfect sense in that the validation-seeking scale asks people directly about whether they are perpetually seeking to validate their worth and whether they feel that their worth is constantly on the line.

But I would also ask what kind of self-conceptions are likely to create a sense of contingent self worth? And I would suggest that the belief that one has fixed traits that are readily judged from one's behavior and performance—that is, an entity theory—is a belief that goes hand-in-hand with both validation seeking *and* a sense of contingent self-worth. Indeed, in later chapters I present research that confirms a strong relationship among implicit theories, goals, and contingent self-worth. I also show that the same treatment can produce all three.

In this chapter, we saw that implicit theories and goals can illuminate not just achievement processes, but even more fundamental processes of the self and even more basic coping processes. They can tell us who, in encountering difficulty in their lives, will maintain and who will lose self-esteem or a sense of worth; who will feel hopeful and who will feel devastated or become depressed; who will cope constructively and who will not. As with achievement, it is ironic that those who care most about proving themselves often act in ways that are least likely to bring that about.

☐ Note

1. As I discuss in Chapter 10, people can hold different implicit theories in different domains. For example, someone can believe that intelligence is a fixed trait but that personality is a quality you can cultivate (or vice versa).

CHAPTER

Why Confidence and Success Are Not Enough

☐ Why Confidence is Not the Answer

One of the reasons we have become so lavish, and perhaps indiscriminate, with our praise of students is that as a society we have come to believe that this will raise students' confidence.[1] And confidence, we believe, is the panacea.

We believe that if students have confidence in their ability all else will follow. They will feel undaunted by difficult tasks, never doubting themselves when they meet obstacles, and they will persist effectively.

Confidence is certainly a good thing to have. But our research has shown us, somewhat unexpectedly, that the confidence students bring to a situation often doesn't help them when they meet with difficulty (e.g., Henderson & Dweck, 1990; Hong et al., 1998). When we looked at students making the transition to junior high school (Henderson & Dweck, 1990), we saw that entity theorists with high confidence in their intelligence showed, as a group, a clear drop in their academic performance. What's more they were just as likely as the entity theorists with low confidence to say that they would question their intelligence (they would think, "Maybe I'm not smart") if they performed poorly in school.

I think the key to understanding this puzzling phenomenon is this: Within an entity-theory framework, no matter what your confidence is, failure and difficulty still imply low intelligence. The whole framework with its emphasis on measurement and judgment gives a *meaning* to negative outcomes (and to effort) that is undermining to students—even if they entered the situation feeling fine about their intelligence.

We have found the same thing in other research. For example, in two studies with college students by Hong et al. (1998, studies 1 and 2), we measured students' theories of intelligence, along with their confidence in their intelligence, and then we looked at the meaning they gave to failure. In both studies, entity

51

theorists with high confidence in their ability were just as likely as those with low confidence to view the failure as a reflection of their intelligence—and were significantly more likely to do this than the incremental theorists.

The entity theorists with high confidence may sometimes be better able than the ones with low confidence to later "rationalize" the failure (for example, by later questioning the validity of the test they failed), but their initial self-doubting response looks no different.

What appears to be important here is not so much the confidence you bring to a situation, as the ability to maintain a confident and nondefensive stance in the face of obstacles. This is much more difficult to do in the entity-theory framework.

Yet there is much research showing that confidence is a good predictor of academic achievement. How can we reconcile this with the findings I've presented?

As a matter of fact, we, too, have research findings showing that students' confidence in their intelligence is a good predictor of their academic achievement *when they are not facing difficulties*. When it is an ordinary school year and things are not much different from the year before, then students' confidence is clearly related to both how well they've done before and how well they will do that year (MacGyvers, 1993). It is when we look at difficult transitions or situations fraught with failure that we find that confidence loses its power to predict (Henderson & Dweck, 1990). It is then that entity theorists with high confidence lose ground. And that incremental theorists with low confidence gain ground.

The case of the incremental theorists is just as interesting. Here we also find that confidence often doesn't make much difference. Incremental students who have *low* confidence in their intelligence simply do not seem hampered by obstacles, and sometimes even look like the most challenge-seeking and persevering group (Bandura & Dweck, 1985; Henderson & Dweck, 1990; see Hong et al., 1995). They are the group that really blossomed during the transition to junior high (Henderson & Dweck, 1990). And in a study with college students they were the group that was least likely to blame their intellectual ability for their failure (Hong et al., 1995).

This is especially intriguing because in order to get placed in the low confidence group, these students had to express uncertainty about their intelligence on the questionnaire that measured confidence. But when they are having difficulty, their intelligence is not what they think of blaming (see also Erdley, Cain, Loomis, Dumas-Hines, & Dweck, 1997).

One reason this group is so hardy is that when you are pursuing learning goals, confidence in your existing ability is not that critical. After all, you are looking to increase your ability, not to demonstrate that you already have it. A modest opinion of your existing skills may even spur more of a desire to increase them.

These findings—the fragility of the confident entity theorists and the hardiness of low-confidence incremental theorists—again support the idea that the two frameworks give different meanings to what happens to students. In the measurement-oriented framework of the entity theory, failure seems to condemn intelligence, even for many students who previously were quite confident about it. In the learning-oriented framework of the incremental theory, failure gives information about how to adjust learning strategies and does not seem to have deeper meaning for the self, even for students who have clear self-doubts going into the situation.

Despite the fact that confidence seems unreliable within the entity framework and in some ways unnecessary within the incremental framework, it's still hard not to think that confidence is a good thing to have. Surely, having confidence feels better than not having confidence. Nevertheless, it is clearly not the panacea it is often assumed to be.

Let's now turn to a related assumption—the assumption that success breeds adaptive beliefs and effective responses to difficulty.

☐ Does Success Build Mastery-Oriented Responses?

An assumption closely allied with the belief that confidence will ensure effective behavior is the assumption that success is the means to this. It is the idea that if students have a history of success, they will have enough faith in their abilities to be able to cope with challenges successfully.

Intuitively, this makes a great deal of sense. After all, students who have succeeded many times should know that they can do it, and this knowledge should serve them well. Students with checkered histories should be more likely to lose heart when things get rough, because they know that things often do not work out.

The Case of Bright Girls

In our research we have found that the students with the most striking history of success are often the *most*, rather than the least, vulnerable. These are the bright girls.

In grade school they are far and away the highest achievers. What's more, this is usually before social prohibitions against females' achievement really gain momentum—before it becomes unbecoming for a girl to be too smart. This is not to say that there are no negative societal messages that reach girls' ears, but it is to say that grade school is the bright girls' arena, and, as a group, they outshine everyone else.

These bright girls may look very confident and well put together as they go about their academic work, and teachers probably do not think of them as vulnerable. This is because these girls can readily master what is asked of them in grade school. Yet as we will see, they are a group that does not want challenge (Licht & Shapiro, 1982). And when they are presented with challenge or obstacles, they are a group that readily blames their ability and falls into a helpless pattern (Licht & Dweck, 1984a, b; Licht, Linden, Brown, & Sexton, 1984; Licht & Shapiro, 1982; cf. Cramer & Oshima, 1992). Although this is not so in every study, it has been found repeatedly.

Bright Girls' Theories and Goals. You will remember the study by Ellen Leggett and me in which we measured students' theories of intelligence and then assessed their goal choices by offering them an array of different tasks to choose from (see Dweck & Leggett, 1988; Leggett, 1985). This was a sample of advanced, upper-track eighth-grade students, and although we will focus mostly on grade-school students here, we were struck by the gender differences that emerged in this study.

First, the girls were significantly more likely than the boys to hold an entity theory of their intelligence.

Second, when students held an entity theory, the girls were far more likely than the boys to choose the task that presented no challenge. Almost *all* of the girls with an entity theory of intelligence chose the performance goal task that was "easy enough so I don't make mistakes." Almost none of the boys did.

Barbara Licht did a series of studies on bright girls' vulnerability and also found that they did not relish intellectual challenge. In a study by Licht & Shapiro (1982) with fifth graders, bright girls explicitly reported that they liked tasks they were sure they could do well on. In contrast, bright boys wanted tasks they would have to work hard to master.

Bright Girls' Helpless Responses.   We first became aware that the bright girls were more vulnerable than the lower achieving girls in a study by Barbara Licht and me that I described earlier (Licht & Dweck, 1984a). This was the study where we taught grade-school students a new unit on psychology and we gave half of the students a confusing passage near the beginning of the unit. We then looked at how this confusion affected students' mastery of the material. Did initial confusion hinder students' ability to learn?

We had IQ scores for the students in that study and so we were able to look at how students' IQs related to their mastery of the material. Now let's assume that IQ tests tap students' current skills and tap skills that are similar to the ones students tend to use in school. If so, we would expect to see a relation between IQ scores and mastery of the material. On average, the higher a student's IQ, the more likely he or she should be to master the material.

This was true for the boys when they encountered confusion. That is, the higher a boy's IQ, the more likely he was to master the material.

The *opposite* was true for the girls who received the confusing passage. Here, hard as it was to believe, the higher the girl's IQ, the *less* likely she was to master the topic. Girls with higher IQs showed clearly poorer performance than the girls with lower IQs. This means that the high IQ girls were so thrown by the period of confusion that they did not learn as successfully as their lower IQ peers.[2]

More evidence of a helpless reaction in bright girls comes from other research by Barbara Licht and her colleagues (Licht, Linden, Brown, & Sexton, 1984). In this research, they took grade-school girls and boys at differing levels of school achievement (A, B, C, and D students) and gave them a helplessness task we described earlier (where success on conceptual problems was followed by difficulty). They monitored the students' changes in performance from the success problems to the failure problems to see which groups showed impairment and which groups showed improvement.

The findings were that the highest-achieving girls (the girls who were A students) showed the most helpless response of any group. They showed the largest drop in the level of their strategies when they went from success to failure. The high-achieving boys, by the way, showed the most improvement.

Don't Bright Girls Know They're Bright?   How can we understand the bright girls? Don't these girls know they are already bright and successful? Of course they do, but only up to a point, for in this self-measurement framework, you're only as good as your last success (see Pomerantz & Ruble, 1998; Ruble, Greulich, Pomerantz, & Gochberg, 1993). This would not be such a problem if life were one large grade school and the tasks it presented to girls were safe-looking and easily mastered by them.[3]

But the game changes dramatically as students go on in school and school begins to favor the risk-takers and persisters. This is when the bright girls will be at a disadvantage. Researchers find, for example, that the discrepancy between boys and girls in math achievement begins in junior high and high school, when new math subjects are introduced—and that it is often the bright girls who are creating much of this discrepancy (Astin, 1974; Fox, 1976). They are the ones who begin to lag farthest behind their male counterparts.

It is clear from our work that making girls' successes more salient to them, giving them more encouragement, or removing societal barriers to achievement, although important, will not be enough. What must be addressed is the whole framework in which these girls are operating, a framework in which challenge is a threat and errors are a condemnation.

The findings from all of this research demonstrate clearly that a history of brightness and success is no guarantee of a mastery-oriented response to challenge.

What if we took vulnerable students who were not high-achieving and showed them by giving them success that they could succeed? Would this lessen their vulnerability and help them be more mastery-oriented? One of my earliest studies addressed this question directly.

The Impact of Success Training

In this study (Dweck, 1975), I identified a number of grade-school students who showed an extreme helpless response to failure. Not only did they blame their ability when they failed, but they also fell into severe impairment. Some of them were so sensitive to failure that they did not recover their prefailure level of performance for several days. Their teachers agreed that these students were particularly wary of challenge and debilitated by failure.

In order to have a baseline I could use to assess change, first I carefully measured these students' responses to difficulty. I did this by giving them sheets of math problems each day until their performance on the problems became stable. Then, one day, on one of the sheets of problems, I inserted a few problems that were a little too difficult for them, and I looked at what happened to their performance. I looked especially at the problems that followed the difficulty. Even though they had been doing these particular problems for days, all of these students took far longer to solve them after the difficulty or even failed to solve them entirely.

I then divided the students into two equivalent groups and gave them each a different kind of training. The training took place over 25 sessions, and at the middle and end of the training I checked for changes in the students' ability to cope with difficulty.

One group received training that consisted largely of success. We did this precisely to test the idea that giving these students a history of success in the situation might build their expectation of success and allow them to cope better with any failure they might encounter. So in each session they received 15 success trials on which they completed new sets of math problems within the allotted time. The time limit always posed something of a challenge, so that the task would remain interesting and the successes would feel meaningful. The students seemed delighted with the experience.

The other group received training in how to interpret their failures. This was called "attribution retraining" because we were teaching a new attribution or explanation for failure. For them, 2 or 3 of the 15 trials in each session were failure trials. On these trials, students failed to finish the required number of problems within the time limit. They were stopped, shown how many problems they had needed in order to succeed on that trial, and told: "You needed [say] six, you only got five. That means you should have tried harder."

Their failure was now interpreted in terms of effort rather than ability. These were students who strongly blamed their ability when they failed, and we were teaching them to focus on effort instead.

In order to make this message credible, I made sure that the students fell short by only one or two problems and I made sure that by the end of the session they had reached the highest number we said they needed. (It is critical that students not feel you are just paying lip service to effort. A pat message to try harder will be tuned out very quickly.)

At the middle and end of training, I checked the effects of the two treatments by putting students back in the original assessment situation. Over several days I reestablished their stable performance on the sheets of math problems and then gave them the sheets that contained the too-difficult problems. How did the failure affect their performance now?

At the middle of training, there was no real change in the group that received the success training. They were no more able to deal with failure than they had been before. However, the group that got the attribution retraining—the group that was given a new meaning for failure—showed real improvement. Their decline in performance when failure occurred was less pronounced than it had been before the training began.

By the end of training, the group that got the success training still showed no improvement. In fact, some of them looked like they were *more* affected by the failure than they had been at the beginning. This group was not given a new meaning for failure, and, we found, still interpreted failure as meaning that they lacked ability. Perhaps in light of their considerable success, the failure, still signaling lack of ability, hit them all the harder.

In contrast, the group that got the attribution retraining improved greatly, to the point where several of them showed *better* performance after failure than they showed before it—just like the mastery-oriented students we described earlier. Also like mastery-oriented students, some of the students in this group spontaneously gave themselves instructions to try harder during the failure trials.

What was perhaps even more fascinating was that these students' teachers told me they had changed in the classroom too. The teachers didn't know which students had received which training, and they wished they could give me favorable reports on all the students we worked with. However, they singled out for special comment those students who were given a new meaning for failure.

They told me that some of these students, who had often been given less work than their classmates so they wouldn't feel overwhelmed, were now requesting more work. They also told me that the students were persisting more appropriately, as well as asking appropriately for help when they needed it instead of just giving up. Although the teachers tried to think of something positive to say about all the students we worked with, they were not able to think of comparable changes for the students in the success group.

Thus, training that gave students just success experiences did not help them to cope with failure, even though they showed confidence and enthusiasm while the success lasted. They still interpreted failure as an indictment of their ability and showed a clear helpless response. In contrast, training that gave students a new meaning for failure succeeded in helping them to cope with failure far more effectively than they had before. Many of them, in fact, began to look quite mastery-oriented. (For subsequent attribution-retraining studies, see Andrews & Debus, 1978; Chapin & Dyck, 1976; Fowler & Peterson, 1981; see also Anderson & Jennings, 1980; Schunk, 1982; for attribution retraining in the realm of social skills, see Hudley & Graham, 1993; see also Anderson, 1983.)

These findings tell us that students who show a helpless response do not simply lack success or confidence. Once again, we find that they are working within a framework where failure represents an indictment of the self—and it was this framework that had to be addressed before they showed more mastery-oriented responses. Just building students up within the same old framework seemed to be ineffective. It may have made them feel good in the short run, but it did not fortify them in the long run.

So what do we have? When students hold an entity theory, confidence and success are not enough. Confidence and success do not seem to breed a desire for challenge or the needed fortification against failure. Success will certainly give students a boost, while they are succeeding. But as long as they remain within the entity-theory framework, the vulnerabilities remain.

Yet so much of our child-rearing and educational efforts are aimed at providing success and boosting confidence within an entity-theory framework. We want to prove to our children that they are the smart ones, because we believe that's what they need to feel good about themselves and to fulfill their potential. But there are better messages we can give our children, better messages about what it means to be smart and about how to get smarter.

What's more, the confidence students need is *not* the confidence that they have a certain level of smartness, or that they have more of it than other students. The confidence they need is the confidence that they, or *anybody* for that matter, can learn if they apply their effort and strategies.

☐ Notes

1. For discussions of the lavish and indiscriminate use of praise to try to raise self-esteem see Damon, 1995; Seligman, Reivich, Jaycox, & Gilham, 1995; see also Berglas, 1990; Meyer, 1982.
2. The high IQ girls who did not receive the confusing passage did fine, and even better than other girls.
3. It may also be the case that the perfection bright girls achieve in grade school backfires. Maybe they come to define themselves by this perfection and then anything less is undermining. Anything less than their usual "A" performance may be a source of threat and self-doubt. In other words, they may come to adopt a framework of self-measurement and one that demands near-perfection for them to feel smart (see Blatt, 1995; cf. Pomerantz & Ruble, 1998).

CHAPTER

What Is IQ and Does It Matter?

☐ What Is an IQ Score?

Some years ago I read about an eminent scientist who, several years after winning the Nobel prize, found out his IQ. Somehow his early school records came into his possession and on them was his IQ score. What struck him immediately was this: The number was too low to have enabled his accomplishments. Someone with that IQ could not possibly have made the groundbreaking discoveries he had made. He freely admitted that had he known his IQ, he would never have dreamed of embarking on his scientific career.

Our first thought is that the test was wrong. It must have mismeasured his real IQ. Maybe it did. But maybe it didn't. Maybe it accurately measured his skills at the time, at least as far as what the IQ test assesses. The fallacy is in thinking that by measuring someone's present skills, you've measured their potential; that by looking at what they can do now, you can predict what they're capable of doing in the future (Ceci, 1990; Resnick, 1983; Sternberg, 1985, 1990).

Alfred Binet, the inventor of the IQ test, knew this wasn't true (Binet, 1909/1973). He invented the IQ test, not to measure children's fixed entities, but to identify children who were not thriving in the Paris public schools. He wanted to devise programs that would get them back on track and help them to blossom intellectually. Far from assuming that these children were irrevocably deficient, he held the view that their intelligence could be nurtured through the proper educational programs. Binet was a card-carrying incremental theorist.

☐ Can We Measure Potential?

Our first thought was that the scientist's mental endowment was mismeasured. The mental powers that were clearly there later must have been there all along.

Yet there are countless examples in the realm of athletic accomplishments of people who did not in fact have the requisite endowment but nonetheless went on to do groundbreaking things.

Take Glenn Cunningham, the record-breaking miler. As a child, he was trapped in a fire, lost part of his foot, and was told he might never walk again.

Or take Pete Gray, who had only one arm, and yet amazingly became a major-league baseball player.

We are not as tempted here to say that their physical endowments were misdiagnosed, that Glenn Cunningham really did have a whole foot, and that Pete Gray really did have a second arm—we just didn't see it at the time.

Why do we feel the need to do this with intelligence? Why do we insist on trying to measure intellectual endowment and predict potential? Why can't we accept that skills can grow, abilities can blossom?

Can we measure intellectual potential? No. We can measure what someone can do right now, and we can use our measurement to *try* to predict what he or she might do in the future, but we cannot really measure potential. What's more, all our predictions have a great margin of error. There's a great deal of error in trying to predict academic achievement from prior IQ scores, and if we want to predict success in life, IQ scores are of very little use (see Sternberg, 1985).

The enormous fuss over whether one group in our society has 5 or 10 more IQ points than another group is, for the most part, senseless. It would make sense to raise a fuss over this only if it spurred us to fight for greater equality of education. But it makes no sense to use this as an index of a group's potential, as an index of what they're capable of accomplishing with the right kinds of motivation and instruction (see Baron & Sternberg, 1987; Brown, 1997; Brown & Campione, 1996; Ceci & Williams, 1997; Howard, 1995; Hunt, 1972, 1979; Nickerson, Perkins, & Smith, 1985; Pintrich, McKeachie, & Lin, 1987; Resnick, 1983; Sternberg, 1985, 1990, 1997; Weinstein & Mayer, 1986).

☐ What Is Intelligence Anyway?

Throughout this book we have been looking at students who believe that intelligence is fixed and comparing them to students who believe that intelligence can be developed. But what do they mean by intelligence? Do entity and incremental theorists mean the same thing by intelligence?

We will certainly not settle the question here of what intelligence *really* is, for there is no agreed-upon answer. This is a topic that has been hotly debated within society and within psychology for decades (see Sternberg & Jensen, 1992). Some psychologists try to isolate pure intelligence, factoring out all personality and motivational factors (e.g., Jensen, 1969). Others see motivation as being part and parcel of intelligence and optimal intellectual functioning (e.g., Wechsler, 1974, the man who devised one of the most widely used IQ tests).

Cultures differ as well in this regard. Asian cultures see effort as being a major and integral part of intelligence, much more so than Americans (Stevenson, Lee, Chen, Stigler, Hsu, & Kitamura, 1990).

What about entity and incremental theorists? Aside from disagreeing on the malleability of intelligence, do they disagree about what intelligence is? Indeed they do.

In a study with college students, Claudia Mueller and I (Mueller & Dweck, 1997) asked the students to define intelligence. When we analyzed students' definitions we found, first, that entity theorists, significantly more often than incremental theorists, defined intelligence as a person's inherent capacity or potential. Incremental theorists significantly more often defined intelligence as a person's skills and knowledge.

Second, many entity theorists explicitly ruled out effort or motivation as part of intelligence or as something that enhances intelligence. Many incremental theorists, on the other hand, explicitly included effort and motivation as integral parts of intelligence.

Here are some examples of how entity theorists complete the sentence "I define intelligence as . . ."

"Inborn ability to learn and evaluate complex ideas. I don't believe it can be learned from books"

"The ability to survive with the least effort while still reaping enormous gains"

"The innate capacity for problem-solving, analysis, and innovation which each human being is born with (at different levels). Hence effort does not affect basic intelligence"

"Something innate. One can go to school to be educated (academically), but one doesn't have to go to school to be smart!"

Incremental theorists, in contrast, said, "I define intelligence as . . ."

"The amount of knowledge one possesses and how they use it"

"How much effort you put in to something and [your] willingness to learn and do all that you can to fully understand it"

"Someone who knows how to work hard and sets out to accomplish a certain task"

"The capacity to understand something and think about it, not just mimicking the facts. Intelligence should be about the effort that goes into opening oneself to the world and new things"

We got just as interesting results when we asked fifth graders to define intelligence (Mueller & Dweck, 1998). Entity theorists told us that intelligence is simply about smartness or IQ:

"What your IQ is or how smart your are"
"Intelligence is how smart you are"
"Very smart, brilliant, or bright"

But incremental theorists, once again, put the emphasis on knowledge and effort:

"I think it's what you know"

"How much you look at a problem and check it over to find stuff wrong"
"I think it is to try your best"
"Studying hard"
"Intelligence is how hard you work to do something"

Claudia Mueller and I (Mueller & Dweck, 1997) also asked college students to complete the equation:

$$\text{Intelligence} = \underline{\hspace{1cm}} \% \text{ effort} + \underline{\hspace{1cm}} \% \text{ ability.}$$

Entity and incremental theorists completed this equation quite differently. The equation, by its very nature, suggested that both factors were part of intelligence, and so virtually everyone filled in something for both effort and ability. However, incremental theorists put a good deal more weight on effort. In fact, for them, *most* of intelligence was effort. They filled in the equation as follows:

$$\text{Intelligence} = 65\% \text{ effort} + 35\% \text{ ability.}$$

Entity theorists, in contrast, put more weight on ability in their intelligence equation. For them it was the just the reverse:

$$\text{Intelligence} = 35\% \text{ effort} + 65\% \text{ ability.}$$

These findings really illuminate students' theories of intelligence. Those who think of intelligence as a fixed trait are the ones who define intelligence as consisting more of innate capacity. Those who think of intelligence as a malleable quality are the ones who define it more in terms of what you know, what you can do, and how hard you try—things that are far more under our personal control than something like innate capacity.

☐ Who's Smarter: Someone Who Works Hard or Someone Who Doesn't?

After our earlier discussion of the meaning of effort, you will not be surprised to learn that we get different answers to this question from entity and incremental theorists. Once again, in several studies where we asked students to judge the intelligence of others, we found that effort is a more important part of intelligence for incremental theorists.

In one study, Claudia Mueller and I (Mueller & Dweck, 1997) asked college students to imagine they were deciding who should be admitted to an elite honors program in a high school. We gave them a number of candidates to rate. Some had high College Board Examination scores (seen by many as reflecting intelligence) but were not working hard or earning high grades. Others had lower College Board scores but were working hard and earning high grades.

Entity and incremental theorists differed strongly in whom they thought should enter the honors program. Entity theorists favored admitting the "higher ability" students even when they were not achieving as well. Incremental theorists favored the students who had worked and achieved higher grades even if their test scores were not as high. Thus entity theorists seemed to care more about the ability students had revealed on a test, whereas incremental theorists seemed to care more about what students had accomplished through their studies.

In another study, by Hong et al. (1998, study 4), college students were told: "Students A and B ranked first and tenth on a class test. Student A was a diligent student; every week he studied what was taught. Student B only studied before the test." They were then asked to indicate which student they thought was more intelligent. This is quite similar to the question I posed at the beginning of the chapter on effort. Entity theorists were significantly more likely than incremental theorists to think that Student B, the last-minute studier, was the smarter student. In fact, the great majority of entity theorists thought that this student, who did pretty well without working hard, was the smarter one.

These findings tell us again that effort is a much more important part of intelligence for incremental theorists than for entity theorists, whereas effortless ability is a much more important part of it for entity theorists.

In sum, students' theories of intelligence and their definitions of intelligence appear to go hand in hand. It is much easier to believe in malleable intelligence when intelligence is about skills, knowledge, and effort—although it is possible to believe in malleable capacity, as Alfred Binet did.

The goal of this book is not really to resolve what intelligence is, but rather to ask: What is the most useful way of thinking about intelligence and what are the consequences of adopting one view over another? I think our research findings speak very clearly to this issue.

CHAPTER

Believing in Fixed Social Traits: Impact on Social Coping

We have seen that people have theories about their intelligence and that these theories have major consequences. But clearly intelligence is not the only attribute people have. They obviously have many others, including personality and social attributes, and people care greatly about these qualities.

Do people hold the different implicit theories about these attributes? Do some people think their personality is a fixed trait, while others think it is a malleable quality? And do the implicit theories carry with them similar consequences? These are questions we were very eager to answer.

☐ Helpless and Mastery-Oriented Patterns in Social Situations

Some years ago, Therese Goetz and I (Goetz & Dweck, 1980) showed that certain children exhibit a helpless response when they meet with a social rejection, whereas others display a more mastery-oriented response—and these responses look very much like the helpless and mastery-oriented responses students show on achievement tasks. Let's take a look at these patterns, and then go on to research that linked these patterns to students' implicit theories and goals.

In the Goetz and Dweck study (1980), fourth- and fifth-grade students one at a time tried out for a pen-pal club. In fact, Goetz formed a real pen-pal club for this study, and all children who participated were later matched with a pen pal, who had similar interests, in another part of the country. To try out for the club, the student composed a sample letter to a pen pal. To help them, we gave students a list of points they might want to put into their letter. This included the kinds of questions they might ask and the types of information about themselves they might want to convey, such as information about their family, their school, or the activities they enjoy. Each child was also given a chance to make some notes and to practice the letter for a while.

When children were ready, their pen-pal letter was recorded and, they were told, transmitted to a representative of the pen-pal club for evaluation. After a pause, children were informed that the representative was not sure yet about their joining the club, but that they should try again. We made this feedback as mild and encouraging as possible. If any children seemed upset, we immediately informed them of their acceptance into the pen-pal club. Otherwise, they composed a second letter to the same person—which gained them immediate and enthusiastic acceptance.

We then analyzed children's second letters, comparing them to their first ones, to see how they responded to the temporary rejection. What would be the adaptive thing to do if you wanted a pen pal, and all the children in the study had indicated that they did? Well, if the first letter didn't quite work, clearly some revisions needed to be done. So, when we looked at the second letter in relation to the first, we looked at how much revising the children did, particularly how much new information was offered.

We found that some of the children sent the same letter over again, without the slightest change, whereas others revised their letters substantially, for example, by including new, self-revealing content and explicitly friendly overtures ("I'd like to be your friend"). There were no differences between these children in the length or quality of their original letters, but there were striking differences in their responses to the social setback.

What's more, as in the achievement situations, these responses were linked to children's attributions for rejection. The children who showed the most severe disruption were the ones who attributed social rejection to their personal incompetence, for example, not being good at making or keeping friends (see Anderson, 1983). This means that just as the helpless children attributed their achievement failures to a lack of ability, so the helpless children attributed their rejections to a lack of social ability. The children who showed the more mastery-oriented responses made a variety of other attributions. Unfortunately, we did not include effort attributions among the attributions children could choose from in this study, so we could not tell whether the mastery-oriented response was most strongly related to these attributions, but we did include such attributions in the next study.

☐ Social Goals

We have now seen that the helpless response in social situations looks very much like the helpless response in achievement situations. Do performance and learning goals play the same role in social situations as they do in achievement situations? The next study (Erdley et al., 1997, study 1) was designed to tell us whether children's social goals can actually create the helpless and mastery-oriented responses.

As in the Dweck and Goetz study (1980), fourth- and fifth-grade students tried out for a pen-pal club. However, before they composed their try-out letter, they were given instructions that emphasized either a performance goal (for half of the students) or a learning goal (for the other half). The students in the performance-goal group were told that the pen pal try-out would give them a chance to make a new friend, but the try-out was presented as a test of their social ability:

> The important thing is, we'd like to see how good you are at making friends. Think of it as a chance to see how good you are at making friends too.

The students in the learning-goal group were also told that the try-out would give them a chance to make a new friend, but here the try-out was presented as an opportunity to improve their social skills:

> The important thing is, this will give you a chance to practice and improve your ways of making friends. So think of it as a chance to work on your skills and maybe learn some new ones.

The students then composed their sample letter and received the mild, temporary rejection (again in the form of the representative's not quite being sure yet), along with the encouragement to try again. After that, they composed their second letter. The question was whether the two groups would now respond differently to the setback. Would the performance-goal group be more vulnerable to a helpless response? Would the learning-goal group show more mastery-oriented responses, as in achievement situations (for example, in the study by Elliott & Dweck, 1988)?

We found that the groups did indeed differ both in their actions following the setback and in their attributions for the setback.

First, although the performance-goal group and the learning-goal group did not differ at all in the length, quality, and general content of their initial letters, the second letters of the two groups looked quite different. The students in the performance-goal group included fewer kinds of information in their second letter than the children in the learning-goal group. (The performance-goal group's letters tended to get shorter after the setback, whereas the learning-goal group's letters tended to get longer.)

In particular, the children in the performance-goal group decreased the information about themselves that they were willing to reveal. In contrast, the children in the learning-goal group not only showed continued willingness to reveal themselves but also showed an increase in their expression of positive feelings (e.g., "I like to meet new people," "I really like talking to you"). Thus the letters of the children in the performance-goal group became more restricted and less personal, whereas the letters of those in the learning-goal group continued to be rich, self-revealing, and openly positive. In short, those children with learning goals appeared to take a more constructive, mastery-oriented stance toward the setback.

Following their enthusiastic acceptance into the pen-pal club, students' attributions for the initial setback were probed. The researcher told them the kinds of things other children had thought about when they first heard that the representative wasn't sure yet ("It made me wonder: Am I a likable person? Am I not so good at making friends? Are we too different? Did I not try hard enough?"), and she asked them to indicate how much they had thought each of the different thoughts. The children in the learning-goal group endorsed the effort choice (wondering if they had not tried hard enough) far more than the children in the performance-goal group. Thus, for the learning-goal group, mastery-oriented behavior was accompanied by a mastery-oriented emphasis on effort.

Students in the performance-goal group differed from their learning-goal counterparts on one of the other choices. Students in the performance-goal group chose the incompatibility attribution ("Are we too different?") significantly more than the students in the learning-goal group. Although this attribution does not condemn the self, incompatibility is a fairly unchangeable thing. It is something that is not likely to be altered by further action, and therefore something that would not encourage persistence.

In summary, when students were focused on a learning goal in a social situation (practicing and improving their social skills), they displayed a more mastery-oriented response to rejection than when they were focused on a performance goal (evaluating their social skills). The goals directly produced the different responses. These results closely paralleled what we had found in achievement situations and led us to take the next step.[1]

☐ Theories of Personality

The next step was to find out whether students' theories about their personality directly predict their goals. Does a belief in fixed personality lead people to be concerned with how they are judged in social situations, so that they focus more on validating themselves? Does a belief that personality is malleable lead people to seek social situations in which they can grow, so that they focus more on developing themselves and their relationships?

In two studies, one with late grade school students (Erdley et al., 1997, study 2) and one with college students (Kamins, Morris, & Dweck, 1996), we addressed these questions. In both studies, we measured students' theories about their personality and their social goals and then looked to see whether they were related.

In the first study, we measured students' theories about their personality by asking them to agree or disagree with statements such as: "You have a certain personality, and it is something that you can't do much about," or, "Either you have a good personality or you don't and there is really very little you can do about it." As with intelligence, those who agreed with this fixed view were classified as entity theorists; those who tended to disagree were classified as incremental theorists.[2]

With a second questionnaire, which contained six hypothetical social situations, we assessed students' social goals. Each scenario vividly depicted a social situation that required a decision, such as which children to invite to a birthday party, what to say to a new classmate at lunch, or which children to send valentines to. At the end of each scenario we listed three goals that could be pursued in that situation, and students rated the extent to which they would pursue each of them. One goal involved learning or developing relationships (for example, inviting the kids you would like to know better, talking honestly about what you like and finding out what the other child likes, or making a valentine for a new child you'd like to know better).

The second goal choice was a high-risk performance goal that, if attained, would gain the child status and approval (for example, inviting the most popular kids in the class, talking about all your friends to try to impress the child with your popularity, making a valentine for the most popular child in the hope that she or he would send you one, too).

The third goal choice was a low-risk performance goal that minimized the risk of rejection (for example, inviting the kids who are sure to say yes, talking about anything the new child wants so that she or he will be sure to like you, or making a valentine for someone who was your valentine before and will definitely send you one).

What was the relation between holding an entity versus incremental theory of your personality and choosing performance versus learning goals to pursue? The learning-goal choices we offered were, unfortunately, too attractive to everyone. Everyone said they wanted very much to develop new relationships. In real life, taking such initiative involves some risk. In our actual achievement experiments there is often real risk in choosing the learning goal, because when they make the choice, the students believe they may really make a lot of mistakes and not look very smart. But here, on the questionnaire, there is no risk, and an attractive choice can draw universally high agreement.

However, there was a highly significant difference between the entity and incremental theorists in their endorsement of the performance goals. Students who believed their personality was a fixed trait were more interested in validating themselves—in courting status and approval and in avoiding rejection—than were students who believed in malleable personality. This was particularly true for the low-risk performance goals; that is, compared with incremental theorists, entity theorists were especially eager to ensure social acceptance and avoid the risk of rejection or negative evaluation.

I should also mention that in the previous study (Erdley et al., study 1) we measured students' theories of their personality before they came into the pen pal try-out. Over and above the differences we found for the different social goals we gave to the students, we found an important difference in the attributions of the entity and incremental theorists. When asked to explain their initial failure, students who held an entity theory of their personality chose the social-incompetence attribution ("Am I not so good at making friends?") significantly more than the students who held an incremental theory. So, just as in the domain of intelligence, students who hold an entity theory of their personality are more likely to condemn an important attribute of the self when they meet with setbacks.

This means that the model that we developed to explain helpless responses to failure in achievement situations can also help to explain helpless responses to rejection in social situations. Students who believe in fixed personality are more likely to endorse performance goals; holding an entity theory and focusing on performance goals make them vulnerable to helpless responses when rejection occurs.

☐ Theories Predict Goals in Intimate Relationships

In our next study, with college students (Kamins, Morris, & Dweck, 1996), we examined students' performance versus learning goals in intimate relationships. We reasoned that some people want mostly to be confirmed and validated in their romantic relationships, whereas others want to be challenged to grow, even if it means being confronted with their weaknesses. So, in this study, we assessed students' goals in their intimate relationships and then looked to see whether students with different theories about themselves had different goals in their relationships.

On the goal questionnaire, we said, "We are interested in students' views on their 'romantic' relationships. Please rate the items below in terms of what is important to you in a relationship." We then presented 16 different items, half describing self-validation concerns (performance goals) and half describing self-growth concerns (learning goals). The self-validation items included: "someone who worships me," "someone who thinks I'm perfect," "elevates me in my parents' eyes," "gives me status on campus," and "makes me look good." The self-growth items included: "someone who challenges me to address my weaknesses," "someone who challenges me to grow," "makes me understand things about myself I should work on," "gives me experience understanding others," and "prompts me to confront and change my faults."

We classified the students as holding an entity or incremental theory of themselves based on a questionnaire that was administered as part of a separate study. Here we used a more general measure that did not refer to any specific attribute of the self but referred instead to the person as a whole. Students were classified as entity or incremental theorists based on whether they consistently agreed or disagreed with such statements as "The kind of person I am is something basic about myself and it can't be changed very much," "I can do things differently, but the important parts of who I am can't really be changed," and "I am a particular kind of person and there is not much that can be done to really change that."

We use this measure when no one particular attribute of the self (such as intelligence or personality) is at issue, but rather more than one attribute can be involved, as is true in romantic relationships. In these relationships, the validation one seeks or the growth one seeks can be for one's character, one's personality, or one's skills in a variety of different areas.

When we looked at how strongly entity and incremental theorists endorsed the performance versus learning goals for their romantic relationships, a very strong difference emerged. Although both entity and incremental theorists endorsed both types of goals, they did so to different degrees. When we looked at the performance goals, we saw that students with an entity theory of themselves were far more interested in gaining validation from a romantic partner than were students with an incremental theory of themselves. When we examined the results for the learning goals, we found that the students with an incremental theory of themselves were far more interested in the growth-promoting aspects of a relationship.

Could it be that students with the two different theories differ in self-esteem? Maybe the entity theorists have lower self-esteem and therefore have greater need of a relationship that boosts their egos. In the same vein, maybe incremental theorists have higher self-esteem and can more easily take and profit from criticism from a partner. Yet just as we saw earlier in our discussion of intelligence and achievement, people's levels of self-esteem are not playing a role here. The entity and incremental theorists in this study did not differ at all in their level of self-esteem.

Could it be that one group is trying to make themselves look good by choosing what seem to them to be the more desirable options, while the other group is being more honest? To test for this possibility, we administered another questionnaire that required students to admit somewhat negative things about themselves in order to be wholly truthful. This "social desirability" questionnaire (Paulhus, 1984) presents actions and feelings that characterize virtually everyone at some point, and it asks students to report whether each is true of them. These are some examples: "Sometimes at elections I vote for candidates I know little about." "Would you declare everything at customs, even if you knew that it would never be found out?" "I am always courteous, even to people who are disagreeable." "I am sometimes irritated by people who ask favors of me."

If people present a positive face on one or two of the items, that is no problem, but if they consistently deny that they ever feel or do negative things and report that they always do and feel positive things, then this becomes suspicious and there is reason to doubt their responses on other measures. When we compared the answers of entity and incremental theorists on this questionnaire, they were entirely the same. This means that they were probably being equally honest in reporting their goals in their romantic relationships.

In summary, self-validation and growth are certainly not mutually exclusive, and, as I noted, both groups endorsed both types of goals to some extent. However, as we predicted, people with a fixed theory about their personal qualities were more concerned than others with validating themselves through a close relationship—having their worth confirmed and gaining status in the eyes of others. In contrast, people who believe in more malleable personal qualities were the ones who were most interested in having relationships that promoted their future growth.

☐ Implicit Theories and Their Impact on Actual Relationships

In my laboratory, we have not yet looked at how implicit theories affect people's motivation and behavior in their actual, ongoing relationships. However, C. Raymond Knee has conducted a fascinating study at the University of Rochester of college students who were involved in romantic relationships (Knee, 1998).

Thus far I have described implicit theories of the self—of intelligence, of personality, and of the person as a whole—and the differences between people who believe in fixed traits versus malleable qualities of the self. In his study, Knee assessed people's theories about relationships. He reasoned that people could have a relatively fixed view of relationships: Relationships have a certain inherent character and they are meant to be or not meant to be. He called this a *destiny* belief.

People could also have a more malleable view of relationships: Relationships develop over time through hard work and successful conflict resolution. This view he called a *growth* belief.

Knee (1998) predicted that the people with a strong destiny belief would test potential partners fairly quickly, make their judgment, and move on if the judgment was negative. In contrast, students with a strong growth belief, he thought, should take a more committed, long-term approach to their dating relationships. He also predicted differences in how people would respond to negative events within a relationship. Those scoring high on the destiny belief should distance themselves or withdraw from the relationship when things go wrong (a relatively helpless response), whereas those scoring high on the growth belief should engage in more active, mastery-oriented coping that would enable them to solve the problem and learn from the experience.

To test these ideas, Knee (1998) first developed a scale that separately assessed the destiny (fixed) versus growth (malleable) beliefs. The destiny beliefs were tapped by items such as: "Potential partners are either destined to get along or they're not" and "Relationships that do not start off well inevitably fail." The growth beliefs were assessed by items such as "A successful relationship evolves through hard work and resolution of incompatibilities" and "Challenges and obstacles in a relationship can make love even stronger." Of course, people can agree with both. They can think that there has to be some compatibility between people to start with, as well as some learning and growth over time. And many people did, but you can still ask whether strong destiny beliefs have the predicted effects and whether strong growth beliefs have their predicted effects.

Knee (1998) then identified undergraduate students who were in romantic relationships and followed them over a period of 6 months. He found, as he had predicted, that people with strong growth beliefs had a more committed, long-term approach to dating: They had fewer one-night stands and, what's more, they dated a particular partner for a longer time compared with people with weak growth beliefs. Also, as he had predicted, those with strong destiny beliefs tested their partners rather quickly and if they found the relationship wanting, moved on. That is, when destiny theorists reported low initial satisfaction with a relationship, that relationship soon ended.

Did destiny and growth beliefs predict how people coped with setbacks or stress within their relationships? To answer this question, Knee (1998) had students describe the most stressful event they had experienced during the semester and then asked them to complete a coping scale that assessed how they responded to the event (Carver, Scheier, & Weintraub, 1989). About a third of the students reported that their most stressful event involved a relationship, such as having a serious argument with their partner or finding out that they had been cheated on. An analysis of the coping strategies of these students showed that those who had strong destiny beliefs were likely to disengage from the relationship or the problem in the face of the negative event. They endorsed items on the coping scale indicating, for example, that they reduced the amount of effort they put into solving the problem as a way of coping with the stress.

In contrast, those with strong growth beliefs engaged in much more active coping designed to solve the problem, strengthen the relationship, and promote personal growth. They endorsed items indicating that they concentrated their efforts on doing something about the problem, made a plan of action, deemphasized competing activities, and tried to learn or grow from the experience.

In summary, this study examined how implicit theories play out in close relationships and yielded strong evidence that those with fixed versus malleable theories of relationships approach their relationships in different ways and respond in different ways to challenges and setbacks within those relationships.

We can now say that the ideas that we originally developed to understand how students think, feel, and act in achievement settings also hold the promise of helping us understand how people think, feel, and act in their social relationships. The ideas that help explain academic success and failure may help explain relationship success and failure.

☐ Notes

1. For other work on the role of social goals in adaptive functioning see Erdley, 1996; Renshaw & Asher, 1983; Wentzel, 1996.
2. Interestingly, a number of students have the same theory about personality as they do about intelligence, but many have different ones. This means, as I mentioned earlier, that someone can think that intelligence is fixed but personality can be developed, or that personality is fixed but intelligence can be developed. See the Appendix for our current Implicit Theories of Personality measure.

CHAPTER

Judging and Labeling Others: Another Effect of Implicit Theories

Is it possible to know people really quickly? Does their behavior give away their underlying intelligence and character? That is, does everyone have an essential self that shows through in their actions? In this view, some people are smarter than others and some people are more moral than others and if we watch them, we'll soon know who's who (see, e.g., Baron & Misovich, 1993).

Or is a person too varied to capture so easily? Does each person vary according to the situation and according to his or her goals, concerns, or state of mind, so that it's simply not possible to know quickly what someone is *really* like (see, e.g., Mischel & Shoda, 1995)? In this view, any behavior, whether it looks smart or dumb, or good or bad, may simply reflect the person's state in *that* situation or at *that* time and may not reveal more enduring qualities. Maybe someone looked dumb because he was nervous, maybe someone looked greedy because she was taking extra for someone else, maybe someone looked boastful and conceited because she was insecure about being taken seriously.

In this chapter, I show how people's entity versus incremental theories affect which of these two views they adopt (see Dweck, 1996b; Dweck, Chiu, & Hong, 1995). In the next chapter I show the consequence of these views.

☐ Judging the Self Versus Judging Others

We saw how people with an entity theory of intelligence quickly measure and judge themselves. They do this to find out how much fixed intelligence they have and to figure out what they have the potential to learn and accomplish. If they decide they have low fixed intelligence—which they might decide from one failure—then they set their sights lower. They may hope to learn and accomplish less than they otherwise might.

People with fixed theories about their personality also measure and judge themselves quickly, labeling themselves as deficient after a social rejection and curtailing their efforts to form a relationship.

This is what people do to themselves when they hold an entity theory. But how do they act toward others? Do they measure and categorize others as readily? And do they decide on that basis what others have the potential to learn?

Let us turn to research in which we assessed people's theories and then looked at how they measured and judged others.

☐ Judging Others' Intelligence from Their Success and Failures

First let's look at how grade-school students judge their classmates and find out whether entity theorists make more sweeping judgments of their classmates' intelligence from their performance. In a study by Gail Heyman and me (Heyman & Dweck, 1998), we asked second graders to explain why their classmates might do well on their schoolwork: "Think of kids in your class who get a lot right on their schoolwork. Why do you think they get a lot right?"

Children who held an entity theory were twice as likely as incremental theorists (54% to 23%) to simply chalk up the success to their classmate's intelligence, saying things like, "They're smarter than the other kids" or "It comes natural."

Children with incremental theories, in contrast, were much more likely to explain their classmates' successful performance in terms of what the students *did*—their study habits, concentration, persistence, or motivation. They said things like, "They practice at home," "They make mistakes and learn from them," "They tell themselves they can do it," or "They don't rush through their work." These incremental children, rather than concluding that their successful classmates simply had superior minds, focused on the processes that led to good performance.

We also asked children how they explained poor academic performance. We said, "I know some children who don't do well on their schoolwork. Do you think this means they are not so smart?" Even though children this age are reluctant to say negative things about their classmate's intelligence, entity theorists were twice as likely as incremental theorists to agree (38% versus 18%) that the poor performance meant a poor intellect.

Thus, when students looked at their classmates' performance, entity theorists were more likely to make decisive judgments of their classmate's intelligence. Incremental theorists preferred to explain performance differences in terms of how students approached their schoolwork—what they did to study, learn, and perform well.

What about older students? Would they see things the same way, with entity theorists making more global judgments of students' intelligence from their performance?

In a study by Ying-Yi Hong (Hong, 1994), college students were given information about the successes and failures of different students (of unspecified age) and were asked to explain why they thought these outcomes occurred. For example, they were told, "Mary got an A on her last two exams," and then they completed the sentence, "This probably occurred because . . ."

Entity theorists were significantly more likely than incremental theorists to explain the outcomes—both successes *and* failures—in terms of the students' intelligence. The students who did well succeeded because they were smart and the students who did poorly did so because they were not.

Incremental theorists took a different stance toward the students they were told about. They were, as before, more likely to explain the outcomes in terms of something the students did, such as how much they studied. They did not take this piece of information as an assessment of the quality of the students' minds.

In another study, C.Y. Chiu, Ying-Yi Hong, and I (Chiu, Hong, & Dweck, 1997) also told college students about the intellectual performance of other students. Here, for example, we told them that one student (Jack) outperformed another student (Joe) on one occasion. We then asked them to predict who would display the better performance in another, completely different, situation (cf. Kunda & Nisbett, 1986).

Entity theorists believed that Jack would win out again. They had apparently decided that he was the more intellectually able student. In sharp contrast, incremental theorists thought the *other* student, Joe, would come out on top in the new situation. Knowing nothing but the one piece of information, incremental theorists were not willing to make general intelligence judgments. They instead decided that the relative performance of the two students would probably even out across different situations.

In our earlier research it was surprising that entity theorists were willing to judge their own intelligence from just a few outcomes, sometimes only one. There, it could have been that their own failures were somehow magnified because of their personal significance. But here we see that entity theorists may also judge others' intelligence on the basis of a poor performance.

This is noteworthy given how very little we told them in each case about the student, the task, or the outcome.

First of all, they knew nothing about the students' motivation or behavior—or anything else about the students that could have affected their success or failure. Maybe the students who did well had worked harder and longer than the ones who did poorly.

Second, we told them nothing about the nature of the tasks. Maybe the student in the first study who did well (Mary, who got As on her last two exams) had taken a really easy course, and maybe the students who did poorly (in other vignettes) had taken really hard ones.

Third, in the study where one student outperformed another on one occasion, we did not say *by how much* the one student had outperformed the other. It could have been by a tiny margin.

Thus, students' theories of intelligence affect the way they see and react to their own successes and failures, *and* the way they see and react to others' successes and failures. In both cases, holding an entity theory leads students to see performance as a direct reflection of intelligence. In the case of their own failures, a judgment of low ability and a helpless reaction may result. In the case of others' failures, a judgment of low ability and a diminished belief in their capacity to learn may follow (see Brown, Palincsar, & Purcell, 1984; Gould, 1981; Wagner & Sternberg, 1984).

Holding an incremental theory of intelligence instead leads students to emphasize the processes that go into intellectual achievement and to recognize the many factors that cause good or poor performance. In the face of their own failures, they are likely to focus on their effort or strategy and to show a mastery-oriented reaction. In the face of others' failures, they are also likely to think about effort or strategy, and, as we will see in the next chapter, to consider what kinds of instruction or remedial actions would help the students overcome their difficulty.

☐ Judging Others' Personalities and Character from Their Behavior

Do entity and incremental theorists differ from each other in the way they judge *other* personal attributes of people, such as their personalities or moral character?

Our first evidence that they did came from a study by Cynthia Erdley and me (Erdley & Dweck, 1993). We showed fourth- and fifth-grade children a narrated slide show of a new boy in school (John), who had moved from another state in the middle of the school year, and who did a number of negative things. When the math lesson that first day began, the new boy felt lost. It was not material he had covered in his old school, so he leaned over and tried to copy from his neighbor.

Next, when he was asked to come up front and tell his new class about himself, he worried that the truth would not be impressive enough. So he made up a story about how his father was a Hollywood producer and how his family had a swimming pool at their house.

Later, when the class was doing its Valentine's Day project, the boy's cut-out hearts came out somewhat mangy and asymmetrical. Another child had left some of his extra, well-formed hearts on the art table, and our boy, eager to have a good-looking valentine, decided to use them for his project.

Finally, in order to finish his valentine, the boy took some magic markers back to his desk that were not supposed to be removed from the art table. Although the teacher announced that if the markers were returned by the end of the day, no one would get in trouble, the boy was too embarrassed to be seen returning them.

None of the boy's actions were malicious or harmed anyone else. And, in each case, the boy wrestled with himself about what to do. It was just that each time he was so eager to make a good impression and not embarrass himself that he chose the less honorable course of action.

We had also measured students' theories about personality. Just as students can have different theories about intelligence, as we noted earlier they can have different theories about personality. We did this by asking them to agree or disagree with statements such as "Someone's personality is something about them that they can't change" or "A person can do things to get people to like them, but they can't change their real personality."

We then compared those who thought people's personalities were fixed entities with those who thought people's personalities were malleable. First we compared them on how they rated the new boy on the basis of his behavior. We wrote "John is . . ." at the top of the page and then gave them a list of adjectives to rate. Everyone was expected to rate John negatively on the more specific ones, such as "dishonest," that related directly to his behavior, and they did. This is important because it shows that incremental theorists are not oblivious to negative behavior. They saw it and they held the boy responsible for it.

But we were particularly interested in how they rated the boy on the more global traits: "bad," "mean," and "nasty." More extreme ratings on these traits would mean that students took the boy's behavior as a sign of his deep, underlying nature. We found that the entity theorists made far more extreme ratings of the boy on these global traits than incremental theorists did. This was true even though the boy's behavior was not malicious or hurtful, and even though the situational pressures on him were emphasized.

In summary, this study was the first to show that when entity and incremental theorists saw someone behaving badly, they differed in how likely they were to attach a global negative label. Does this mean that entity theorists tend to be more mean-spirited, more misanthropic, more likely to dwell on other people's flaws? Our next studies showed that this was not the case: Entity theorists are also quicker than incremental theorists to attach global *positive* labels.

☐ More About Quick Judgments

We will now revisit two of the studies I presented earlier (Chiu et al., 1997; Hong, 1994). I used them to illustrate entity theorists' more rapid judgments of people's intelligence, but the studies also contained questions about personality and morality.

In the study by Hong (1994), you may remember, college students were given information about people's successes and failures and then were asked to complete the sentence: "This probably happened because . . ." These students were also given information about some positive and negative actions people had performed, ones that could reflect on personality or morality, and were asked to explain the actions by completing the same sentence. The positive behaviors included things such as "Arthur brought his colleagues some souvenirs from a trip," and the negative behaviors included "Alexis stole some bread from a bakery" and "Anna poured some orange juice over her classmate's painting."

Hong then coded students' explanations to see who thought the behaviors reflected more deep-seated personality traits and who thought the behaviors reflected psychological processes in the person (what she or he needed, felt, believed in, wanted, feared, liked, valued, etc.). She found that although both groups gave both kinds of explanations, they still differed significantly on both. Entity theorists gave significantly more global trait explanations, both positive and negative ones, than incremental theorists did. For example, entity theorists more often said that Arthur was good-hearted, or that Anna was mean, or that

Alexis was a thief. In other words, they were more likely than the incremental theorists to draw a conclusion about the kind of person someone was—good or bad—from one of their actions.[1] This means that entity theorists don't simply have chips on their shoulders, since they are quick to arrive at positive labels as well as negative ones.

In the study by Chiu et al. (1997), we saw that when college students were told that Jack had outperformed Joe on an academic task in one situation, entity theorists predicted that Jack would do so again in a completely different situation. We also asked students similar questions relating to personality (friendliness) and morality (honesty): "Suppose you observed Mary and Jane in one particular situation and found that Mary was more friendly [honest] than Jane. What do you suppose is the probability that in a completely different situation, you would also find Mary to be more friendly [honest] than Jane?" As with the intelligence scenario, entity theorists, unlike incremental theorists, expected the same person to be the honest or friendly one in a very different situation. Again, they seemed to have arrived at a trait from knowing a single behavior.

Is this because entity theorists are imagining a more extreme action than incremental theorists are? That is, when entity theorists are told about how a person behaved (stole bread, brought gifts, acted friendly), do they imagine that more bread was stolen, or more wonderful gifts were brought, or more expansive friendly behavior was displayed? Or, on the other hand, do entity theorists imagine that the same thing was done but put a more positive or negative evaluation on the act? In this case, the two groups would imagine that the bread that was stolen was the same bread, but the entity theorists would think that this was a much more negative behavior.

In fact, neither of these explanations is true. In several studies (Chiu et al., 1997; Levy & Dweck, 1998; Levy, Stroessner, & Dweck, 1998), we gave entity and incremental students (both grade-school students and college students) long lists of behaviors to rate. For example, in the study by Chiu et al., we gave college students a list of 35 behaviors to rate. Some of them were clearly positive ("risking one's life for another"), some were mildly positive ("making one's bed in the morning"), some were mildly negative ("interrupting someone who is speaking"), and some were clearly negative ("stealing a car"). When we compared the ratings that the entity and incremental theorists gave these actions, we found that their ratings were identical. In fact, the two groups did not differ on any of the 35 items. So when entity theorists attach a trait label to a person, this is not because they evaluate the behaviors as being more positive or more negative than incremental theorists do.

We (Chiu et al., 1997) then took the 35 behaviors, presented them to different students, and asked the students to tell us how much they thought each behavior was indicative of the goodness or badness of a person. In other words, how much did such an action reflect the underlying moral character of the person who performed it? Here we found a very clear difference between students who held different implicit theories. Entity theorists, significantly more than incremental theorists, believed that a person's underlying character could be revealed by a single behavior. This difference was true for the strongly positive and negative acts *and* for the weak ones.

☐ Do Implicit Theories *Cause* Differences in Judging and Labeling?

Is holding a particular implicit theory actually the cause of these differences? I have been talking as though it is, but it was important to address this question directly. So in the research by Chiu et al. (1997), we changed people's implicit theories and then looked to see if we also altered their tendency to form rapid trait judgments.

How can you change someone's theory about human nature in an experiment when these beliefs are often firmly held? As I have stressed before, people's beliefs, goals, or behavioral tendencies can be rather strong, but personality is dynamic. When a situation strongly highlights a different belief, goal, or mode of action, it can "tip" the person in that direction, at least temporarily. We saw this process in action in the studies I described earlier in which we manipulated students' attributions, goals, and theories of intelligence.

In the present experiment (Chiu et al., 1997, study 5), we oriented college students toward either an incremental or an entity theory of human attributes by having them read a vivid and compelling scientific article that espoused and documented one theory or the other. The articles, which were in truth written by Ying-Yi Hong, presented a variety of research evidence to support the idea either that people possessed a small set of rather fixed traits or that people possessed dynamic potentialities that could be developed over a lifetime. (The two articles are described in greater detail in the next chapter, on stereotyping.) Would reading these persuasive articles influence how students now judged others? For example, would those who read the entity-theory article now show a tendency to form more rapid trait judgments, compared with those who read the incremental-theory article?

Each student in the study read one of the articles and answered questions about it. This part of the experiment was said to be a study of comprehension of and memory for person-relevant information. The trait-judgment task, later presented as a third and separate experiment, contained some of the same trait-judgment measures we had used in our previous research.

For example, students were told that someone behaved in a more honest (or friendly, aggressive, or defensive) way than someone else and then were asked whether, in a completely different situation, the same person would still be the more honest one. They were also given a series of six behaviors (half positive, half negative) and asked to tell us how much each behavior was indicative of the goodness or badness of the person who performed it.

On both trait-judgment measures, the students who had read the entity-theory article made significantly stronger trait judgments than those who had read the incremental-theory article. That is, they made stronger predictions from a person's present behavior to his or her future behaviors, and they thought that a single behavior was a surer sign of someone's underlying moral character.

This study showed that holding an entity versus incremental theory can play a direct causal role in fostering trait judgments. When we learn that personality and character are unchangeable, we may quickly come to believe that how people act on one occasion tells us about their deeper traits. When we instead learn that personality and character are more fluid and more able to be cultivated, we are less certain that an action bespeaks a person's entire character and tells us how that person will be in the future.

Of course, we all tend to form some impression of people from our initial encounter with them, regardless of whether we hold an entity or an incremental theory. For example, when we experience someone behaving badly, we form a more negative impression and are more wary of the person in the future. Incremental theorists don't ignore negative behavior or think it is uninformative—this would be highly maladaptive. What differs for entity and incremental theorists is *how* negative that first impression is, how much they condemn the person's character, and, as we will develop later, how negative they expect the person to be in the future.

☐ The Belief that Traits Are Easy to Judge

Lisa Sorich and I were fascinated by entity theorists' more rapid judgments, so we decided to find out more (Sorich & Dweck, 1996). Did entity theorists make rapid judgments but really believe that it was better to wait and gather more extensive information? Or did they really believe that people's traits are transparent enough to be assessed swiftly?

To find this out we asked entity and incremental theorists to rate the truth of a series of statements. These statements depicted people's moral character as something that could be accurately judged quickly and easily: "Each person has a basic character, and you can tell what kind of person someone is even by details of their behavior or appearance." "A single act often tells you alot about a person's fundamental character." "It's fairly easy to tell what kind of person someone is by observing them on one or two occasions."

Entity and incremental theorists differed significantly on this issue: Entity theorists agreed with these statements and incremental theorists disagreed with them.

This means that the quick judgments entity theorists make are not impulsive ones that they are likely to think better of later. Rather, these judgments seem to grow out of a belief in character as a unitary thing that permeates virtually all actions and displays itself with great consistency. If this is true, then little time or effort is needed to decide what someone is made of. Thus entity theorists do not think they are making unwarranted snap judgments. They think they are reading others' traits from reliable information.

It might sometimes be good or even necessary to make rapid judgments, and when it is, someone who can make them may be at a real advantage. However, if you've made a snap judgment, you should probably be willing to revise it in the face of new information. If so, then a first impression, even if it were extreme, would be only a first impression. Yet our research indicates that entity theorists, once they have formed an impression, are often less sensitive to new, contradictory information (Erdley & Dweck, 1993; Plaks & Dweck, 1997) and may even try to avoid it (Plaks & Dweck, 1997). This may well be for the reasons we have examined—that entity theorists believe they are judging permanent traits that reliably express themselves in people's behavior.

Sheri Levy thought that perhaps there was yet another reason that entity theorists felt they were judging something deep and permanent about people. She thought that maybe entity theorists saw traits not simply as more fixed but also as more innate than incremental theorists did. This would mean that those holding an entity theory indeed believed they were judging something deep-seated when they formed an impression.

☐ Note

1. Entity theorists also draw stronger conclusions about people's personality and moral character from their appearance (Gervey, Chiu, Hong, & Dweck, 1998).

12

CHAPTER

Belief in the Potential to Change

In this chapter we spotlight people's belief in the potential for change. Although the belief about the potential for change is at the heart of the entity-incremental distinction (and is indeed the definition of the incremental versus entity theory), there were still questions to be answered about the basis and the consequences of these beliefs.

We will start with entity and incremental theorists' beliefs about the innateness of human traits: Are traits largely biologically based and innate or are they largely determined by environment and experience? Although entity theorists, by definition, believe that traits are more fixed, this doesn't necessarily mean they think traits are more innate. It could be that they are molded by experience over time, and only at some later point do they become set.

We have seen that entity theorists form rapid and often global trait judgments based on a small amount of information, but this doesn't mean that they decide about people's future potential so quickly.

We will also examine beliefs about how to deal with people who perform poorly or behave inappropriately: Should we try to educate, counsel, and rehabilitate them (that is, try to change them), or is this a fruitless endeavor?

☐ The Belief that Traits Are Innate

Sheri Levy told college students that she was interested in the extent to which people's characteristics could be explained by two kinds of factors—*innate* or *biological* factors and *social* or *environmental* factors (Levy & Dweck, 1996). She then gave them a list of 12 characteristics, including intelligence, criminal behavior, self-discipline, moral character, and friendliness. For each one, she asked students to rate how much they thought the characteristic was explained by innate versus environmental factors.

We got some hint earlier that entity and incremental theorists thought differently about this issue. In the studies where we looked at entity and incremental theorists differing definitions of intelligence (Mueller & Dweck, 1997, 1998), we saw that entity theorists more often asserted in their definitions that intelligence was innate.

In the present study, Levy and I found that entity and incremental theorists differed significantly in the importance they assigned to heredity and environment. Although both groups granted influence to both factors, entity theorists thought the traits were more innate than incremental theorists did, while incremental theorists thought they were more a result of experience than entity theorists did.

☐ Young Children's Views of Heredity and Environment

Even much younger students have strong views about where traits, such as intelligence, come from—whether they are a product of a child's genes or a child's environment and experience. This was beautifully demonstrated in a study by Gail Heyman and Susan Gelman (Heyman & Gelman, 1997), who looked at grade-school students' beliefs about fixed, innate intelligence versus malleable, acquirable intelligence. They did this by telling children a story about babies who were switched at birth (see Hirschfeld, 1995).

Children were asked to imagine, for example, that a baby was born to one set of parents "who were not so smart" but, because of a mistake made at the hospital, grew up with another set of parents who *were* smart. Children were then asked to decide which couple the child would turn out to be like, and to explain why they thought so.

Children's answers clearly reflected two opposing views. Some confidently maintained the fixed, innate view—the view that the child would be just like the biological parents:

> "The family would try but the baby would always stay not very smart."
> "It will have trouble. It's in its genes."
> "You can change the way you act, but you can't change the brain. If the child was born to not so smart people, it couldn't learn things as well because it has a low IQ."

Other children just as confidently expressed the malleable, environmental view—the view that the child would be smart, like the parents he or she grew up with:

> "She learns how to be smart. The more you read, the smarter you get."
> "The parents would read all the time and they would see what the parents are doing and would read along."
> "It grew up with people who encourage learning."

Thus even grade-school students can have the view that traits are fixed and innate. And when they do, they seem to make decisions about what it is that children are capable of learning—no matter how enriched their childhood environments are.

Those who believe in acquirable traits do not talk about the insurmountable limitations the child will face. Instead they talk much more about the processes through which parents can encourage the development of a child's potential—which brings us to our next point.

Once you have decided that someone has innate, fixed, low intelligence (or other traits), you have also decided—in advance—what they can and cannot learn. And this may dramatically affect what and how you try to teach them (Brown et al., 1984; Howard, 1995; Rosenthal & Jacobson, 1968).

In contrast, when you decide that someone is lacking in skills and knowledge, even severely lacking, you do not pass judgment on their potential for learning. It may take time and tremendous effort to get someone on track, but in an incremental framework currently low skills do not preclude future high skills.

Is there direct evidence that incremental theorists retain a greater belief in people's potential to learn or grow despite currently poor performance or behavior?

☐ The Potential for Change

We were fascinated by this question because although the potential for change or growth is part and parcel of an incremental theory, we wanted to know whether those with an incremental theory really held onto this belief when they were confronted with evidence of deficient performance or behavior.

In a study by Heyman and Dweck (1998), young students were asked to give advice to a floundering fellow student on how to improve academically. We told children:

> Imagine a child you know keeps getting lots and lots wrong on their schoolwork and asks you for your help. What would you say or do?

When you assume that "it comes natural or it doesn't," there is not much you can recommend for other students who are doing poorly: They simply don't have the potential. And, in fact, many entity theorists offered minimal advice or, in some cases, simply expressed sympathy.

When, however, students assume that achievement is the end point of a process, they have lots of advice to offer their classmates: Poor performance is a problem to be solved. Thus, in response to this question, incremental theorists gave much more extensive instructions about what precisely the students should do. Here is one example:

> Do you quit a lot? Do you think for a minute and then stop? If you do, you should think for a long time—two minutes maybe and if you can't get it you should read the problem again. If you can't get it then, you should raise your hand and ask the teacher.

It's a lucky classmate who goes to this student for advice.

Earlier, we described a study by Erdley and Dweck (1993) in which students watched a narrated slide show about a new boy in school who misbehaved because he was nervous about making a good impression. As we saw, entity theorists rated the boy more negatively on global traits (like bad, mean, and nasty) than incremental theorists did.

Here we ask: Did students grant the boy the potential to change? We assessed this by asking them how they thought John would be in the future. First, we asked about the short-term future: "Suppose you saw John again in a few weeks. Do you think he would seem pretty much the same or very different?" Presumably the few weeks would give him some time to acclimate to his new classroom and perhaps to pull himself together. The two groups differed significantly in what they thought they would see on their return visit. On a scale that ranged from "pretty much the same" to "very different," incremental theorists thought that John was, in fact, likely to look somewhat different after a few weeks. However, entity theorists thought he would be somewhat the same.

We also asked about the longer-term future: "How will John be in the future? Do you think he will be a troublemaker in eighth grade?" Again the groups differed significantly in what they thought the future held. The answers of incremental theorists fell on the "no" half of the scale (more specifically in the region marked "sort of no"), whereas those of the entity theorists fell on the "yes" half of the scale (in the region marked "sort of yes"). Once again, the students with an incremental theory granted the boy a greater likelihood of changing. They did not think he would definitely change, so in that sense they were not unrealistically optimistic. Nor did the entity theorists say he would definitely *not* change. However, on the basis of what they saw the entity theorists formed a stronger negative expectation than the incremental theorists did.

Of course, this finding is in a way what you might expect given the two theories. The incremental theory is defined by the belief in the potential for personal change, whereas the entity theory is defined by the belief that basic change is not a real possibility. What may be unexpected is how quickly entity theorists can decide what a person is like and then predict that person's future.

☐ What Should Happen to a Wrongdoer?

We continued to explore the idea of potential for change by asking entity and incremental theorists to tell us the appropriate ways to treat a wrongdoer.

What should happen to a wrongdoer? Some answers to this question imply a belief in the potential to learn, grow, or change, while other answers do not. If you believe in the potential to grow, then wrongdoing simply becomes a problem to be solved: One attempts to educate the offender. Depending on the level or seriousness of the offense, this can take the form of reasoning with the person, having the person receive counseling, or having the person undergo some kind of rehabilitation program. If you do not believe in the potential for fundamental change, then these forms of intervention are ineffective and wasteful. Instead, you might simply wish to make the offenders pay for their crimes and perhaps try to deter them from future crimes by making their payment harsh (for even if you can't change their fundamental nature, maybe you can scare them into controlling themselves).

We expected the incremental theorists to favor the education route, and not only because the potential for change is the basis of an incremental theory. You will also remember how those holding an incremental theory explained people's behavior, that is, in terms of their psychological processes (Hong, 1994). Compared with entity theorists, they thought that people acted the way they did because of such things as what they believed, felt, or knew how to do in a given situation and not because of deep-seated character traits. Well, these psychological processes should be more amenable to education than deeper-seated or more global character traits. In other words, it seems easier to think that you can change someone's ideas about how to behave appropriately and teach someone new strategies for behaving appropriately than it is to think that you can change a bad person into a good person.

We have conducted several studies so far of how people respond to wrongdoers. In one (Chiu, Dweck, Tong, & Fu, 1997, study 4), students were asked to imagine the following wrongdoing on the part of their professor:

> At the beginning of an introductory calculus class, the professor told the class that they would be given eight problem sets throughout the course, each contributing 12.5% to the final grade. The professor also promised to set the cut-off point for an A grade at 80. After the seventh problem set was given back to the students, you found that you had already accumulated 81 points. Therefore, you did not finish the last problem set and spent your time preparing for the finals in other courses. It turned out that the professor raised the cut-off point to 85 because too many students scored above 80. Consequently, you only got a B+ for the course.

We then asked students to describe how they would feel and what they would do in this situation. Entity and incremental theorists were equally likely to say they would take some action (although entity theorists were more likely to say they would persist if their initial action didn't work). But the nature of the action they would take differed. Incremental theorists were more likely to say they would try to educate this wrongdoer: They would try to convince him of why it was wrong to go back on his word. As an example, one incremental theorist said, "I would confront the professor and remind him that he promised not to raise the cut-off and that it was unfair of him to do it." Incremental theorists thus granted the professor the capacity to understand what he had done wrong and to amend his injustice.

None of the entity theorists said they would try to educate the professor (as opposed to 35% of the incremental theorists, who spontaneously reported that they would try to educate him). The entity theorists were certainly angry about the injustice and eager to react to it, but for them it took a different course. Not granting the professor the potential to change, they instead attempted to vent their anger at him, make him pay, or get the higher-ups to force him to honor his word. For example, entity theorists said, "I think the professor is a junk [sic] and I would tell him" or "I'd be ticked as hell and be in the Dean's office at 9:00 the next morning." None of the incremental theorists planned a response of this nature (versus 21% of the entity theorists who spontaneously proposed such a response). Thus although both entity and incremental theorists agreed that the professor had done wrong, they differed significantly in what exactly they planned to do about it.

In another study, by Israela Loeb and me (Loeb & Dweck, 1994), we were interested in how people would react to being victimized. College students read three scenarios that depicted them in very important situations, and in each of the situations, other people's actions hurt them.

In the first scenario students were asked to imagine that after some time in college they had finally found a wonderful relationship that they hoped would become permanent. The relationship had been happy for quite a while and they were now living with their partner but returned home one day to find a note. The partner had left without any real explanation.

In the second scenario, students were asked to suppose that they had been preparing for some time for an exam that was crucial for their future. One day, not long before the exam, they were studying in the library, left for a moment, and returned to find that all of their notes had been stolen. The librarian reported that some students had run into the library and had quickly run out again laughing.

In the third scenario, students were told to imagine that they had been experiencing unusual symptoms and went to the doctor for a checkup and some tests. Due to the negligence of the medical laboratory, the results of the lab tests did not come back for some time. By the time they did, some permanent physical damage—which could have been prevented—had taken place.

After each scenario, students were asked a number of questions about what their reactions to these situations would be. Specifically, each question asked them to rate on a 5-point scale how likely they were to react to the events in a particular way. Entity and incremental theorists differed consistently in how they said they would react, with entity more than incremental theorists focusing on punishment and revenge, and incremental more than entity theorists focusing on understanding, forgiving, and educating the perpetrators.

For example, entity theorists were significantly more likely than incremental theorists to harbor negative and aggressive wishes toward the perpetrators, agreeing more strongly with statements such as, "I would spend time fantasizing about how miserable the partner would hopefully become," "I would wish the perpetrators a real bad life," and, "Frankly, I would try to hurt the partner when an opportunity comes along." When we asked them about their overall goal, they also said, more than incremental theorists, that a major goal of theirs would be "to punish the perpetrators for my suffering and loss." This was the least-endorsed goal of incremental theorists.

In contrast, incremental theorists, more than entity theorists, said, "I would try to understand why the perpetrators behaved the way they did and I would try to forgive them." In fact, when *they* were questioned directly about the goals in this situation, a major goal of theirs was to educate the perpetrators about why what they did was wrong and how they could improve. This was the goal least-endorsed by entity theorists.

As part of another study (Gervey, Chiu, Hong, & Dweck, 1999), people were asked to tell us what, in their opinion, was the primary purpose of imprisonment. Both entity and incremental theorists agreed that a major purpose of imprisoning wrongdoers was to protect society. But after that they differed. Entity theorists thought, far more than incremental theorists, that the primary purpose was to punish the wrongdoer. Incremental theorists thought, far more than entity theorists, that the primary purpose of imprisonment was (or should be) to rehabilitate the wrongdoer—that is, to develop his or her potential for leading a moral and productive life.

In the earlier chapters we saw how entity theorists gave up on themselves when they failed. They condemned themselves, lost self-esteem, fell into a depressed state, and lost confidence in their future performance. Now we find that they give up on others too. Simply put, entity theorists don't grant people the potential to grow—not themselves and not others.

Incremental theorists, on the other hand, see their own failures as problems to be solved, and they see other people's failings that way as well. To them, people can make mistakes, follow the wrong paths, or do harm to others, but they are also capable, with the proper motivation and guidance, of going beyond this. We might ask: Are all people, even criminals, capable of change or is this a naively optimistic point of view? As I will argue, it is often a constructive first hypothesis.

13 CHAPTER

Holding and Forming Stereotypes

Entity theorists believe in fixed traits that can be judged readily from behavior or performance, and, as we saw, this applies to themselves and to other individuals. Given this, Sheri Levy wondered whether this might also apply to groups: Do entity theorists think good and bad traits belong to some groups more than others?

For example, we know that some groups may, on the whole, tend to achieve academically more than others. What does this mean? If you are willing to judge underlying intelligence from these outcomes then you may conclude that some groups have more intelligence than others. On the other hand, if you look at environment, experience, academic preparation, schools, peer values, study habits, and study skills (not to mention beliefs about intelligence), then it may be less clear what the achievement gap means.

Levy and her colleagues have now done over a dozen studies of stereotyping in students (both college aged and grade-school aged) who come from diverse ethnic backgrounds and socioeconomic levels, finding in each study that those holding entity theories exhibit higher levels of stereotyping (Levy, 1998; Levy & Dweck, 1998; Levy et al., 1998; Levy, Freitas, & Dweck, 1998). This is true for positive as well as negative stereotypes, and for existing groups (such as ethnic, racial, gender, and occupational groups) as well as novel groups (about which they have just learned). Does this mean that entity theorists are simply more bigoted than incremental theorists? I think that when we understand the process behind the stereotyping, this is not the conclusion we draw.

In other words, we know that entity theorists simply believe that what they perceive on the outside reflects what people are like on the inside. They judge themselves this way (and we don't say that they are bigoted against themselves), they judge other individuals this way (and we don't say that they are bigoted against other individual people), and they judge groups this way, too. What this means is that their stereotyping is in some ways a natural outgrowth of their beliefs about human beings—what they're made of (fixed traits) and how you come to know them (very readily from a sample of their overt behavior).

That stereotyping can result directly from the way entity theorists think about people may seem like bad news. However, it can also be seen as good news, for if stereotyping results, at least in part, from people's implicit theories, then we should be able to change their level of stereotyping by changing their theory.

In what follows, I briefly review some of the studies that revealed higher levels of stereotyping among entity theorists, and then I turn to studies that altered people's implicit theories to see if this altered their stereotyping.

In the first study on this issue, Levy et al. (1998, study 1) had college students list all the stereotypes they could think of for a number of racial, ethnic, or religious groups: African Americans, Asian Americans, Jews, and Latinos. They then asked them to go back over what they had listed and rate how true they thought each of the stereotypes was. So first students simply reported what they thought society's stereotypes were, but then they told us what theirs were. Across the traits and across the ethnic groups, entity theorists gave more credence to societal stereotypes.

In a second study, Levy et al. (1998, study 2) had students rate the truth of stereotypes of African Americans, and again entity theorists ascribed more truth to the stereotypes, both the positive and the negative ones. In a third study (Levy et al., 1998, study 3), we gave college students information about a new group of people, one that they had no knowledge of before. Half of the students were told about a group in which many (two thirds) of the members had performed negative behaviors (such as pushing to the front of the line in a movie theater); the remaining one third performed neutral behaviors. The other half of the students were told about a group in which many of the members had performed positive behaviors (such as offering to share an umbrella with a stranger); the rest, as in the negative group, performed neutral behaviors. They then rated the groups as a whole on a number of trait dimensions, including bad-good, immoral-moral, rude-polite, considerate-inconsiderate, and evil-virtuous.

We found that compared with incremental theorists, entity theorists made consistently more positive ratings of the positive group and consistently more negative ratings of the negative group. Entity theorists also saw the groups as more homogeneous than incremental theorists did. That is, entity theorists rated the group members as being quite similar to one another, even though in each group one third of them had behaved differently from the rest. And finally, entity theorists thought that the information they had received (one behavior per group member) was far more sufficient for forming their impression than incremental theorists did. As when they are judging individuals, entity theorists saw behaviors more readily as reflecting the underlying traits of a group.

Levy then replicated (and extended) all of these findings with younger students (Levy, 1998; Levy & Dweck, 1998). In a series of studies with fifth graders, she showed that entity theorists held stereotypes more strongly and formed them more quickly. In the studies of stereotype formation, where young students formed impressions of novel groups, Levy and Dweck (1998) also asked them to explain why they thought the group members had behaved the way it did. Just as in our studies of how entity and incremental theorists explain individuals' behavior, those who were entity theorists explained the behavior chiefly in terms of the children's traits. Incremental theorists explained the behavior mostly in terms of the children's mental and emotional processes and their social environment.

In addition, students were asked to suppose that one of the children had been absent from school on the day that the group members' behaviors had been observed. What would that student be like? Entity theorists believed, significantly more strongly than incremental theorists, that the absent boy would be like the misbehaving school mates they read about.

Do these stereotypes affect behavior? Sheri Levy, Antonio Freitas, and I have shown that they do (Levy et al., 1999). For example, in a game that could be either competitive or cooperative, entity theorists (college students) played more competitively than incremental theorists when they thought their opponent was a law student. The two groups played equally competitively or cooperatively against a student whose affiliation wasn't specified. This means that entity theorists protected themselves when they thought the other party was a lawyer-in-the-making who would compete against them. Incremental theorists probably did not invoke a strong stereotype and saw no reason to treat an anonymous law student differently from any other student. Did entity theorists do the right thing by protecting themselves or did incremental theorists do the right thing by withholding judgment and giving a cooperative strategy a chance?

In another study (Levy et al., 1999, study 2), when asked to grade students' assignments, entity theorists (again college students) varied the grades they gave depending on the ethnicity of the student. That is, they gave higher grades to the same paper when they thought the student belonged to one ethnic group versus another. Incremental theorists did not.

Finally, in the studies by Levy where children formed impressions of novel groups (Levy, 1998; Levy & Dweck, 1998), most children said they'd like to meet and get to know the children in the "positive" group (the group in which many of the children had performed a positive behavior), and most children said they would not care to make the acquaintance of the children in the "negative" group. However, entity theorists were *more* eager than incremental theorists to make friends with the children in the "positive" group and were *less* willing than the incremental theorists to make friends with the children in the "negative" group.

It does seem, then, that entity theorists not only hold stronger stereotypes but are also willing to act on those stereotypes.

☐ Does an Entity Theory Cause Stereotyping?

We then asked the same question we had asked earlier about trait judgments: Does holding an entity or an incremental theory directly *cause* stereotyping? If we changed someone's theory would we change their belief in stereotypes?

To find this out, Sheri Levy and colleagues (1998) taught college students to believe in an entity or an incremental theory (temporarily, of course). This was done by having half of the students read a highly compelling (but fictitious) scientific article that presented conclusive evidence for the entity theory. It reviewed scientific research and case studies showing that people's traits cannot be changed.

The other half read an equally compelling article that presented conclusive evidence for the incremental theory. This article reviewed the same kinds of scientific research and case studies but this time showed that people's traits are malleable. (The articles were from Chiu et al., 1997.)

Both groups of students were equivalent before the start of the study, but the articles turned one group toward the entity theory and the other toward the incremental theory.

The entity-theory article stressed the point that personal traits, "like plaster," are pretty stable over time. It reviewed research showing that people's characteristics "seem to be rather fixed and to develop consistently along the same path over time" and that although people "age and develop . . . they do so on the foundation of enduring dispositions."

The article also described a large research program, "one of the most ambitious and exciting intervention programs ever conceived," that tried to counsel predelinquent boys into productive careers and lives. The intervention included extensive, long-term caseworker involvement in families, tutoring in academic subjects, medical and psychiatric attention, and social and recreational resources.

According to the entity-theory article:

> Despite the huge investment of effort and money, the results of the intervention were disappointing. Compared to the youngsters who were also "at risk" but were not in the program, those who had the intervention were equally likely to commit juvenile offenses. Later, in their adulthood, many of them committed crimes—roughly 15–20 percent of them committed serious offenses against people or property, while over 50 percent of them committed minor offenses. . . . Many other research intervention programs have yielded similar results.

The article went on to discuss how many significant figures in history displayed their key characteristics at an early age, giving the example of Mother Teresa:

> According to the people who knew her as a child . . . she often took care of other children, even those who were older than she. Also, instead of playing with other children, she spent most of her time volunteering at a local clinic. Mother Teresa, even when she was very young, displayed strong empathy for others' feelings and a willingness to help even when self-sacrifice was needed. These characteristics of hers seems to have guided her life mission of helping those who suffered.

The incremental-theory article presented much of the same research but provided different findings and drew different conclusions. This article stressed that personal traits are changeable and can be developed. It defined personal traits as "basically a bundle of potentialities that wait to be developed and cultivated" and provided evidence that at almost any time in a person's life his or her personal characteristics can be shaped.

It, too, described the large-scale intervention study, but instead of the disappointing results, reported:

> The results of the intervention were rewarding. Compared to the youngsters who were also "at risk" but were not in the program, those who had the intervention showed dramatic differences as adults. Among the youngsters who were not in the

program, 23 percent went on to commit serious offenses against people or property, and over two-thirds of them committed at least minor offenses. In contrast, almost none of the youngsters who experienced the intervention committed a serious offense and less than ten percent of them even a minor offense. In fact, most of them graduated from high school, and then found and kept steady employment. . . . Many other research intervention programs have yielded similar results.

The incremental-theory article went on to discuss case studies of historical figures, saying that "many significant figures in history developed their key personality characteristics over their childhood and young adulthood." It talked about how Mother Teresa was not at all a model child, but how, through her experiences, she developed her strong empathy for others and her capacity for self-sacrifice.

After reading the assigned article and answering some questions about it, students went on to another task that they thought was unrelated. This next task was the assessment of stereotyping. Here, we presented students with a number of ethnic groups (African Americans, Asians, Latinos) and occupational groups (lawyers, doctors, politicians, teachers), and we asked them to rate each group on a number of traits. We then looked at the extent to which they endorsed traits that were stereotypes of each group.

Could something as simple as what we did possibly affect something as complex as stereotyping? We thought it was a long shot, but certainly worth a try—and we were not disappointed. Our results showed that we had indeed affected stereotyping. Students who were exposed to the entity theory agreed significantly more with stereotyped traits than students who were given the incremental theory.

Levy (1998) then conducted a similar study with fifth graders. In this study, students were taught either an entity or incremental theory through an engaging oral presentation. After the presentation, as part of another study, they were asked to form an impression of a novel group of children from another school. Students who had been taught the entity theory formed significantly stronger stereotypes than those who were taught the incremental theory.

This means that students who adopted the entity theory began to take group differences in behavior as evidence of deeply rooted characterological truths, compared to students who adopted the incremental theory.

After the studies, students were all thoroughly informed of the purpose of the research. They were told about both viewpoints and the implications of both were discussed. These students are now aware of the theories they carry around and how these theories affect the way they see people. Unfortunately, most of us don't have this awareness. We simply think we are seeing reality.

☐ Are Stereotypes Wrong?

Is it wrong to hold stereotypes? Don't groups in fact often differ from each other in important ways? In my view it is not wrong to recognize that groups may differ from each other in notable ways. In some places or at some times, one group on average may have higher levels of academic achievement or better jobs or lower crime rates than another group. But it is also important to recognize the many factors that may be influencing a group to facilitate or impair its overall success. And, as many people have pointed out, it is important to keep in mind that a group is composed of individuals, who can differ greatly from one another (see e.g., Hamilton & Sherman, 1996).

Dangers arise when people lose sight of this complexity and go beyond the evidence to conclude that some groups are inherently superior or inferior to others, or that most members of a group share the same qualities. Dangers can also arise when people draw strong conclusions about groups from too little evidence. Holding an entity theory appears to raise the chance of this happening.

Holding an incremental theory does not have to prevent people from seeing the facts. In our novel-group studies, incremental theorists rated the negative group as being negative and the positive group as being positive. Yet they still saw variability within the group, and they explained the negative behaviors in a way that left room for growth and change.

14

How Does It All Begin?
Young Children's Theories
About Goodness and Badness

So far we've talked about seasoned students, and we've seen how believing in fixed intelligence can create vulnerabilities for them. What about young children, say preschoolers or kindergartners? Do they have theories about themselves and do they have vulnerabilities?

For a long time many researchers didn't think so (see Dweck, 1991, 1998; Dweck & Elliott, 1983). We believed that young children were pretty much protected from the negative effects of failure. Why did we think this? First, it didn't look as though children younger than 8 years or so were advanced enough to understand the idea of fixed intelligence (Nicholls, 1984). It wasn't even clear that young children knew what intelligence was. Therefore, when they failed, they shouldn't doubt their (fixed) intelligence and experience the resulting vulnerability.

Next, there were studies showing that young children didn't display helpless reactions when they confronted the same failures that evoked helpless reactions in older children (e.g., Miller, 1985). Instead of wilting, the young children appeared to remain optimistic and engaged (Parsons & Ruble, 1977; see Stipek, 1984).

In sum, we didn't think young children understood intelligence and failure in ways that would lead to negative self-judgments and helpless reactions. We also believed this because it made a good deal of sense. Young children, learning to walk and talk, are learning the most important tasks of a lifetime. Isn't it adaptive for the species if our young are protected from vulnerability as they attempt to master these tasks? Imagine what would happen if youngsters decided not to persist in their attempts to locomote or speak after initial mistakes and setbacks. What if they thought their difficulties reflected on their ability to master these tasks and decided to cease their efforts? What if they thought continued errors

95

and setbacks reflected badly on them and chose instead to remain mute and sedentary? Thankfully, this is not what occurs. Children forge ahead on these tasks despite frequent and sometimes painful errors.

Wouldn't it be even better if this invulnerability lasted over the early years of school, as children embarked on their academic pursuits? This would enable them to tackle a series of difficult new tasks, like reading and writing, in a purely mastery-oriented fashion.

Unfortunately, it does not. Despite our earlier beliefs, our research has now shown that young children can display *every* aspect of the helpless response when they confront failure: self-blame, negative feelings, plummeting expectations, low persistence, and a lack of constructive strategies (Cain & Dweck, 1995; Hebert & Dweck, 1985; Heyman, Dweck, & Cain, 1992; Kamins & Dweck, 1998; Smiley & Dweck, 1994; see Heckhausen, 1987; Lewis, Alessandri, & Sullivan, 1992; Stipek, 1995; Stipek, Recchia, & McClintic, 1992). We have found helpless responses in children as young as 3½ years old (the youngest age we've tested), and we have found them in a sizable proportion of young children.

Why were we able to find helpless responses in young children when others were not? First, we realized that to gauge young children's true response to difficulty, they had to recognize that they were having difficulty. You had to give them tasks that were meaningful to them and ones on which poor performance was totally obvious. In some past research, for example, children were asked to find 10 hidden pictures in a scene, when in fact there were two. Yet, young children may be delighted to find the two, and the rest of the hidden pictures are, after all, hidden. Older children who are vulnerable to a helpless response will feel as though they have failed whenever they believe they haven't reached a standard, but young children may need visible evidence.

In another past study, different-colored lights came on depending on whether children got the right or wrong answers (Harter, 1975). Many older children were disconcerted when the light signaling a wrong answer came on. But Harter reports that young children seemed pleased that they were turning on lights and producing interesting effects, regardless of the color of the light and what it was meant to signify.

Thus, we realized that in past research, young children might have looked immune to the effects of difficulty because the difficulty didn't register.

However, the most important reason we found the helpless response in young children is that we began to believe it was there, but in a different place. Despite the fact that some parents worry from the start about how smart their offspring are, we realized that intelligence was not *the* burning issue for children in the early years.

Intelligence is an issue that gains importance over the school years, as children pursue their academic studies, experience successes and failures, observe the successes and failures of their peers, and observe the reactions of their own parents to their academic efforts.

Young children, on the other hand, are in the thick of being socialized. They are being taught what is right and wrong or good and bad. They are being schooled in the complex world of rules and expectations; what it means to be a good child and not a bad one (see, e.g., Hoffman, 1970; Kagan & Lamb, 1987). Many of the stories they're told teach about good guys and bad guys and what happens to them (Paley, 1988).

Maybe *this* is their issue, we thought. Maybe young children are grappling with questions of their goodness and badness—and vulnerable children are the ones who see failure as meaning they are bad or unworthy. So we set out to see if this was the case.

In this chapter I first present evidence of clear helpless responses in young children. I'll then describe research that links this helpless response to children's feelings of badness. What we'll see is that vulnerable young children do indeed feel they're bad when they encounter failure or criticism. And—just like older children with intelligence—they think badness is a stable trait.

☐ Evidence for Helpless Reactions in Young Children

The first of our studies to look for, and find, helpless responses in young children was a study by Charlene Hebert and me (Hebert & Dweck, 1985; see Dweck, 1991). In this study, we gave preschool children (aged 3.5 to 5 years) four jigsaw puzzles to solve. The puzzles were large and colorful, and all depicted children's favorite cartoon characters. With a jigsaw puzzle, it is abundantly clear when you have completed it or failed to complete it.

The first three of these puzzles were too difficult to solve within the allotted time, although all of the children made good progress on them. The fourth puzzle was of the same type, but we made sure that all the children solved the fourth one successfully. (Again, extreme care was taken to make sure that all children left the situation feeling proud of themselves and their performance, and at the end of the session, children were given mastery experiences on all of the puzzles.)

The first thing we were interested in was whether children would show persistence in trying to solve the unsolved puzzles. So after they had worked on the four puzzles (three unsolved and one solved), we asked children which one they wished to rework. We told them that we had some extra time and that they could choose any of the puzzles to work on again. We assured them that any choice was fine, and that in the past, different children had made all kinds of choices.

If the children selected one of the unsolved ones, we considered this to indicate persistence, because they were trying to pursue the task to completion. If children selected the puzzle they had already solved, we considered this to be the nonpersistent choice. In this study, 37% of the children made the nonpersistent choice. Interestingly, children of this age do not yet feel inhibited about choosing the one they've already done. A few years later, even children who sorely wish to avoid challenge are too embarrassed to declare this as their choice.

Could it be that these nonpersistent children found the already-solved puzzle to be challenging or that they wanted to practice a little more on this puzzle before moving on to the more challenging ones?

We tested for these possibilities in two subsequent studies that used very similar procedures, one by Pat Smiley and me (Smiley & Dweck, 1994) and one by Kathleen Cain and me (Cain & Dweck, 1995). In these studies, after children selected a puzzle to work on again, we asked them to explain their choices. We said,

"Good choice! Why'd you pick that one?" Not one of the nonpersistent children (those who chose to redo the already completed puzzle) *ever* gave a challenge-seeking reason for their choice or ever indicated that they thought this was a good way to practice their skills. Instead, the great majority of them clearly said they were picking this one because it was easy or because they didn't know how to do the other ones. Their answers to the question "Why did you choose that one?" included statements such as, "Because he was the easiest" or "Because I already know how to do it."

In contrast, a large proportion of the persistent children gave clear challenge-seeking reasons for their puzzle choice, stressing, for example, that they were eager to see if they could do it or that they wanted to try a hard one. They gave answers such as, "Because I wanna see if I can try him again" or "Because I didn't hardly do any of 'em."

In one of the studies (Smiley & Dweck, 1994) we even asked children to make yet another choice—to see if the nonpersistent children would now be ready for a challenge. After their initial choice, we said, "Suppose we had even more time and you could work on another puzzle after that one. Which would you choose?" Much to our amazement, a great many of the nonpersistent children chose the same, already completed puzzle once again. This means that they preferred to work the same puzzle three times rather than risk a confrontation with difficulty. This was true even though many of them had made good progress on the incomplete puzzles.

In striking contrast, almost all of the persistent children, when given this option, chose a different incomplete puzzle to attempt.

Could it be that the nonpersistent children were simply not as good at puzzles as the persistent children, and this was the reason they hesitated to take on a challenge? To check for this possibility, in several of the studies, all children were tested in a previous session on their ability to do this kind of puzzle. In this previous session, we gave them puzzles that were very similar to the ones they were later asked to solve, and we timed how long it took them to complete them. There was absolutely no difference between the nonpersistent and the persistent children in how well they solved these puzzles. This means that their later choice to avoid or confront a challenge had nothing to do with how good they actually were at the puzzles.

Could it be that the nonpersistent children *thought* they were not good at puzzles and therefore approached the puzzle task with less confidence? To examine this possibility, we asked all of the children (in a session that was prior to the "difficulty") to tell us whether they thought they were good at puzzles or not good at puzzles. There were no differences between the persistent and the nonpersistent children. Both groups overwhelmingly and emphatically saw themselves as being good at puzzles—before they encountered difficulty.

We now had a procedure we could use to identify persistent and nonpersistent responses. The next question was whether the children who showed nonpersistence would show the other characteristics of the helpless pattern, such as the negative self-judgments, the negative expectations, and the negative emotion.

In two of the studies (Hebert & Dweck, 1985; Smiley & Dweck, 1994), we asked the children to talk out loud as they worked on the puzzles. We then analyzed their statements and found that, in both studies, the nonpersistent children made significantly more negative statements about their performance and their expectations than the persistent children did. The nonpersistent children said things such as:

> "I can't do it. These are too hard."
> "There's a lot of pieces. I bet I can't make this puzzle."
> "I can do easy puzzles, but I can't do hard ones."
> "Don't think I'll be able to get this puzzle at all."
> "You shouldn't have mixed up the pieces cuz then I'll never know how to do it."
> To distract the adult: "Did you ever see *Star Wars?* That's my favorite movie."

We also asked children about their expectations of future success and their explanations for their failures. In the study with Charlene Hebert (Hebert & Dweck, 1985), referring to the incomplete puzzles, we asked, "If you tried very hard right now—your very hardest—do you think you could do any of these puzzles? Yes or no?" We also asked, "If you had lots of time right now, do you think you could finish any of these puzzles—or are you just not good enough at puzzles?"

Again there were strong differences. As the quotes above suggest, the nonpersistent children had much lower expectations of being able to solve any of the puzzles and, unlike before the failure, expressed a poorer opinion of their puzzle abilities. The majority of the helpless children reported that even with more time or effort they would not be able to solve any of the puzzles. The majority of the mastery-oriented children were certain that with time and effort they could conquer the puzzles.

Finally, in all of the studies, we monitored children's feelings. We either asked them to rate how happy or sad they felt while doing the puzzles or we coded their facial expressions for emotion. Not surprisingly, the nonpersistent children conveyed significantly more negative emotion than their persistent counterparts.

Thus, in terms of persistence, negative judgments, plunging expectancies, and negative affect, young children were displaying the full helpless response. But did they see themselves as bad?

☐ Helplessness and Expectations of Punishment

As a first attempt to find out whether young children who display a helpless response view themselves as bad for failing, Charlene Hebert and I had them role-play teachers' and parents' reactions to their failure (Hebert & Dweck, 1985). Would the vulnerable children role-play more criticism and punishment for their failures?

Children were given a doll that represented themselves and were shown dolls representing their teacher, their mother, and their father. They were then taken through four scenarios. In the first three, the adult dolls, in turn, look over the incomplete puzzles, which are arrayed in full view. Each time the experimenter said something like: "This is your mother. She looks at what you've done. What does she say? What does she do?"

After the child's response to this question, the child doll asked the adult doll: "Are you happy with me?" "Are you mad at me?" And for the final probe, the child doll asked, "Will you punish me?"

For the fourth scenario, we introduced another prop, a telephone. This time, the mother looked over the work and called the father on the phone to report. This in fact was the scenario that prompted the most copious responses.

When we coded children's responses for criticism and punishment from the adults, a truly striking difference emerged. Most of the children who had shown a persistent, mastery-oriented response on the puzzles role-played little or no criticism or punishment from the adults. On the contrary, they role-played a great deal of praise, encouragement, and constructive suggestions from them. Here are examples of what these mastery-oriented children had the adult dolls say:

> "She did the puzzles beautiful."
> "He worked hard but he just couldn't finish them. He wants to try them again later."
> "You did the best you could. Come sit on my lap."
> "He didn't work hard enough. He can try again after lunch."

To be sure, the mastery-oriented children had the adults say many nice things. But what is most notable to me in these responses is the extent to which they had the adults issue suggestions for how they could improve through effort and persistence. Is this how the children learned constructive responses to setbacks?

Unfortunately, as we suspected might happen, the children who had shown a helpless response on the puzzles role-played an alarming amount of harsh criticism and punishment. The majority of them role-played clear criticism and punishment on at least some of the scenarios and many of them (50%) role-played clear criticism or punishment in the majority of the four scenarios. Here is a sampling of what they had the adults say:

> "She didn't finish the puzzles. I spanked her but she keeps on hiding."
> "You better do nothing but sit in your room."
> "He did one good one and three bad ones. He's punished."
> "He's punished because he can't do them and he didn't finish."
> "Daddy's gonna be very mad and spank her."

Some of these reactions seem a little extreme, and it's not likely that in real life these parents would go all out to punish a puzzle failure. But what is so compelling to me is that these children seem to feel that what they've done is reprehensible and that they deserve punishment for it.

☐ Helpless Responses to Criticism

We found this and more in another study. Here, Gail Heyman, Kathleen Cain, and I wanted to see whether young (kindergarten) children would show a helpless response to *criticism* (Heyman, Dweck, & Cain, 1992). We also wanted to see whether helpless children themselves thought they were bad when they failed and weren't just role-playing disapproval and punishment from others.

Because we didn't want to criticize children directly, Heyman invented a role-playing procedure in which the experimenter vividly narrated a series of scenarios and, armed with props, the child acted them out.

In each scenario, the child pretended to create something nice as a surprise for the teacher. In one scenario, the child pretended to draw a picture of a family, in another to build a house of blocks, and in a third to write out the numbers 1 through 10. The child then called the teacher over to bestow the product on her, but before she arrived the child noticed a mistake: A child in the drawing had no feet, the house had no windows, and the number 8 was missing from the array! Here is one of the scenarios that the experimenter read aloud as children acted it out with the appropriate props:

> You spend a lot of time painting a picture of a family to give to your teacher. You pick out colors you think are nice and carefully draw each person. As you are about to give it to your teacher you say to yourself, "Uh oh, one of the kids has no feet." But you worked really hard on the picture and want to give it to her. You say, "Teacher, here's a picture for you."

When we stopped the stories here and asked children to evaluate their product, virtually all of them still thought their product was dandy, despite its flaw. A year or two later, children are harder on themselves and are not at all satisfied with a faulty product. But for kindergarten children a small mistake is fine—unless it is criticized.

For some of the scenarios, the action continued and the pretend teacher criticized the flaw: "What, no feet? I don't call this drawing the right way. I'm disappointed." Children were then asked to rate their product, their emotions, and their desire to persist. They were also to generate an ending for the scenario so we could see whether they came up with constructive solutions to the problematic situation. These measures were designed to detect helpless reactions.

In addition, to judge children's sense of wrongdoing, we asked them to role-play their parents' reactions to their flawed product. We said, "If you took this home and showed it to your parents, what would they say?"

Finally, to see whether they themselves felt like they were bad or deficient, we asked them questions about each of the scenarios. We said, for example,

> Think about everything that happened with the picture. Did everything that happened with the picture make you feel like you were a good girl/boy or not a good girl/boy? [Child's answer.] Did everything that happened with the picture make you feel like you were nice or not nice? Did everything that happened with the picture make you feel like you were smart or not smart?

Once again, we found clear evidence of a helpless response in a sizable proportion of the children. Thirty-nine percent of the children responded to the criticism by lowering their evaluation of their product. What they had been quite happy with before the criticism they were considerably less happy with afterward. These same children reported much more negative emotion than the others, were less willing to persist on the task, and came up with far fewer constructive solutions to the problem. They thus showed every aspect of a helpless reaction.

The constructive-solution measure, where children were asked to take the dolls and finish the story, was an interesting one. We said to the children, "Please hold your dolls and finish off what would happen next in the story."

The mastery-oriented children came up with a myriad of ways to fix the picture, the house, or the numbers and to leave everyone feeling happy. Many of their responses were dissertations on the efficacy of practice and effort, much like the following:

Teacher: *You are a good girl but you missed the 8.*

Child: *That's OK because I didn't have time, but I'll finish it for homework.*

The child then acted out bringing the completed work to a pleased teacher.

In this next one, the child acted out finishing her work in the extra time her teacher gave her. Then she had the teacher say,

> I really like your painting, and I know you worked very hard at it, and I'm glad I gave you extra time, and it's fun having paintings even when they aren't already done, and you have to spend some extra time, but I know that I still really like your painting.

In contrast, the helpless children seemed paralyzed by the situation. They often failed to come up with any useful solution at all and tended to leave the players mired in negative emotions. They role-played things like going to get a Kleenex for crying or going home to throw away their work.

What is so remarkable to me about this is that to fix the situation, they didn't really have to do much of anything. They just had to wave the dolls in the air, say they corrected the product, and declare everyone happy. It was not a task on which they had to gather their resources to meet a real challenge or solve a difficult problem. Yet the helpless children were paralyzed by the criticism, seeing it as insurmountable, to the point where many of them could not even initiate the little that was required to make things better. It was as though they had been judged and they considered the judgment to be final.

☐ Punishment Expectations

Once again the helpless children role-played significantly more criticism and negative evaluation from their parents and teachers, suggesting that they viewed their actions as reprehensible. The helpless children role-played their parents and teachers saying things such as:

> "You are very bad."
> "I hate those numbers."
> "You did a very bad job."
> "That's bad work."
> "We are throwing this out."
> "How could you do this? This is not a very good building. I don't like it!"

What did the mastery-oriented children role-play as their parents' and teachers' reactions? Here is a sample:

"Did you do those terrific numbers?"
"That's a very nice picture. Why don't you put some feet on that picture?"

These findings continue to suggest that, for young children, the key issue is goodness, and that their mistakes and failures are seen in that light. These children are grappling with questions about what makes someone good and what makes someone bad. Do good intentions, effort, and partial mastery make a child good? Or does a flawed or criticized product make a child bad? In this study, we intentionally put these things in conflict—the children had good intentions, they tried hard, and did fairly well, but their work had a flaw and was criticized. Our findings show that helpless and mastery-oriented children resolve this dilemma in different ways.

One child, who will remain in our memories forever, experienced this conflict acutely and enacted it in his role-playing of his parents' reactions to his work. In his role playing, each parent took a different stance, one implying that effort made him good and the other that the flaw made him bad:

Mother: *Hello. What are you sad about?*

Boy: *I gave my teacher some numbers and I skipped the number 8 and now I'm feeling sad.*

Mother: *Well there's one thing that can cheer you up.*

Boy: *What?*

Mother: *If you really tell your teacher that you tried your best, she wouldn't be mad at you. [Turning to father:] We're not mad at him, are we?*

Father: *Oh yes we are! Son, you better go right to your room.*

Unfortunately, the boy gave greater weight to his father's point of view. He rated his work and himself very poorly across the board. But at least he knew that grown-ups can hold both points of view, as opposed to many other helpless children who were quite certain that their mistakes would bring universal condemnation.

☐ Self-Ratings of Badness

But the new measure in this study was the one that asked children directly how *they* felt about themselves, given what had happened. We said, for example,

Think about everything that happened with the painting. Did everything that happened make you feel like you were a good or not good girl? [Child's answer] Did it make you feel like you were a nice or not nice girl? [Child's answer]

When asked whether they felt they were good or not good, nice or not nice, very few of the mastery-oriented children (fewer than 10%) said they felt not good or not nice based on what happened in the scenarios. The very idea that they should feel different about themselves because they received some criticism seemed very odd to many of them.

In contrast, 60% of the helpless children said they felt they were not good kids as a result of what happened. Even more striking was the fact that 40% of them said they felt that they were not nice. What is noteworthy about this is that the whole point of their endeavor was to create a nice surprise for their teacher. Yet the criticism was so undermining to them that for many it erased their good intention and left them feeling culpable.

The other noteworthy thing is that this was pretend criticism given by a pretend teacher to a doll representing the child. Why should it have this impact? As I have been arguing all along, failure has a certain meaning for helpless children—a meaning about their adequacy—and it is through this meaning that it produces its impact. Thus the medium through which it is delivered may be less important than the message it conveys.

But couldn't it just be the case that helpless children think adults are always right, and that an adult's opinion is more valid than their own? Maybe that's why the teacher's criticism had such impact on them.

To find this out, we asked children to imagine the following: "You are having fun listening to some new music you really like. You tell your father,[1] I really like that music.' Your father says, 'I don't like that music one bit.' Who is right?"

There was no significant difference in the responses of the helpless and mastery-oriented children to this question: 76% of the helpless children and 69% of the mastery-oriented children thought that their own judgment was correct and that their father was wrong. Thus it couldn't be that helpless children were adversely affected by the teacher's criticism because they put more stock in adults' opinions. Instead, these findings support the idea that failure and criticism for mistakes have different meanings for helpless and mastery-oriented children. For one group they send an undermining message, for the other they send a motivating one.

We can see from these studies that young children who are prone to a helpless response do indeed see failure and criticism as meaning they're bad. Do they have beliefs that go along with this—maybe a theory of badness?

☐ Young Children's Theories of Badness

Older students who are prone to a helpless response have a set of beliefs, like their theory of intelligence, that foster vulnerability. Do younger children have analogous beliefs? In this study with Gail Heyman we looked at two beliefs we thought might create vulnerability in young children.

One is the belief that mistakes mean a child is bad. We saw a moment ago that vulnerable young children felt they were bad after making a mistake and receiving criticism. But they were in the heat of a situation, perhaps filled with emotions. Would they really think mistakes mean a child is bad if they were asked this question in a more low-key situation and if the question did not make reference to them in particular? Yes, they would.

In a session several days prior to the one in which children went through the mistake and criticism scenarios they were asked a number of questions including the following:

> Imagine a new boy [or girl] is in your class. You look over at his schoolwork and see that he got lots and lots wrong and has a big frown on his paper. Does this mean that he is bad?

Very few of the mastery-oriented children thought that the mistakes in any way meant that the new child was bad. However, a substantial number of the helpless children took the mistakes to be a sign of badness. This means that it is not just in the heat of a failure experience that young children think mistakes imply badness. This is a belief that they seem to carry around with them.

The other belief we examined was the belief that badness is a stable trait. For older students we can just ask directly whether they think a trait is fixed or malleable. But this doesn't work for young children. They don't have experience pondering abstract internal personal qualities and answering questions about the true nature of these qualities. Instead, they need questions that portray concrete behaviors (to represent the trait) and that ask them to decide if these behaviors will persist through time.

So we said to them,

> Imagine a new girl [or boy] is in your class. She steals your crayons, scribbles on your paper, and spills your juice. Then she teases you and calls you names. Do you think this new girl will always act this way?

Again, very few of the mastery-oriented children thought that this badness would be stable. After all, this is a new child in school, and besides, how can you know how someone will be for all time? This did not deter the helpless children. A full 50% of them confidently said that this new boy or girl would always act the same way.

In later studies, Gail Heyman and I confirmed this significant relation between the helpless response and this belief in fixed badness (Heyman & Dweck, 1998).

This means that many young vulnerable children have the same kinds of beliefs as older vulnerable students—the belief that your traits can be measured from your failures and that your traits are for all time.

How lasting are these early beliefs and responses? We informally followed the young children from two of our studies (Heyman et al., 1992; Smiley & Dweck, 1994) for 2 years and found significant stability in their beliefs about badness and in their helpless versus mastery-oriented response to failure. This stability makes it even more important for us to understand where these beliefs and patterns come from and how they can be influenced.

☐ Thoughts on Badness

It's important to keep in mind that most young children, not just the vulnerable ones, are deeply involved in, intrigued by, and even obsessed with issues of goodness and badness. It permeates their games, their stories, and their questions (Paley, 1988). In their role playing, the mastery-oriented children mentioned goodness all the time. (Interestingly, nobody at this age mentioned intelligence or ability.)

In current research on child development (Damon, 1996), and in traditional theories of personality development (e.g., Erikson, 1950), issues of goodness are seen as being critical to young children's self-concepts. Later on, when children go to school and become increasingly involved with their peers, academic and social success loom larger. But in the early years, when a major goal in life is to draw love and esteem from your parents, goodness is the ticket.

If both mastery-oriented and helpless young children are vitally involved in issues of goodness, what's the difference between them? Our most recent research (Kamins & Dweck, 1998; see also Heyman et al., 1992) has shown that mastery-oriented children have a sense that they are good, and setbacks and criticism don't disrupt that sense of goodness. In fact, in their role playing, they have adults confirm their goodness despite the errors.

Most helpless children also have a sense that they are good, until something happens (Kamins & Dweck, 1998)—that is, until failure undermines this sense by telling them they're bad or unworthy, and possibly irrevocably so.

In other words, most young children go around feeling pretty good about themselves. The difference between vulnerable children and hardy children is in how "contingent" this sense of goodness is, whether it comes and goes depending on what happens. Hardy children recognize that they are good and worthy even though they might have done something wrong. Vulnerable children lose the sense that they're good or worthy when things go wrong.

How might children come to have a contingent sense of goodness? One way might be through parents who react to their behavior in a judgmental way. What the helpless children might have been telling us when they role-played harsh criticism and punishment from their parents is that they feel deeply judged by their parents when they transgress.

Again, I don't believe that these parents mete out punishment for a puzzle error or for the omission of feet from a picture. But they might evaluate the child's goodness (or judge the child as a whole) for true transgressions, and the child may not yet distinguish between task errors and conduct errors.

Is it possible that the helpless response arises in young children when they are treated in a judgmental way, as when their traits or their entire selves are evaluated from their behavior? Is this how they learn to judge themselves from their failures? We set out to answer this question.

Now, you might think that what these children need is more praise for their ability and their goodness—to counteract the negative judgments and to prevent them from doubting themselves so quickly—but you'd be wrong.

15 CHAPTER

Kinds of Praise and Criticism: The Origins of Vulnerability

In the last chapter we looked closely at vulnerabilities of young children, and saw that even children as young as 3½ years old can show clear evidence of a helpless response, including nonpersistence, lowered expectations, negative self-evaluations, negative emotions, and feelings of badness. Where do these responses come from? How do children develop these feelings, expectations, and reactions? Do they simply come this way, with some children being naturally mastery-oriented and others being more inclined to react helplessly?

It's possible that some children come with temperaments that incline them one way or the other—some being more natural risk takers and others inclined to be more cautious or easily frustrated (see Kagan & Snidman, 1991). But our research has shown clearly that the kind of feedback children get from adults can directly cause these different patterns—no matter what inclinations the children come with. These patterns can be strongly molded by the child's environment. In a series of experiments, with Melissa Kamins and Claudia Mueller (Kamins & Dweck, in press; Mueller & Dweck, 1998), we showed that different kinds of criticism and praise from adults can directly create mastery-oriented hardiness or helpless vulnerability. Here is how we showed this.

First, we pinpointed different kinds of criticism and praise. We did this by looking at what children said when they role-played their parents' and teachers' reactions to their work, by examining the findings in the childrearing literature, and by observing parent-child interactions. We chose types of criticism and praise that parents and teachers might frequently use and that we thought, from our previous work, would play a role in setting up mastery-oriented and helpless responses.

We then designed several experiments, in which children worked on tasks and were given a certain type of feedback. Each child was given only one type of feedback, and we evaluated how that feedback affected his or her ability to cope with later setbacks. The question was: Did children receiving some types of feedback

107

show a more mastery-oriented response when they later encountered difficulty or criticism, and did children receiving other types of feedback show a more helpless response?

It is important to understand that in these studies children are randomly assigned to feedback groups. This means that at the start of an experiment each group consists of a mixture of helpless and mastery-oriented children, and we assume that each group has roughly the same mixture. We then observe the impact of the feedback—whether each group as whole becomes more helpless or more mastery-oriented than other groups in its responses to setbacks.

What studies like this show is that no matter what tendencies children enter a situation with, if the situation is powerful it can mold their patterns of reaction. It can make them, for the moment, more helpless or more mastery-oriented in their reactions.

Our predictions for the types of *criticism* that would promote helplessness and mastery-orientation were fairly straightforward: Criticism that measured the child's traits or judged the child as a whole would make children more vulnerable when they later encountered setbacks. They would learn to measure themselves from their performance, and, in the presence of poor performance, they would come to negative conclusions. In contrast, we predicted that criticism that focused children on effort or strategies would promote a mastery-oriented response to later difficulties.

But we also thought that *praise* could create vulnerability. After all, praise can judge the child's traits or the child as a whole, for example by telling children they're smart or they're good children when they do well. Couldn't this, too, teach children that they can measure themselves from their behavior or performance?

That is, praising children's traits or selves when they do well may tell them that their basic attributes can be readily judged by what they do. If they take this message to heart, they may also judge themselves thoroughly when they later fail.

It is commonly believed that adults can do nothing more beneficial for children than praising their traits when they do well. Our past research led us to doubt this conventional wisdom. Thus our hypotheses for the types of praise that would create vulnerability versus hardiness were novel and perhaps a little startling. But first let us examine the effects of criticism.

☐ Criticism and Helpless Versus Mastery-Oriented Responses

In a study, by Melissa Kamins and me (Kamins & Dweck, in press), kindergarten children pretended to perform a series of four tasks for their teacher (much as in the study by Heyman et al. 1992, that I described previously), but in each case the task was not completed appropriately, and the teacher delivered some criticism. As before, the pretend task was enacted in a vivid way, with the use of toy dolls representing the child and his or her teacher. Also as before, we used a pretend task so that no criticism would be leveled at the child directly. After each of the four tasks, the toy teacher pointed out the problem with the child's work and delivered the critical feedback to the toy child.

For example, in one task children were asked to pretend that when they finished fingerpainting the teacher asked them to clean up the painting area and to clean themselves off. After they thought they had completed the task and after they had called the teacher over, they noticed that their hands were still messy and that the table still had paint on it. The teacher pointed this out and then delivered the feedback.

For one group, she delivered feedback that oriented the child toward different strategies, saying, for example, "Your hands are still messy and the table still has paint on it. Maybe you should think of another way to do it." This was based on our observation that mastery-oriented young children often role-played strategy suggestions from their parents, and also on our findings that mastery-oriented children tend to focus on strategies when they encounter difficulty.

To a second group of children, she directed the feedback toward the appropriateness of the specific behavior, saying, for example, "That's not what I call doing it the right way" or "That's not what I call doing it the right way because there is still paint all over." This group was designed to test the often repeated childrearing advice that we should aim our criticism at the behavior and not at the child.

The third and final group was given criticism that reflected more on the child as a whole. We didn't feel that it was appropriate even in a pretend situation to tell children they were bad for what they did, even though many parents may do this as a matter of course. Instead, for this group, we had the toy teacher express disappointment in the toy child as she surveyed the incomplete task.

It is important to point out again that, as in all of our studies, extensive precautions were taken so that children would leave the situation feeling pleased with themselves and their performance. For example, in this study, after the feedback and test stories, an additional story was told in which the child performed a laudable act and received praise from the teacher. In addition, the experimenter went back through every one of the feedback stories with each child and helped the child generate successful endings, with the teacher giving positive feedback for the child's successful resolution of the mistake. Thus, each child was trained in mastery-oriented strategies for dealing with problems.

After the four stories with feedback came the test for the effects of the feedback (again, modeled on Heyman et al.). All children were told a fifth story in which they pretended to build a house but forgot to put in any windows. The teacher looked at the house and pointed out the mistake—"That house has no windows"—but she did not issue any further criticism.

So all groups were given the exact same experience on this last task, and our question, again, was: How would children react to this last mistake based on the previous feedback they had received from the teacher?

Even though all children received identical feedback on the last story, they were expected to cope differently with the mistake because of the feedback they had received on the previous stories. In our view, the feedback on the previous stories had taught them what mistakes mean and how they should be interpreted. Do mistakes mean you should just adjust your strategy? Do they mean your behavior was off the mark? Or do they, more globally, reflect on you as a person?

Our findings were extremely clear. The group that received the person-oriented criticism showed the strongest helpless reaction of any group, whereas the group that received the strategy feedback showed the most mastery-oriented response of any group. Let's look at the results in more detail.

First, how did the children in the different groups rate their product in the final story, the house with no windows? Children who had received the strategy feedback gave their windowless house a very high rating, an average rating of almost 5 on a 6-point scale, with 6 being the highest rating. In contrast, the children who received the person-oriented feedback gave their house a rating of only 3. (The other group fell right in between, as they did on most of the measures, and so we focus our discussion on the difference between the strategy group and the person-oriented group.) Thus, even though the groups were rating the exact same house, children who had received person-oriented criticism saw their work as inferior.

Second, children were asked how everything that happened with the house made them feel. Those children who had received the strategy feedback expressed significantly more positive affect than those who had received the person-oriented disapproval. This was true even though the two groups received identical feedback on this final story.

Third, the children were asked to finish the story, and we looked at whether they generated constructive solutions to the problem. The children in the strategy-feedback group were much more likely than those in the global-feedback group to generate a constructive solution. In fact, most of the children in the strategy group thought of a way to fix their product and solve the problem, whereas most of the children in the global-feedback condition did not come up with endings that resolved the situation in a satisfactory way.

This was true even though the groups were presumably equal in their ability to come up with solutions. Also, as I mentioned in the previous chapter, it's not very difficult to take the toy dolls and concoct a constructive, satisfying ending. Yet when children fall into a helpless mode of responding, they become far less likely to do so. It is as though they have lost faith in their ability to solve problems effectively.

Fourth, children were asked to think back to everything that happened with the house, and to tell us whether everything that had happened with the house made them feel like they were a smart boy or girl or not a smart boy or girl, a good girl or boy or not a good girl or boy, and a nice girl or boy or not a nice girl or boy. Each question was asked separately. Children who had received the strategy feedback answered most of the time in the positive way, whereas the children in the person-oriented feedback group answered most of the time in the negative way, creating a highly significant difference between the groups.

Finally, we wanted to see whether the different kinds of feedback affected how the children thought about badness. Would person-oriented feedback make children think that badness can be judged from mistakes and that badness is a stable quality? Would strategy feedback, on the other hand, make them feel that mistakes don't equal badness and that bad behavior is not necessarily permanent?

So we asked children, as in the earlier study, whether they thought a child who got lots wrong on his or her schoolwork and got a big frown on his or her paper is bad, and whether a child who performed a series of naughty behaviors would always act this way. We did not have a strong expectation that the feedback children had received would affect these general beliefs about badness, but it did.

Children who had received the person-oriented feedback were significantly more likely to agree with these ideas than were the children who had received the strategy feedback. How could global feedback change children's beliefs about badness, making them think that badness can be inferred from very specific performance and that badness is a stable trait? It's as though the person-oriented disapproval taught children that, based on their behavior, an adult can look deeply into them and judge a permanent quality. Perhaps, in this way, it taught them that permanent traits can be read from performance, and this is exactly what they did themselves on the final scenario—they read their ability, their goodness, and their niceness from their mistakes.

In short, criticism that reflected on the child as a whole created the entire helpless pattern of self-blame, negative affect, and a lack of constructive solutions, as well as the general beliefs (such as the belief in stable badness) that accompany the helpless pattern.

In contrast, critical feedback that focused the child on alternative strategies produced the most mastery-oriented pattern.

The feedback group where the criticism focused on the child's specific behavior (e.g., "That's not what I call doing it the right way") fell in the middle. These children generally fared considerably better than the global-feedback group, but not as well as the strategy-feedback group. They were not taught a negative meaning for mistakes, but they were not taught the most positive one either.

This study showed that giving children experience with certain types of feedback can lead directly to more helpless or more mastery-oriented responses. Because children were randomly assigned to the feedback groups, we can assume that all of the groups were essentially the same before they experienced the different types of feedback. Each had a mix of helpless and mastery-oriented children. Yet after the feedback experiences the group looked dramatically different in how they interpreted and reacted to setbacks.

This shows that some of the common feedback practices that parents employ can have a powerful effect on children's coping skills. Indeed, in our study children received only four instances of feedback in a small set of situations, and still we found very strong effects. Parental practices will be experienced by a child every day and in many situations.

☐ Praise and Helpless Versus Mastery-Oriented Responses

After seeing these effects, we became very interested in finding out whether different types of praise might have similar impact. We saw that with criticism, negative feedback that called attention to children's underlying traits had a negative effect on their ability to cope with later setbacks. What about *praise* that calls attention to children's traits—for example, telling children they are smart or good when they perform well? Will this, too, teach children to read their traits from their performance so that, even though they might feel wonderful at the time, they will later read negative traits when they display poor performance?

This possibility runs counter to the deepest intuitions of people in our culture. Much of education and childrearing today is based on the assumption that giving children lots of praise at every opportunity, and *particularly* praise that reflects on them globally as a person, will make them feel good about their abilities and boost their self-esteem. This, in turn, will make them eager to pursue challenges and will make them hardy in the face of setbacks.

There is also some excellent research showing that when you give children trait-oriented praise, such as praise for their ability, it does raise their sense of efficacy and it does boost their performance—while they are succeeding. But research has not investigated what happens when that student hits difficulty.

Nor has it looked at whether children, after getting praised for their ability, want to take on challenging (i.e., risky) learning tasks—or whether they just want to keep on looking smart.

The question here, then, is whether delivering praise that tells children they are good or smart or wonderful when they succeed makes them vulnerable to a helpless response later on when they don't succeed. Again, this is not what common wisdom would have us believe, but it is precisely what our research led us to suspect, for across studies we saw that children who read their abilities or goodness from their performance were vulnerable. And we believed that praise, not just criticism, could teach children to do this.

So we designed several studies to find out whether our fears were well founded. In these studies, we gave children different types of praise that parents or teachers might commonly use, and we assessed the impact of the praise on children's helpless versus mastery-oriented responses.

In another study by Melissa Kamins and me (Kamins & Dweck, in press, study 2), kindergarten children again pretended to work on tasks for their teacher and again acted out the scenarios with a toy child and a toy teacher. All children were entirely successful on the first four tasks, and they received praise from the toy teacher each time.

As in the last study, children received person-oriented feedback, outcome feedback, or strategy/effort feedback, but we added some new kinds of person-oriented feedback and a new kind of effort feedback.

There were six groups in all, and each received a different form of praise: Three of the groups received a kind of person- or trait-oriented praise, one received outcome praise, and two received a kind of effort or strategy praise.

For the first three groups, the praise reflected on the child as a whole or on the child's traits. In these groups, children were told after each success that they had completed the task appropriately and then either, "You're a good boy/girl" (group 1), "I'm proud of you" (group 2), or "You're very good at this" (group 3). This is the kind of person- or trait-oriented praise that we believed might make children vulnerable to later failure or criticism, even though it is the kind of praise that may make them delighted and confident when they receive it.

A fourth group received a more specific kind of praise that was focused on the child's outcome, but not the strategy or effort. Here, after their success was noted, children were told, "That's the right way to do it" (group 4).

The final two groups were focused on either their effort or their strategy. After each success they were told, "You really tried hard" (group 5), or, "You found a good way to do it; could you think of other ways that would also work?" (group 6). These groups were expected to look the most mastery-oriented since a hallmark of the mastery-oriented response is a focus on effort and strategy as the way to bring about success.

Incidentally, we checked up on the groups after three successes to see how they were faring, and we found them all to be equally positive about their work on the tasks, in their mood, and in their ratings of themselves.

After the four episodes of success and praise, we looked at how the children in the different groups would cope with setbacks.

All children now encountered two pretend scenarios in which they made mistakes. For example, in one scenario, they built a house of blocks but the house had no windows. These mistakes were pointed out by the teacher, who said, for example, "That house has no windows," but no criticism was given.

Following the second mistake scenario, children were asked a series of questions designed to see how the setback affected their self-assessments, their emotions, their persistence, and their beliefs about badness.

The findings were again very clear. The groups that had received the person-oriented praise on the success scenarios ("You're a good girl/boy," "I'm proud of you," or "You're really good at this") were the ones who were most vulnerable to the effects of failure. These three groups showed the most helpless pattern of all six groups, and the three looked about equally helpless on our measures. This means that the groups that were most "deeply" praised were the groups that were later most vulnerable.

In contrast, the two groups that had gotten the effort and strategy praise looked the most mastery-oriented.

The group that was given specific outcome information was again in the middle, and we will not focus on them as we review our findings.

Let's examine the results in more detail. First, when children were asked to rate their product on the scenario with setbacks, children in the strategy-praise groups gave their product a significantly higher rating than those in the person-praise groups. In fact, the strategy-praise groups gave their house a positive rating, despite its lack of windows, while the person-praise groups gave their windowless house a negative rating.

How did the children rate themselves? For this measure, children were asked to think of what happened in the window scenario and to rate how they felt about themselves on several dimensions. Did they feel as though they were smart or not smart, a good boy or girl or not a good boy or girl, and a nice boy or girl or not a nice boy or girl? Children who had received the strategy praise rated themselves significantly more positively on these questions than did children who had received the person praise. In other words, those who were told they were good or had high ability when they succeeded now thought they were less good and had lower ability when they failed.

Next, when we looked at children's ratings of their emotions on the last scenario, we found the same pattern. On this measure, children were asked to select a face that represented how they felt, ranging from a big sad face to a big happy face. Children in the effort-strategy groups felt okay about their setback—they chose a face in the happy-face range. Children in the person and trait groups felt significantly worse and tended to choose a face in the sad-face range.

We had four measures of persistence. We asked children which task they would like to do the next day—one of the success tasks or the failure task. We asked them which they would like to do the day after that. These were designed to see whether children wanted to keep at the failure task until they could succeed. Another question asked them how much they wanted to try the failure task again (a little, a medium amount, or a lot). A final persistence question asked them to finish the story, and we looked at the extent to which they came up with constructive solutions. We then averaged the scores from the four measures to form an index of persistence.

Once again, the children in the strategy-praise groups looked more mastery-oriented: They were significantly more persistent and constructive than the children in the person-praise groups. Thus, those children who were told they were good, that they were good at the tasks, or that the teacher was proud of them were the same children who were not inclined to persist when they encountered obstacles.

Finally, children were asked whether they believed that a child who got a lot wrong on their schoolwork was a bad child and whether a child who performed a series of negative behaviors would always act that way. Children in the person and trait groups were significantly more likely to say "yes" to these questions. This means that their experience with person-oriented feedback led them to believe that global judgments could readily be made and that the traits that were judged were lasting ones. Even though they had learned this lesson from positive feedback applied to positive traits, they readily transferred the lesson to negative traits.

In short, children who had received what might seem like the most ego-boosting forms of praise ("You're a good girl/boy," "I'm proud of you," and "You're very good at this") were at a clear disadvantage when it came to later coping with setbacks. In contrast, children whose positive feedback focused on their effort or their strategy were in the best position to cope with obstacles.

Not only did the children in the person-oriented praise groups show poorer affect and lower persistence when they performed poorly, they also showed more self-denigration. In other words, if you learn from person praise that success means you're a good or able person, then you also seem to learn that failure means you are a bad or inept person. If you learn from praise that your good performance merits wholesale pride, you also seem to learn that poor performance merits shame.

☐ Contingent Self-Worth

In a sense, the person-oriented feedback seems to be instilling a sense of "contingent self-worth." When people have a sense of contingent self-worth, they feel like worthy people only when they have succeeded, and they feel deficient or worthless when they fail. This concept forms the core of several traditional personality theories, such as those of Carl Rogers (1961) and Karen Horney (1937, 1945, 1950). In these theories, some parents' reactions to their children teach the children that the parents consider them worthy of love and respect only when they behave a certain way or meet a certain standard. Children then adopt the idea that they are persons of worth only under those circumstances.

It had struck us before that the helpless young children in our earlier studies (Hebert & Dweck, 1985; Heyman et al., 1992) were displaying a clear sense of contingent self-worth (see Baldwin & Sinclair, 1996; Burhans & Dweck, 1995; Covington, 1992; Dykman, 1998; Harter, 1990). They behaved very much as though they expected major rejection from their parents (and their teachers) for their failures. And they told us that they themselves felt as though they were not good kids as a result of making a mistake or receiving criticism.

Now we see that the person criticism and the person praise can actually create this by leading children to be proud and happy with themselves only when they succeeded and to be globally self-denigrating and unhappy with themselves when they erred.

Melissa Kamins and I have continued to explore the idea that contingent self-worth and helplessness go hand in hand. In a recent study with kindergarten children (Kamins & Dweck, 1998), we assessed children's sense of contingent self-worth via a series of questions and scenarios. These were designed to tap whether children found themselves to be deserving and worthy all of the time or only when they behaved in a certain way. We then gave children the Hebert and Dweck (1985) puzzle task, in which they experienced difficulty, and checked for signs of helplessness. As we predicted, the children who had expressed a sense of contingent self-worth were significantly more helpless on virtually all of the measures of helplessness than were the children who asserted that they were worthy and deserving people all of the time.

In a study with college students, by Michael Chafets-Gitin, Melissa Kamins, and me, we looked at the relation between students' theories of intelligence, their achievement goals, and their sense of contingent self-worth. We wondered whether a sense of contingent worth was linked to an entity theory (the idea that you had a fixed trait that could be judged to determine your worth) and to a preference for performance goals (a need to validate your intelligence; in a sense, a need to prove your worth by performing well). We found a highly significant relation among the three.

Although this work is very new, we are fascinated by the idea that an entity theory, performance goals, helplessness, and contingent versus noncontingent self-worth may go together, and that the same kinds of praise and criticism can promote all of them.

To summarize this chapter, we succeeded in showing that no matter how good person praise or trait praise may make children feel at the time it is given, it carries with it a host of dangers.

Is it just that young children, being young children, are unusually susceptible to the messages that adult feedback conveys? Was it just something about this particular experiment that produced these odd results? Given that our findings run so counter to conventional beliefs, we realized that we needed to test the ideas again in a different way.

The next studies, with older children, extend these findings. They show once again that person or trait-oriented praise has a host of negative effects and that some of these unwanted effects can be seen even before failure occurs.

Praising Intelligence:
More Praise that Backfires

At the same time that Melissa Kamins and I were studying the effects of praise on kindergarten students, Claudia Mueller and I were studying the impact of praise on older, fifth-grade children (Mueller & Dweck, 1998). We were very interested in the commonly advocated practice of praising students for their intelligence. In fact, we had found in our previous research that 85% of parents believe that praising children's ability when they do well is something that is necessary for children's self-esteem (Mueller & Dweck, 1996). Why might this be?

Well, for one thing, it's very intuitively appealing. Telling children they're smart should make them believe they're smart, and believing they're smart should make them confident about taking on challenges and seeing them through.

Another reason that this belief is so widespread stems from research by Rosenthal and Jacobson (1968) on the "Pygmalion" or teacher-expectancy effect. In this research, grade-school teachers were given positive expectations for certain children in their classes at the beginning of the school year. The teachers were told that tests indicated these children would bloom over the coming school year. In fact, the children had been designated at random from the children in their class. Yet these children made greater gains in achievement over that year than did comparable children for whom teachers were not given high expectancies.

These findings were taken to mean that when teachers think children are smart and convey this to them, children thrive. The lesson that was derived from this was that we should convey to children, at every opportunity, that they are smart, and this will aid their achievement.

But notice that Rosenthal and Jacobson did not simply tell teachers that certain children were smart or had high IQs. They told them that these children were likely to bloom; in other words, they conveyed that these children were open to learning, were ready to grow, could profit from teaching. What this message probably did was lead teachers to work more effectively with these children, and not simply to praise their intelligence.

At the same time, more and more attention was given to the adverse effects of negative labeling. Practices that conveyed to children that they had low levels of intelligence were receiving a great deal of scrutiny, and educators took pains to prevent students from feeling so labeled. This too, I believe, fed the idea that positive labeling was the answer. Rather than switching students *out* of the entity framework, in which intelligence is evaluated and labeled, many believed that the answer lay in making children feel good about their intelligence within that framework.

Yet another stream of research led to the belief in praising intelligence. This was research showing the many beneficial effects of "positive reinforcement." Rewarding children when they did good things was supposed to make them want to do those things more and more (but see Cordova & Lepper, 1996; Deci & Ryan, 1985; Lepper, Aspinwall, Mumme, & Chabay, 1990). Therefore, praising children when they got right answers or did good work was supposed to make them more eager achievers.

Thus a host of things came together to create the widespread belief in the efficacy of praising children's intelligence when they succeed. As you know, we believed that this practice might backfire when children later hit obstacles. But we also thought that praising children for their intelligence might backfire even before children hit obstacles.

We thought that praise for intelligence might quickly make children shy away from challenging learning tasks that could jeopardize this positive judgment. Instead they might gravitate toward easier tasks that would confirm the positive judgment. After all, if someone looked at your performance and told you you were really smart, would that make you eager for challenges that might show your deficiencies? Or would that make you want to keep on performing well and keep your label "smart"?

In our research, Claudia Mueller and I (Mueller & Dweck, 1998) gave students a problem-solving task to work on. On the first set of problems, all students did very well and were told, "Wow, you got [however many] problems correct. That's a very good score!"

For students in the control group, the feedback stopped there. For students in the intelligence-praise group, the feedback continued with, "You must be really smart at these." For students in the effort-praise group, the feedback continued with, "You must have worked hard."

Immediately following the praise, students' goals were assessed. Did students want to perform a task that ensured further success and allowed them to keep showing they were smart (a performance-goal task)? Or did they want to tackle a task that they'd learn a lot from even if they didn't look so smart (a learning-goal task)?

The groups looked completely different in their goal choice. The group that had received praise for their intelligence wanted the performance-goal task. Two thirds of them opted for the task that would ensure that they would keep on looking smart.

In contrast, over 90% of the students who received effort praise chose the learning-goal task. They were not interested in ensuring success; they were interested in pursuing a potentially fruitful challenge. (The students in the control group were split evenly between the two goals.)

This means that even before failure occurred, students' goals were dramatically affected by the feedback they received: Most of the children who were praised for their intelligence were no longer interested in challenge and learning.

After the first set of problems, the students went onto a second set. They performed more poorly on these and were informed of this by the experimenter, who proceeded to ask them a series of questions (a) about their enjoyment of the problems ("How much did you like working on these problems?" "How much fun were the problems overall?"); (b) about their desire to persist in trying to master the problems ("How much would you like to take some of the problems home to work on?"); and (c) about their explanations for their failure ("I didn't work hard enough" versus "I'm not good at these problems" or "I'm not smart enough").

They then went on to work a third set of problems so we could see the effect of the failure on their subsequent performance.

Again, the groups looked very different. The group that had been praised for their intelligence now, after failure, reported the least enjoyment of the problems of any of the groups. Those praised for their effort reported the most enjoyment.

In terms of their desire to persist in trying to master the problems, those who had been praised for their intelligence after their success were the ones who were now least likely to want to persist by taking the problems home to work on. Perhaps they now found the problems aversive and wanted nothing further to do with them. Or perhaps, if performance on the task was for them a matter of ability, they thought that further effort would not help.

How did the different groups explain their failure? First, the group that had been praised for intelligence was least likely of all the groups to think that the failure was due to their effort. This was the most strongly endorsed explanation for the other two groups but was the least strongly endorsed explanation for this group. So, it seems that praising children for their intelligence almost rules out effort as an explanation of their outcomes.

Second, the group that was told they had high ability were the very ones who condemned their ability in the face of failure. They were the ones who now, after failure, were most likely to say that the failure meant they wre *not* good at these problems (or not smart). In other words, as we have been suggesting, when you teach children to measure themselves from their success, they then measure themselves from their failure as well.

Finally, when we looked at the performance on the last set of problems, we saw that the group that had been praised for its intelligence showed the worst performance of any group. In fact, they showed a significant decline in their performance from the first to the last problem set. The failure was clearly a debilitating experience for them. In contrast, the effort group showed the best performance of any of the groups on the last problem set, and they showed significant improvement in performance from the first to the last problem set. Failure did not appear to hamper the students in this group and might well have spurred them on.

In summary, when children are praised for their intelligence after a job well done, this can create vulnerability. Some of that vulnerability may show right away, as seen in this group's preference for assured success over a challenging learning task. But some of the vulnerability might show only after a failure experience.

Indeed, as another part of the research (Mueller & Dweck, 1998, studies 2 and 4) we took two more groups of students. We gave them only the first (success) set of problems, we gave them the three types of feedback, and we asked them a series of questions about their enjoyment and desire to persist. Those who received praise for their intelligence expressed just as much enjoyment of the task and expressed just as much desire to persist on the task as the other groups. Thus these aspects of their motivation did not look impaired at all after their success experience. It was only after failure that their enjoyment and persistence plummeted, as did their assessment of their ability and their performance.

Because the results of this research were so striking, we thought it was important to repeat the whole experiment with a new group of students. We did, and we found the same thing.

In all, we did it three more times, with students in different parts of the country and with students of very different ethnic and racial backgrounds. We still found the same thing. And we found other things as well. First, we found that intelligence praise makes students so oriented toward performance goals that they will lie about their failure.

In one of the studies (Mueller & Dweck, 1998, study 3), we told students that we would be conducting the same study at another school, and that children at the new school might like to hear a little about the task from children who had already worked on it. We gave students a sheet on which they could record their thoughts about the task. On the sheet was a question that asked them to say how many problems they had gotten right on each problem set. Would they tell the truth or would they glorify their performance to the outside world?

When we looked at the children who had received effort praise, we found that almost all of them told the truth about their performance. Only one child in that group doctored his score for public consumption. In contrast, a full 40% of the children in the intelligence group lied about their scores. Doing well was so important to them that they felt compelled to distort their performance in order to impress unknown peers.

We also wondered whether praise for intelligence versus effort would influence children's theories of intelligence. Would intelligence praise teach students that intelligence is an entity within them that is reflected in their performance? Would effort praise instead orient students toward the view that abilities are malleable qualities developed through effort? So in two of the studies, we probed students' theories about their intelligence (Mueller & Dweck, 1998, studies 4 and 5).

Although students' theories of intelligence are relatively stable beliefs, a powerful situation can highlight one view over the other, and influence students' beliefs at that moment. These situations can also give us insight into the kinds of situations that, if experienced repeatedly, might mold students' theories in a more permanent way.

We found that the praise students received did in fact influence their theory of intelligence in the situation. Those students who received praise for their intelligence were significantly more likely to endorse an entity theory of intelligence than were students who were praised for their effort. This was true whether we assessed their theories of intelligence after their initial success (study 4) or whether we assessed them after their failure trial (study 5).

Maybe the students who received intelligence praise were even eager to buy into an entity theory after the first trial. They had just succeeded and had just been told they were smart. Why *not* buy into a theory that tells you this is a stable entity? However, later on, when they were not feeling very good about their performance or their intelligence, they still held the entity theory significantly more than the students who had received effort praise.

In this research, we also wanted to make sure that intelligence and effort praise still had the same effect on later coping if we changed to a new task after the praise, or if we changed the experimenter after the praise. In other words, we wanted to make sure that the praise gave students a message that they would carry with them to new tasks given by new people—that they weren't just learning, for example, that a particular task measured their intelligence or that a particular person's feedback measured their intelligence. And indeed we found that even when we switched students to a new task (study 6) or to a new experimenter (study 5) after the praise, intelligence praise still created the same vulnerability and effort praise still created the same hardiness.

In all, we performed six studies of intelligence praise with a great variety of students, students from various ethnic groups and from places as diverse as New York City and rural Indiana. In each case we found that intelligence praise for a job well done carried with it a host of drawbacks: It made students too performance-oriented, to the point where they would sacrifice learning or lie about their performance in order to look better. It made them vulnerable to failure so that after they encountered a setback their persistence and enjoyment dwindled, their performance suffered, and their faith in their ability plummeted. This means that the very students whose intelligence was hailed was the group that ended up with the lowest opinion of their ability.

Finally, intelligence praise appeared to foster the theory of fixed intelligence, a belief we know is associated with vulnerability. Effort praise, in sharp contrast, promoted a host of desirable outcomes.

I am not saying that intelligence praise is the worst thing you can do to a child. Heaven knows there are many worse things, but as this work shows there are also clearly better things.

☐ Implications of Intelligence and Effort Praise: Is Effort Praise Enough?

Anyone who has been in the presence of children who are doing really well at something knows that there is an almost irresistible urge to tell them how good, talented, or smart they are at what they're doing. We are at a loss for other ways to show our delight and admiration. Effort praise hardly seems like an adequate substitute.

But effort and strategy praise when given in the right way can be highly appreciative of a child's accomplishments. If a child paints a lovely picture we can ask about and admire how he or she selected the colors, formed the images, or created textures. If a child solves a series of difficult math problems, we can ask with admiration what strategies she or he used and we can admire the concentration that went into it. If children write wonderful stories, we can ask them with admiration how they came up with the interesting characters and story line. We can ask them how they made certain decisions at different points, and we can speculate with them about what might happen next.

In many ways, this kind of "process" discussion is much more appreciative of what the child has done than person praise. Person praise essentially ignores the essence, the true merit, of what was accomplished, and appreciates the work only as a reflection of some ability.

What about times when there is no effort to praise? A student has done something quickly, easily, and perfectly. This is really a time when we are sorely tempted to give intelligence praise. But instead, as I suggested earlier, we should apologize to the student for wasting his or her time with something that was not challenging enough to learn anything from. We should not make easy successes into the pinnacle of accomplishment and we should not be teaching our children that low-effort products are what they should be most proud of. We should direct them into more profitable activities where their time will be better invested.

☐ Implications for Encouraging Achievement

Low Achievers

For decades we worried about the effects that negative labels could have. For example, we worried that low-achieving students would be labeled as unintelligent, and that this label could undermine them further. This concern was entirely appropriate, because negative labels can indeed be harmful. It has been well documented by research, and we've also seen it from the way that helpless children label themselves when they fail and become demoralized.

However, a clear implication of our findings is that positive labeling is not the answer. Intelligence labels, good or bad, have undermining effects. Both teach children that their underlying intelligence can be readily judged from their performance.

In other words, it is not a good idea to try to encourage the achievement of underachieving groups by praising their intelligence when they succeed—even though it may be very tempting to try to boost their faith in themselves in this way. Instead, our results suggest that when students succeed, attention and approval should be directed at their efforts or their strategies. This teaches them the importance of effort and strategies as a means to success and keeps them focused on effort and strategies as a means of overcoming failures.

It is especially important for students who are having difficulty in school to learn this lesson. They don't need inflating praise as much as they need to know how to interpret setbacks and what to do when they occur. Because they will be confronted with challenge upon challenge, they must learn that challenge is something that promotes learning, not something that indicts their ability.

High-Achieving Students

Our findings have implications for high-achieving students as well, especially for the labeling of children as talented or gifted (see Dweck, in press). Again, we may feel that we are giving children's self-esteem a boost by letting them know they are considered to be gifted. But even the term "gifted" conjures up an entity theory. It implies that some entity, a large amount of intelligence, has been magically bestowed upon students, making them special.

Thus, when students are so labeled, some may become overconcerned with justifying that label, and less concerned with seeking challenges that enhance their skills—like the students in our studies who received intelligence praise. They may also begin to react more poorly to setbacks, worrying that mistakes, confusions, or failures mean that they don't deserve the coveted label. If being gifted makes them special, then losing the label may mean to them that they are "ordinary" and somehow less worthy.

A friend of mine had a brother who was a math prodigy. He took college courses when he was in junior high school, and each summer he was whisked away to study with one or another math guru. The whole family was focused on his mathematical talent. He began to feel he was a superior being and often made fun of other people's intellects. Yet, as the challenges grew greater, he grew more fearful of not making the grade and retreated from the more difficult problems he might have tackled. Today he has a rather ordinary job and is quite bitter that lesser mortals have outstripped him in achievement. In short, in order to protect his gifted status, he shrank from true challenges and never really fulfilled his potential.

Each Fall, without fail, hundreds of gifted students show up for college, all of them having been the stars of their high schools. What does it mean to them that a very large proportion of their classmates are equally gifted? For some it can be exhilarating to be in such a stimulating new environment with so many accomplished peers to interact with and learn from. But for others it is devastating to realize that their claim to fame—being smarter than everyone else—has disappeared.

Some of these students may display a strong helpless reaction. They may decide they are not smart after all, and instead of working particularly hard to master the challenges of their new environment, they may give up on their academic aspirations and settle for mediocre achievement.

As I pointed out in a previous chapter, more than a few minority students may fall into this trap. They may have been academic superstars in their high schools and hailed by the faculty for their intelligence. But as they confront their new college environment, they may quickly become demoralized. For example, Steele (1997a), in a study of African American students who enrolled at the University of Michigan, found that a large number dropped out in their freshman year. Was it because they were not well prepared for the rigors of a top college? Steele's data suggest that this was not the reason. What was startling was that the African American students with really high Scholastic Aptitude Test scores (averaging 700 and above) were *just* as likely to drop out as the ones with lower scores (averaging in the 500s).

If we can take these scores, for the moment, as an index of academic preparation, this means that the highly prepared students were dropping out just as frequently as their less-prepared classmates. This sounds very much like what I've been saying all along: The helpless response is not a matter of a student's present ability. Very skilled students are just as likely as less-skilled students to respond to difficulty by blaming their abilities and giving up. In fact, as I have been suggesting, some of our practices—such as bestowing gifted labels—may make the most skilled students even more vulnerable than they might have been.

I am by no means suggesting that we should gloss over students' unusual achievements or in any way fail to recognize our students who have accomplished exceptional things. I am suggesting that it may be extremely important for these students that we keep the emphasis on seeking challenges, applying effort, and searching for strategies (see Aronson & Fried, 1998). This way, when they later hit obstacles, they will not feel they have toppled from the ranks of the intelligent. Instead, they will know how to cope.

High-Achieving Girls

These findings may also help us understand one of the most puzzling findings in our research—the paradox of bright girls. We described earlier how bright girls are the highest achieving group in grade school: They earn the highest grades, they exceed bright boys in reading achievement, and they equal bright boys in math achievement. Moreover, teachers agree that these girls are the stars.

Nevertheless, when we and others look at bright girls in our studies, we find that they are the group with the greatest vulnerability to helplessness. They are more likely than boys to hold an entity theory of their intelligence (Leggett, 1985), they are more likely to want tasks they are sure they can do well at (low-challenge performance goals) (Leggett, 1985; Licht & Shapiro, 1982), and they are more likely to blame their abilities and show impairment when they encounter difficulties (Licht & Dweck, 1984; Licht et al., 1984; Licht & Shapiro, 1982; see also Burgner & Hewstone, 1993; Cramer & Oshima, 1992; Seegers & Boekaerts, 1996; Stipek & Gralinski, 1991). Moreover, when school begins to get more challenging, as it does in junior high school, these girls traditionally have begun to fall behind their male counterparts in achievement, especially in math and science achievement (Astin, 1974; Fox, 1976).

Our findings show how praise for intelligence and praise for goodness can create just these vulnerabilities, and they lead to a hypothesis about why these vulnerabilities might occur.

It is likely that bright young girls receive lots of approval for their goodness— they are much better behaved and self-regulated than young boys (see Dweck, Davidson, Nelson, & Enna, 1978). They may thereby receive early training that they can measure their traits from the outcomes and the feedback they receive (see Roberts, 1991; Roberts & Nolen-Hoeksema, 1994; see also Pomerantz & Ruble, 1998). And the irony here would be that girls' earlier maturation and self-regulatory abilities may set them up for their later motivational vulnerability (see Maccoby, 1998; Whiting and Whiting, 1975).

What about intelligence praise? For many years, we worried, appropriately, that girls might be getting *negative* messages about their ability. That is, we knew that there were longstanding stereotypes in our society that females were less competent than males, especially in certain areas such as math. We worried that society imparted these stereotypes to girls and, by doing so, harmed their achievement. My great concern is that in our attempt to counteract these stereotypes and build girls' confidence in their intellectual abilities, we now heap intelligence praise on them.

As we saw in the studies of intelligence praise, these experiences can encourage an entity theory, performance goals, challenge avoidance, and helpless responses to later difficulties. The diet of early success and praise may even make girls eager to buy into the entity theory, and now we have a recipe for trouble.

Bright girls are not hampered in obvious ways in grade school, where the material may not yet confront them with difficulty or confusion, but we can already see the vulnerability in our experiments when we do confront them with difficulty (e.g., Licht & Dweck, 1984a).

Moreover, after grade school, the game changes. Now, students who are challenge-seeking and persistent and can tolerate periods of confusion have the advantage. This is because the work becomes more rigorous, as new and different subjects, such as algebra and geometry, are introduced. If bright girls doubt their ability when they encounter challenging tasks, then the occasions for ability doubting and helpless responses will become more numerous.

There is another factor that can also contribute to the lag in achievement. As students go on in school, they are given more and more choice as to what courses they will pursue (Eccles, 1984). If bright girls are most attracted to tasks they're sure they'll do well at (so they can keep on feeling intelligent), then they may opt for easier programs of study, avoiding advanced math and science because these may feel too risky.

These motivational patterns, then, can help us understand why girls, who are the stars in grade school, have not traditionally been the stars in the later world of achievement. Notice that this analysis does not assume that any achievement lag is because of less ability on the part of girls. It simply assumes that some girls develop motivational patterns that lead them to dislike challenge and that leave them vulnerable to helpless reactions. Our analysis further suggests that one factor in the development of these patterns may be bright girls' early successes, which undoubtedly bring them acclaim from their teachers and parents for their intelligence and their goodness. This may teach them a framework that can limit their later achievement.

Girls' traditional lag in achievement has most often been attributed to other factors. One, as I mentioned, is society's stereotype of females as less competent, and another is society's prohibition against high achievement for women, which is seen as unfeminine. There is no denying that these societal beliefs have been problematic for women. However, what is extremely interesting to me is that girls' vulnerability is seen as early as grade school, where achievement is, if anything, a girl thing, not a boy thing; where teachers are often less imbued with expectations about girls' limitations; and where girls are actually outachieving boys very consistently. Although I would not deny the impact of stereotypes on achievement, these findings of early vulnerability despite early achievement lend credibility to our motivational analysis as an important underpinning of girls' vulnerability.

I have voiced concern that efforts to combat harmful stereotypes and to encourage girls' achievement may have led people to escalate their praise of girls' intelligence. Our analysis implies instead that an emphasis on challenge, effort, and strategy is absolutely essential for girls. Their successes should indeed be praised, but for the effort and the strategies that went into them. They should be taught that challenges are exciting and should be praised for taking on challenges and sticking with them. They must learn that the hallmark of intelligence is not immediate perfection, but rather the habit of embracing new tasks that stretch your skills and build your knowledge.

Why aren't bright boys subject to the same vulnerabilities? Some may well be, but on the whole bright boys seem as a group to be quite mastery-oriented (Licht & Dweck, 1984a; Licht & Shapiro, 1982; Licht et al., 1984). Part of the reason, paradoxically, is that boys do not seem to take to grade school as well as girls do. Boys misbehave a great deal more, and they are often less diligent and attentive. This leads teachers, and perhaps parents as well, to place more emphasis on effort for boys (Dweck et al., 1978). For example, teachers will exhort boys to pay attention and will tell them repeatedly that they'd do better if they put in more effort. Although all the criticism and exhortations boys receive may make grade school a less pleasant place for them, they are learning a valuable lesson about effort that will serve them well later.

☐ Is Intelligence Praise Always Bad?

We have seen how intelligence praise fosters an entity theory, performance goals, and helpless responses. But what if intelligence praise were given within an *incremental* framework? Would that be all right?

Within an incremental framework intelligence means different things and different behaviors reflect it. For example, if a student really worked very hard and tried a number of strategies in mastering a new task, this could be called intelligent. We would not be evoking some hidden trait inside the student; we would be acknowledging that high effort and the use of multiple strategies was intelligent behavior.

I will confess that not long ago, I slipped up and gave intelligence praise. My husband had just done something so ingenious that before I could stop myself out of my mouth popped, "You're brilliant!" Knowing about our intelligence praise work and seeing the horrified look spread across my face as I realized what I had done, he sought to comfort me. "I know you meant that in a purely incremental way," he told me. "You knew I had given this a lot of thought and tried a lot of different strategies, and that's what you meant."

So it may be that when you are typically operating within an incremental-theory framework, intelligence praise can be seen in that light. I suppose one could even use intelligence praise in a way that explicitly teaches an incremental theory of intelligence—that emphasizes challenge, effort, strategies, skills, and knowledge. But we still have to be careful not to set ourselves up as judges of intelligence and not to orient students toward gaining our favorable judgments of their intelligence. It seems advisable to stick to effort and strategy praise—because that's what we'd be trying to convey anyway.

Our research has shown that adults' praise conveys powerful messages to students. As a society we've had the best of intentions in the messages we've sent. We've wanted to send our students messages of respect and encouragement, ones that would arm them with confidence and allow them to go out into the world and succeed.

The intentions were impeccable, but the way they were put into practice was faulty. In many ways, these practices were based on erroneous beliefs about what self-esteem is, how it works, and how to build it.

We return to this issue later.

Misconceptions About Self-Esteem and About How to Foster It

Let's return to the things adults do to instill mastery-oriented characteristics in students. So many of the well-meant but misguided practices I've been talking about come from a limited view of what self-esteem is. Self-esteem is too often seen as a thing that children have or don't have, where having it leads to good things and not having it leads to bad things.

These practices also come from a limited view of how self-esteem is instilled. It is often portrayed as something we give to children by telling them they have a host of good things inside of them, like high intelligence.

These beliefs lead us as adults to lie to children—to exaggerate positives, to sugar-coat negatives, or to hide negative information entirely. We fear that negative information or criticism will damage self-esteem.

It's as though we've bought into the entity theory, in which children require constant success to feel good about themselves and in which failures send a negative message about intelligence and worth. We are in fact operating within this theory when we attempt to puff children up and boost their egos instead of boosting their effort, when we try to hide their deficiencies instead of helping them overcome them, and when we try to eliminate obstacles instead of teaching them how to cope with them.

These practices also convey an entity theory of intelligence to our children. They tell them that having intelligence is the most important thing, and that not having it is so shameful that errors and deficiencies need to be hidden from them.

This kind of treatment may "work" in some ways. Telling children they're smart and giving them constant successes may in fact make them feel good and it may instill a kind of worth—the kind we call entitlement. We may be teaching them to feel entitled to a life of easy successes and lavish praise for minor efforts (Damon, 1995; Seligman et al., 1995). They may feel entitled to all that society has to offer without putting in the effort to earn it, for when were they taught that anything required effort? This kind of "self-esteem" is not what our students need and it is not what our society needs.

Moreover, it's a recipe for anger, bitterness, and self-doubt when the world doesn't fall over itself trying to make them feel good the way parents and teachers did, or when the world doesn't accept them quite as they are, or when the world makes harsh demands before it gives up its rewards (see, e.g., Bushman & Baumeister, 1998). And what about setbacks, failures, and rejections—all the things that often precede success in the real world? How can they possibly know what to do with these?

Recently, on the subway, I overheard a startling conversation among three undergraduate women, all of whom were highly attractive, appealing, and articulate. They were discussing whether they would ever find a good relationship with a man or whether they should just give up and sit home weekend nights enjoying cookies and videos with friends.

At first I couldn't imagine what could have happened to these young women to make them so pessimistic, but then I realized they must have had some disappointing experiences. With a history of low-effort successes and the belief that if you've got what it takes then things should come easily, a few setbacks are enough to make you flee the arena.

You'd think everyone would know that anything worthwhile—careers, relationships—will involve failed attempts at some point. Are we doing anyone a favor by hiding this? I am certainly not advocating early failure as a training regime for our young, for within an entity-theory framework failure is demoralizing. I am advocating teaching our students an alternative framework in which effort is expected and enjoyed, and setbacks are informative and challenging.

☐ A Different View of Self-Esteem

We want our children to have a basic sense of worth and to know that they have our respect and love, but after that self-esteem is not something we give them. It is something that they are in charge of, and we can simply teach them how to live their lives so that they will experience themselves in positive ways.

In this view, self-esteem is not a thing that you have or don't have. It is a way of experiencing yourself when you are using your resources well—to master challenges, to learn, to help others.

We saw this in the answers of incremental theorists to the question about when they felt smart. Whereas entity theorists' intellectual self-esteem was high when they did things quickly, easily, in an error-free way, and better than others, incremental theorists told us something quite different. They felt smart when they were trying hard to understand something new, when they mastered things independently, and when they used their knowledge to help other students.

Within an incremental framework, self-esteem is how you feel when you are striving wholeheartedly for worthwhile things; it's how you experience yourself when you are using your abilities to the fullest in the service of what you deeply value. It's not about displaying your traits advantageously or showing that yours are better than someone else's. Moreover, in an incremental framework, what feeds your esteem—meeting challenges with high effort and using your abilities to help others—is also what makes for a productive and constructive life.

How can we as adults facilitate this kind of self-esteem? It won't come as news when I say, by emphasizing learning, challenges, effort, and strategies. We can show children how we relish a challenge by waxing enthusiastic when something is hard; we can talk about how good an effortful task feels; we can model the exciting search for new strategies and report the information we have gleaned from the strategy that failed. And when children are working on their own tasks, we can encourage these attitudes in them.

What's more, in this framework we can tell students the truth. When they don't have skills or knowledge, or they're behind other students, this is not a sign of a deep, shameful deficit. It's a sign that they need to study harder or find new learning strategies. If some students don't pick up a subject as quickly as other students do at the moment, that means they have to work harder than the others if they want to achieve as much. In other words, we can be frank with students about what they lack and what they need to do to get it.

Within an entity-theory framework, what we do with students who learn more slowly than others at a given point in time is to relegate them, secretly, to a lower level of intelligence, assign them easier things to learn, and try to make them feel smart learning the easier things—to protect their self-esteem. In this way, we doom them to fall further and further behind.

Within an incremental framework, we give students an honest choice. If they want to get ahead they have to put in what it takes. But we also have to be prepared to help them learn what it takes.

I have been truly aghast at the number of highly intelligent and even intellectual adults who didn't have a clue, when they were in school, about what it meant to study. They would read things through once, maybe twice, and then go take the test. They had no idea about making outlines, testing themselves on the material, or other such study skills. I have taught at the best universities in the country and still many of the students don't know how to approach learning in ways that maximize understanding and retention.

This is how we can help our students have high self-esteem. We can be candid about what their skills are now, about what skills they will need to pursue their goals in school and in life, about what they need to do to build those skills—and then we can offer our aid in equipping them with the attitudes, work habits, and learning strategies they need.

In summary, one view of self-esteem is that it is something we give to students by making sure they succeed and by telling them they're smart. But this ensures that they will feel smart mainly when they can do things easily and succeed constantly.

Another, more fruitful, view is that self-esteem is something students experience when they engage in something fully and use their resources fully, as when they are striving to master something new. It is not an object we can hand them on a silver platter, but it is something we can facilitate, and by doing so we help ensure that challenge and effort are things that enhance self-esteem, not threats to the ego.

☐ Implications of the Two Different Views of Self-Esteem

Telling the Truth

I've noted that one important difference between the two views of self-esteem is that in one we feel compelled to distort reality and in the other we are able to tell the truth. In fact, in the latter view we *need* to tell the truth in order for students to make informed choices. If they want to learn and achieve, this is what they have to do: expend effort, study, acquire new learning strategies. We must provide the appropriate tutoring, we must model and teach the appropriate attitudes and habits, but then it's basically up to them.

One of the greatest controversies in education involves the issue of "ability grouping"—grouping students according to their present achievement level, with more advanced students in one group or class, and less advanced students in another.

Proponents of ability grouping argue that mixing students of different ability levels holds back the more advanced students by forcing teachers to teach at a lower level than these students need. They argue that it also harms the less advanced students because they are struggling to understand what their peers already know. In short, their idea is that in heterogeneous grouping, no group of students is really focused on in the way that it needs.

Opponents of ability grouping argue very simply that it stigmatizes the children who are placed in the lower groups. It is, they claim, essentially a badge of stupidity. And within an entity-theory system this is true.

I am not enough of an expert on these aspects of educational practice to endorse or oppose ability grouping. What I can say is that within an incremental theory system, there is no stigma to being behind. It is simply a fact: Student A does not read as fluently as student B at this time; student C is not as advanced in math as student D at this time. What do we do with this fact?

In the entity-theory framework, as I've discussed, we try to camouflage it, while privately believing that students A and C are poorer students and will always be poorer students. In the incremental-theory framework, we acknowledge the fact that the different students are now at different levels (without seeing this as a reflection of a fixed ability), and we turn everyone's attention to the task of learning. It is in this effortful, involving learning process that students experience self-esteem, not from attempts to camouflage their skill level.

Thus, an incremental-theory framework, and our view of self-esteem within that framework, allows us and compels us to tell the truth. It is a truth about present levels of skills and knowledge, (not about permanent ability), and about how to work toward higher levels of skills and knowledge.

☐ Attitudes Toward Peers

Within the entity-theory framework your peers are competitors for self-esteem. When we asked students when they felt smart, entity theorists told us they felt smart when they did better than other students, when other students messed up on a test but they themselves "aced" it. Some college students even said they felt smart when other students made jerks out of themselves. So here others' misfortunes feed students' self-esteem.

Actually, when you are measuring an internal, invisible quality like intelligence, one of the major ways of measuring it is by comparing yourself to others (Butler, 1988, 1992; Nicholls, 1984). If you do better, especially with low effort, then you're smarter. That's why your peers are your rivals.

However, when your self-esteem is derived from your own striving, from the use of your efforts and abilities, it is not in conflict with anyone else's self-esteem. As you may recall, incremental theorists told us they felt smart, not only when they were striving to master new tasks, but also when they put their knowledge to use to help their peers learn. Thus within this framework, rather than being rivals for self-esteem, peers can gain self-esteem by cooperating and by facilitating each other's learning.

The entity theory, I believe, has had another profoundly damaging effect on students' achievement and on students' attitudes toward their peers. It has led many groups of adolescents to glorify a norm of low achievement, and to punish peers who insist on doing well (Covington, 1992; Juvenon, 1995; see also Ogbu, 1991).

The entity theory creates a system of winners and losers, where there are a few winners at the top and a large number of losers under them. Many groups of adolescents have, understandably, rebelled against this by creating their own rule system in which working hard and getting good grades meets with strong disapproval.

This is how students have conspired to undermine a system that designates winners and losers. Through peer pressure they seek to eliminate the winners. Then, those who would have been the losers no longer stand apart from the others. The norm of low effort also means that students' feelings about their intelligence are further protected (see Chapter 6). If they don't try, a poor grade doesn't mean they're not intelligent.

Unfortunately, by creating a norm of low effort and low achievement, students are undermining themselves and limiting their future opportunities.

I would be very surprised if this peer norm were to arise within an incremental system, where effort is a core value, where using your abilities to the fullest is the basis of self-esteem, and where peers are not rivals for a finite amount of intelligence and self-regard.

☐ Summary

In this chapter, I have presented two views of self-esteem. In one, low effort, easy success, and others' failures make students feel good about themselves. As if this weren't problematic enough, students find self-defeating ways of opting out of this system.

In the other, facing challenges, working hard, stretching their abilities, and using their skills and knowledge to help others make students feel good about themselves.

You can decide which serves our students and our society best.

18

CHAPTER

Personality, Motivation, Development, and the Self: Theoretical Reflections

We all have belief systems that give structure to our world and meaning to our experiences. We would be lost without them.

Some beliefs portray a dynamic self and a dynamic world, capable of growth. These beliefs, as we have seen, help us move forward with determination: They encourage us to look for ways to remedy our deficiencies and to solve our problems. They also encourage us to look for the potential in others.

Other beliefs portray a more static self and world with inherent, fixed qualities. These beliefs may have some advantages, for they portray a simpler world that is potentially easy to know, and there may be a great deal of security in that. As George Kelly (1955) pointed out, one of the primary functions of belief systems is to give us the sense that we can predict what will happen. But, as I have shown, entity beliefs can lead us to make more rigid judgments, sometimes blinding ourselves to our own capabilities and limiting the paths we pursue. They can also encourage us to see people as falling into categories: those who have intelligence, character, or worth versus those who don't.

It is not that one system is more "logical," "rational," "advanced" or "developmentally mature." They can both be internally consistent and they are both widely held by people at all levels of education and from all walks of life.

What does the research on these belief systems tell us about human motivation and personality? First, as I reported earlier, the beliefs are fairly stable in the populations that have been tracked over time (young children and college-aged individuals), at least over the 2- to 4-year periods that have been studied. This means that they are a real part of people's personality, intertwined with such things as their identity, self-concept, and self-esteem (cf. Epstein, 1990).

These beliefs are also an integral part of people's motivational systems in that they can strongly influence the goals people choose to pursue, how intrinsic ver-

132

sus extrinsic their motivation tends to be, the interest they maintain in an activity over time, the vigor with which they pursue the tasks in their lives, and much more.

Yet these beliefs can be influenced or changed. This can be done directly by an explicit message (Aronson & Fried, 1998; Bergen, 1992; Chiu et al., 1997; Levy, 1998; Levy et al., 1998) or indirectly by messages inherent in the feedback someone is given (for example, the person praise or trait praise in the studies by Kamins & Dweck [in press] and Mueller & Dweck [1998]). Some of these changes in "mindset" may last only as long as you are in the situation that is delivering the message, but long-term changes may also be induced by a compelling or continuing message (see Aronson & Fried, 1998; Jones, 1990).

This means that although these beliefs are relatively stable individual differences, they are also highly dynamic. It means that although most of us may favor one theory over another, we also understand the opposing view and sometimes operate in accordance with it.

This, in my view, is how personality works. We bring relatively stable tendencies into a situation with us, but the situation can modify these tendencies, most often temporarily but sometimes more permanently (see Mischel & Shoda, 1995).

How does this approach fit in with existing theories of personality and motivation? The rest of the chapter addresses this question.

What follows is in no way a comprehensive survey of personality and motivational theories. It is a highly selective discussion intended to highlight some of the important features of the present model. I also make no claim for the model as a complete theory of motivation or personality, but rather I wish to portray it as an example of an approach.

☐ Theories of Personality and Motivation

Trait Theories

Many influential personality theories describe personality as a set of traits (Costa & McCrae 1994b; Goldberg, 1990; McCrae & John, 1992). For them, each person has a profile of traits. For example, someone may be highly agreeable and open to experience, but not very conscientious.

These traits are one way to describe people's behavior. But they don't tell us about the *why* of behavior. They don't tell us what situations might trigger the behaviors, or the psychological reasons for the behavior (see Mischel, 1990; Pervin, 1994a,b; see also Block, 1995). This whole book has been about psychological reasons for people's behavior—about the beliefs and goals people bring to a situation that cause them to act in certain ways.

Because trait theories tell us very little about the psychology behind people's behavior, they tell us very little about how people can change. In fact, many trait theorists don't really believe much in personal change and tend to think that our basic traits are rooted in our biology (Eysenck, 1982; Loehlin, 1992; see also Costa & McCrae, 1994a,b). While it may be the case that some emotional or temperamental tendencies are indeed rooted in our biology (see Buss, 1989), there is compelling evidence that these tendencies and the way they express themselves are greatly influenced by experience (Bronfenbrenner & Ceci, 1994; Kagan & Snidman, 1991; see also Higley & Suomi, 1996; Suomi, 1977). Moreover, we have shown quite clearly in our research that much of behavior is influenced not by deeply seated traits but by the beliefs and goals people hold. And we have shown quite clearly that these beliefs and goals can be changed.

Thus, trait theories may describe and summarize behavior, but they don't explain behavior. They don't tell us how people work and how they change.

Motive Theories

One of the first research-based theories of motivation was founded on the idea of motives: that there are certain motives that are basic to human functioning and that people possess them in differing degrees (Murray, 1938). The motives are conceived of as affective, drive-like forces that are shaped by experience. McClelland and Atkinson, in their seminal work, took these motives—such as the need for achievement and the need for affiliation—and spelled out their theory of how behavior is initiated, driven, and directed by them (McClelland, 1961; McClelland, Atkinson, Clark, & Lowell, 1953).

In my view, it remains an impressive theory, but it lacks the power and precision of an approach that incorporates goals and cognitions (such as beliefs and attributions) (see Dweck & Elliott, 1983; Molden & Dweck, in press; see also Dweck, 1986). First, an approach that does not include goals does not deal with the different purposes that achievement strivings can serve. It does not tell us, for example, whether someone is trying to validate their intelligence or to challenge themselves and learn something new. As we saw, these different goal orientations can have very different characteristics and consequences.

Next, an approach that does not include cognitions, such as attributions, cannot deal fully with the mechanisms of persistence. What's more, an approach that does not include beliefs, such as self-theories, cannot deal fully with what children (or adults) take with them from their experiences and bring to new situations. A critical factor in the McClelland-Atkinson theory is the fear of failure. But why would someone fear failure? What does failure mean to them? What do they believe it means about the self? The esteem of others? Their future success?

Thus, for me, the motive approach does not deal in a satisfying way with development. Or with change. If someone has a lot or a little of a motive, what are the implications for change? If you don't specify the precise mechanisms or mediators of a phenomenon, how do we know how to bring about desired change?

How does a motive approach deal with the dynamic and often domain-specific nature of achievement patterns? An approach that deals with broad motives has a harder time than a cognitive-goal approach in explaining how achievement behavior is so context-sensitive (remember how we created the different patterns in our various studies) and how people can be mastery-oriented in one domain but more helpless in another.

Recently, Andrew Elliot proposed a wonderful integration between the motive approach and the goal approach (Elliot, 1997). He suggested that achievement motives are the underlying personality factors that orient people toward different achievement goals, and in his elegant research he has shown how "achievement motive" measures can be used to predict achievement goal orientation. I believe that this is a very exciting and valuable contribution. Yet I still believe that we must include cognitive variables to gain a full understanding of mechanisms, development, and change.

Biological Theories of Personality

How much of our personality is biologically determined? Some psychologists argue that a great deal of it is programmed in our genes (e.g., Eysenck, 1982; Loehlin, 1992). The reason that parents make a big difference, they believe, is mostly because they give us our genes, and not so much because of how they treat us.

There is abundant evidence that children are born with different temperaments, that is, different emotional personalities (Kagan & Snidman, 1991). However, there is also abundant evidence that environment and parenting make an enormous difference in how that temperament is expressed (Bronfenbrenner & Ceci, 1994; Higley & Suomi, 1996; Kagan & Snidman, 1991). Steven Suomi, at the National Institute of Mental Health, conducted some stunning experiments with monkeys to show this (Suomi, 1977). Some of the monkeys were bred for extremely shy and inhibited temperament. Under normal circumstances, these monkeys have difficulty. They are easily frightened and easily bullied by others, and they tend to end up quite low on the dominance hierarchy. However, when these monkeys were reared by supercompetent mothers, they became supercompetent themselves and tended to end up at the *top* of the dominance hierarchy. In fact, they looked even better than "normal" monkeys who were reared by the supercompetent mothers. In other words when they had the right environment, their heightened social sensitivity became an asset, not a liability.

Bronfenbrenner and Ceci (1994) review a great deal of evidence that this is the case with humans as well. We come with a temperament, but how we are treated by our parents, teachers, siblings and peers determines how that temperament expresses itself in our lives. Some temperaments, like a cheerful disposition, may tend to be assets and others, like an irritable one, may tend to be a liability. But the research is very clear that temperament is not destiny. Then why do some researchers continue to insist that personality is largely inherited and environment is not very important?

Because they look at temperament-type characteristics, like how extroverted people tend to be, and show that people who share more genes are more similar. But they don't look at how these temperamental characteristics play themselves out in people's lives. They don't look at adaptive functioning.

If basic temperament were all there was to personality, then *maybe* we could be satisfied with genetic explanations of where it comes from. But if we care about how people lead their lives—whether they lead constructive lives, how effectively they can cope when it matters, whether they can attain their goals, how they treat others—then there is plenty wrong with the genetic story. If we care about whether people can sustain successful relationships, succeed in school, and hold meaningful jobs, then environment matters greatly. These depend on things we learn (Bolger, Caspi, Downey, & Moorehouse, 1988; Coyne & Downey, 1991; Downey & Walker, 1992; Lewis & Feinman, 1991; Maccoby, 1992). It may be that some temperaments make it easier to learn adaptive skills, but under the right circumstances virtually everyone can. What matters is that we come to understand those circumstances.

In this book I have shown that the beliefs people hold are a large part of their personality and play an important role in their adaptive functioning. Our research has dramatically demonstrated that these beliefs can be taught.

Freudian Theory

Classic Freudian theory is based on people's desire to seek pleasure and avoid pain (Freud, 1923/1960, 1940/1949). For pleasure, the emphasis is on physical pleasure (libidinal, instinctual pleasure). For pain, the emphasis is on avoiding the punishment and anxiety that comes from desiring and seeking such pleasure. So they can maximize their pleasure and minimize their pain, people internalize society's do's and don'ts. They also develop a network of defenses that help them ward off anxiety and channel their impulses into socially approved activities.

Without denying the importance of pleasure and pain in people's lives, our approach differs from this in several important ways. First, in classical Freudian theory there is no inherent impetus toward growth. All of development, including the development of the mind, takes place in the service of pleasure and pain. Yet we know that the desire to explore and learn is a major force in humans from birth (Berlyne, 1978; Hunt, 1961; White, 1959). This is one reason that learning goals have such a prominent place in our model.

Next, in Freud's theory, an individual has no goals that relate specifically to the self. None of a person's concerns relate directly to establishing, validating, or expanding the self. Yet, as children develop a sense of self, motivations involving the self come into play. For example, they seek to think of themselves in certain ways (as competent, good, worthy) and to be thought of by others in certain ways. The self and one's beliefs about the self become important in their own right, not just as means of bringing instinctual rewards and avoiding punishment. Our model is very much about the self. The implicit theories are theories about the nature of the self and the goals are about validating and expanding the self—and about maintaining self-esteem. We have also discussed how certain patterns of feedback may foster a sense of contingent self-worth, leading to a need to continually validate the self.

Finally, all achievement in Freud's theory comes through defenses: What people *really* want is to satisfy their basic (mainly sexual) drives. But society and people's defenses will not really allow this, so the defenses offer them compromises by allowing them to channel these powerful instincts in other ways. Great discoveries and great works of art are simply compromises, socially approved ways of channeling instinctual energy. In our model, two very powerful goals drive achievement directly: the desire to validate one's competence and the desire to learn and master new things.

Dissatisfied with some of these very things in Freud's theory, a number of Freud's followers proposed theories that expanded upon his by including an inherent tendency toward growth and development (Erikson, 1950, 1959; Horney, 1937, 1945, 1950; Jung, 1933) and by placing a greater emphasis on the self (e.g., Erikson, 1950, 1959; Horney, 1937; Kohut, 1971, 1977).

Growth-Oriented Personality Theories

Some of Freud's disciples grew particularly disenchanted with his focus on sexual drives as the primary basis of personality and its development. They believed that human nature was not simply about the wish to fulfill physical instincts, and they believed that achievement came not just as a substitute for other, unacceptable outlets for the instincts.

Thus there emerged theories that proposed other sorts of strivings as inherent to human nature. Erikson (1950, 1959), Jung (1933), Horney (1938)—and from a very different perspective, Carol Rogers (1961) and Abraham Maslow (1955, 1962)—all proposed that some form of striving for growth or self-development was part and parcel of human nature.

Several of these theories (Erikson, Horney, and Rogers) also proposed that the growth or self-development instinct could be thwarted by harsh, disrespectful, or rejecting parental treatment. These might be practices that led the child into shame or guilt (Erikson) or by practices that made the child more concerned with winning the parents' approval than with personal growth or self-expression (Horney and Rogers).

Our model gives self-development a central role in personality, motivation, and development as well. However, rather than dealing with one large motive toward growth or self-development that acts in the same way across all situations and all domains of the self, our model talks about more specific goals. Children's experiences with their parents, teachers, siblings, or peers can indeed turn them away from learning goals and lead them to be overconcerned with approval and self-validation, but this can be specific to a given domain of the self (e.g., intelligence versus personality), or a social milieu (e.g., involving family versus peers versus teachers).

In addition, our formulation allows for the individual to remain responsive to new situations and not just play out the same personality tendency over and over. As we have seen, when a situation gives strong cues toward learning or performance goals, individuals are responsive to these cues. Thus our approach allows for a much more specific and dynamic understanding of behavior.

Our model, with its clearer specification of the beliefs and goals that guide behavior also gives a clearer blueprint for personal change.

The model, moreover, adds some new dimensions to existing theories of motivation and personality. For example, we have shown how people's implicit theories affect not only how they think of themselves, judge themselves, and react to personal events. They also affect how they think of others, judge others, and treat others. These are issues that are often not dealt with in a specific way in theories of motivation or personality, yet how we judge and react to people is a central part of our lives.

As I have noted, most past theories have addressed how children may be undermined by negative treatment from their socializers. While not denying that negative treatment can have negative consequences, our research has shown that some forms of positive treatment can also have negative consequences. Person praise or trait praise (such as intelligence praise) is often heartfelt, respectful, and well intentioned; yet it can divert children from learning goals and lead to self-denigration and helpless reactions in the face of difficulty. This shows that once we understand the specific beliefs and goals that underlie behavior, we can begin to understand the ways in which socialization practices feed into these beliefs and goals. And it may not always be what we intuitively expected.

Theories About the Self

Many of the theories after Freud's, whether they grew out of the Freudian tradition or arose from different traditions, have given the "self" a central role in motivation, personality, and development. These theories (Erikson, Horney, Rogers, Kohut, Maslow) all deal in their own way with how individuals forge their identities.

They acknowledge that we share with other animals a concern with pleasure and pain. But they point out that unlike most or all other animals, we develop representations or ideas about the self that have tremendous motivational power. These ideas are so powerful that they sometimes become more important than life itself. Think about people who commit suicide after an experience that brings shame upon the self. They would rather die than live with such a diminished view of themselves (Baumeister, 1990). Think about anorexia nervosa. In the service of ideas about the perfect self, young women starve themselves often to the point of death.

Our model is also built around the self, but it does not portray the self as one monolithic thing. Instead it focuses on the self-beliefs and self-relevant goals that people develop, and these, I have stressed, can be domain-specific, situation-sensitive, and malleable over time. (For current theories of the self and identity see Ashmore & Jussim, 1997; Deaux, 1993; Epstein, 1990; Greenwald & Pratkanis, 1984; Markus & Cross, 1990; see also Brown, 1998).

In addition, our model highlights the *processes* that people engage in as they pursue self-relevant goals in their daily lives (cf. Breckler & Greenwald, 1986; Cantor, Markus, Niedenthal, & Nurius, 1986; Deci & Ryan, 1991; Epstein, 1990; Gollwitzer & Wicklund, 1985). That is, it identifies the specific cognitive, affective, and behavioral processes they engage in as they strive to validate or expand their attributes and competencies.

It also depicts self-esteem in process terms. We do not portray self-esteem as something that people have or don't have, but as something that people seek, something they strive to attain and maintain (cf. Cantor, 1990; Maslow, 1962). Moreover, we attempt to specify the different goals through which people seek self-esteem and to pinpoint ways of seeking self-esteem that may be more effective, more constructive, and more lasting.

Social-Cognitive Theory: A "Meaning System" Approach

Our approach is part of what has been called the "social-cognitive" approach to motivation, personality, and the self. One branch of the social-cognitive approach addresses, in a fine-grained way, how social information is processed. The other branch—the one I work in primarily—addresses how people's beliefs, values, and goals set up a meaning system within which they define themselves and operate (Cantor & Zirkel, 1984, 1990; Downey & Feldman, 1996; Epstein, 1990; Higgins, 1989; Markus, 1977; Markus & Cross, 1990; Markus & Ruvolo, 1989; Mischel, 1973; Mischel & Shoda, 1995; Pervin, 1983).

The emphasis on cognition in the social-cognitive approach does not mean that we deny the great importance of emotion, but rather that we see most important emotions as being tied into cognitions. That is, people tend to feel positive or negative emotions because of the meaning they give to something that has happened (Lazarus, 1991; Weiner, 1984). These meanings may not be conscious. None of the theories, attributions, expectancies, hopes, fears, or goals that we have talked about need be conscious thoughts that people are aware of (Andersen, Reznik, & Chen, 1997; Bargh, 1997; Greenwald, 1992; Greenwald & Banaji, 1995; Kihlstrom, 1987; Nisbett & Wilson, 1977; Stern, 1987; Uleman & Bargh, 1989; see Dweck & Leggett, 1988). They are things that we can *become* aware of, but at any given moment we may not realize that they're present and how they are affecting us.

This "meaning system" branch of the social-cognitive approach can be traced to George Kelly. In his book, *The Psychology of Personal Constructs,* he called the field's attention to the fact that people create meaning systems for themselves. He proposed that through the concepts they acquire, people make sense of their world, and become able to predict and understand the things that happen to them. Walter Mischel (1973), building on the work of Kelly, wrote the landmark paper that defined the social cognitive approach and brought it into the mainstream. He enumerated the social-cognitive variables—such as people's interpretations of situations and events, their expectations, their goals—that mediate and regulate behavior. In doing so, he redefined personality and challenged psychologists to engage in a more process-focused analysis of personality.

Although Kelly's theory of personal constructs has been widely hailed and influential, few people have set about identifying core personal constructs—ones that many people share and that have important consequences for how people think, feel, and act in important areas (see Dweck et al., 1995; Epstein, 1990; Janoff-Bulman, 1992; Lerner, 1980; Rotter, 1966). We have attempted to do this by identifying the implicit theories that people hold and showing the many consequences of these beliefs.

The social-cognitive approach has permitted researchers to begin to capture many of the processes that classic personality theories attempted to capture, but to do so in a way that is more differentiated, more specified, and more amenable to rigorous research.

Attribution Theory, Learned Helplessness, and Learned Optimism

A closely allied, and tremendously influential, theory has been "attribution theory" (Heider, 1958; Jones, Kanouse, Kelley, Nisbett, Valins, & Weiner, 1972). Attribution theory also deals with how people make sense of their world, particularly with how they explain the things that they observe and experience. Perhaps the most important line of work in this field was pioneered by Weiner, who showed that the attributions people make for their successes and failures (i.e., the way they explain them) will determine the impact of those successes and failures (Weiner, 1984; Weiner, Heckhausen, & Meyer, 1972; Weiner & Kukla, 1970). For example, explaining a failure in terms of a more variable factor, like luck or effort, will leave you more optimistic about future success than explaining the failure in terms of a more stable factor, like task difficulty or ability. That is, some explanations leave you with a greater hope of success than do others.

The importance of this insight cannot be overestimated. Weiner's contribution brought new vigor to the field of motivation and ushered in an era in which deep and important motivational processes could be studied in rigorous and precise ways. It allowed researchers to begin to probe systematically into how people's beliefs shaped their motivation.

Weiner's work in attribution theory formed the basis for my work on learned helplessness (e.g., Dweck, 1975; Dweck & Reppucci, 1973), as well as for Seligman and his colleagues' work on explanatory styles, learned helplessness in humans, and learned optimism (Abramson, Garber, & Seligman, 1980; Abramson, Seligman, & Teasdale, 1978; Seligman, Kamen, & Nolen-Hoeksema, 1988; Seligman et al., 1995). Specifically, Seligman and his colleagues set about assessing individual differences in the kinds of causal explanations that people tend to make for negative events in their lives. They called these "explanatory styles." Some people tend to focus on more pessimistic explanations for negative events, blaming more global and stable factors, while others tend to focus on more optimistic explanations, blaming more specific and temporary ones. They then went on to dramatically demonstrate the power of a helpless, pessimistic explanatory style to predict such things as depression, and the power of an optimistic explanatory style to predict mental and physical health (Abramson, Metalsky, & Alloy, 1989; Nolen-Hoeksema et al., 1992; Peterson & Seligman, 1984; Seligman & Nolen-Hoeksema, 1987; cf. Scheier & Carver, 1987).

How is our model related to attribution theory and to learned helplessness or its happier counterpart, learned optimism? Helpless and mastery-oriented attributions and the consequences of these attributions formed the basis of our model and are still an important part of it. I continue to believe that attributions are fundamental motivational variables and critical motivators of persistence. However, our current model attempts to go beyond the attributional approach in several important ways. First, and perhaps most important, our model delineates the meaning system in which the different attributions or explanatory styles occur. That is, it spells out the personal theories and the goals that set up the explanatory styles.

In the attribution-theory and learned-optimism approaches people have simply learned different explanations, and these explanations are called forth when an outcome occurs. In those approaches people are basically the same before that outcome occurs. But in our work we have shown that people are not the same beforehand. They have different self-theories and different goals that orient them toward different explanations. For example, we have shown how an entity theory sets up an emphasis on measuring fixed traits and thereby creates a tendency to make global, stable trait attributions for actions and outcomes. In contrast, holding an incremental theory leads people to focus on more dynamic (specific, unstable) processes as the mediators of behaviors and the causes of outcomes.

A second major difference between our model and these others is that in attribution theory and learned optimism, motivation does not truly begin until people encounter an outcome to explain. But what brings people to a situation in the first place? What are they trying to achieve there? How are they trying to achieve it? A complete theory of motivation must deal with what motivates people to initiate behavior and what determines the direction, character, and intensity of that behavior even before an explicit outcome is experienced. In our model, people have goals. These goals lead them to initiate behavior and influence the nature of their behavior, as well as what they think about and feel as they pursue and engage in this behavior.

Yet another difference is that attribution theory designates some causal variables, like ability, as stable and others, like luck, as unstable. However, the crucial thing for a person's motivation is how these variable are seen by that individual. If a person blames a lack of ability for a failure but sees that ability as readily acquirable, then that person will remain optimistic. And we know that many people see abilities as acquirable. Thus, a lack of ability attribution made by an incremental theorist may be very different from a lack of ability attribution made by an entity theorist (Stone, 1998). In a related vein, we have shown in our research (Zhao et al., 1998) that some people have an entity theory about their luck. That is, they believe in a fixed fate or destiny. So when something happens to them and they attribute it to luck, they may not see this as something temporary that they can surmount. This means that people's implicit theories may influence not only which attributions people make, but also what a given attribution means.

In short, attributions and attributional styles remain a central part of our model, but they are seen as existing within the context of people's self-theories and goals.

Goal Theories of Personality

In the past two decades, there have emerged several theories of personality and social behavior that are built around people's goals (Cantor & Zirkel, 1990; Emmons, 1986; Frese & Sabini, 1985; Geen, 1995; Klinger, 1977; Little, 1989; Read & Miller, 1989; see Dweck, 1996a; Grant & Dweck, in press; Pervin, 1989). Taken together, they show ways in which people's goals and concerns can shape their thoughts, feelings, and actions to affect their achievement, social relationships, and feelings of well-being. Needless to say, I find much that is congenial in these theories. In particular, they demonstrate the dynamic nature of personality and reaffirm the importance of understanding people's motivation to understand their adjustment. Our work adds to this tradition by pinpointing certain classes of goals that we believe are central to people's functioning in their intellectual and social lives. Our research also links these goals to people's beliefs, showing how certain self-theories can increase the importance of one class of goals relative to the other. Finally, our research links the goals to specific experiences that foster them.

☐ Implications for Development

Motivational researchers used to believe that vulnerability was rare among young children (see Dweck & Elliott, 1983; Stipek, 1984). This view was in part a legacy of Piaget's theory of cognitive development. In this theory, many cognitive skills, built over long periods of time, were necessary before children could understand what to us seem like simple things. For example, Piaget believed that not until children directly explored and acted on their physical environment for much of their first year of life could they form mental representations. And not until then could they realize that an object that was out of their sight (be it their toy or their mother) continued to exist.

This was the received wisdom for a long time until infant researchers like Renee Baillargeon (Baillargeon, 1995; Baillargeon & DeVos, 1991) showed that infants as young as 3 and 4 months old knew perfectly well that objects that were out of sight continued to exist. Piaget, it turns out, had required infants to perform an action (retrieving the object from its hiding place) to show that they knew a hidden object existed. It was knowledge of how to perform the action that they lacked, not the knowledge that the hidden object still existed.

Researchers who studied the development of motivation were steeped in this tradition. They (myself included) thought about all of the cognitive skills that were necessary for children to understand ideas about personal traits and about intelligence in particular. They thought about how a helpless reaction required children to understand that a failure reflected on their intelligence, and they believed that not until late grade school was this possible.

Many researchers who studied the self were also steeped in the Piagetian tradition. Based on interviews with children of various ages, they concluded that young children had a "physicalistic" rather than a "psychological" sense of self. This was because, in response to questions asking children to describe themselves, young school children described such concrete things as what they looked like, who their brothers and sisters were, or what new toys they had. Researchers therefore decided that the more psychological aspects of the self-concept, such as ideas about personal attributes, came later.

Much developmental research in the past 10 to 15 years has shown that children can do things much earlier than was previously thought. Sometimes this is because researchers originally used the wrong tasks to assess children's cognitive competence, and sometimes this is because children don't in fact need all the skills we thought they did in order to accomplish something.

In our case, both were true. Some of the tasks and assessments underestimated children's knowledge (see Cain & Heyman, 1993). And, as we showed in our research, children do not really need to know much about intelligence to feel bad about themselves when they fail. So what can we now say about children's development?

First, we can say that important conceptions about the self are operative in early childhood, even though children may not be able to talk cogently about them when asked a global question about themselves. The presence of early self-conceptions comes as no surprise to anyone from the psychoanalytic tradition, where it is taken as a given that important self-representations develop over the first few years of life.

We saw that children as young as those in preschool already had elaborate notions about their goodness and badness, including whether or not these were stable traits. They had criteria for judging themselves as good or bad, and clear ideas about what should happen to them if they were good or bad. We also saw that the more vulnerable children had a different set of beliefs about goodness and badness than the more mastery-oriented ones. These findings suggest that beliefs about the self are an important part of children's personality from a young age and that they play a central role in their motivation.

How do these beliefs arise? The work by Kamins and Dweck (in press) on criticism and praise shows one way that feedback can mold these beliefs. Specifically, we showed that person-oriented versus process-focused praise and criticism taught children different beliefs about goodness and badness and led to different responses to setbacks. But many, many questions remain.

What is the importance of this early learning about the self? What effect do these early self-conceptions have on the development of later ones? We know that over the grade-school years children come to differentiate more among different domains, for example making sharper distinctions between social and intellectual successes and failures (Benenson & Dweck, 1986; Ruble & Dweck, 1995). How do their earlier ideas about goodness and badness affect their later ideas about intelligence and social abilities? We know that over time peers become increasingly important to children. What role do peers play in shaping self-theories?

Are these ideas more malleable in early life than they are in later life? By later life, have people built more elaborate belief systems that they are more invested in? We have shown that implicit theories of the self can be influenced in college students, as well as in children. But does it becomes harder to do so in a broad and lasting way?

In all of our work, one thing that has struck me time and again is how attuned people (both children and adults) are to messages about the self. It never ceases to amaze me how our experiments, in one session, can teach people a "new" view of the self, influencing their motivation and behavior (see Jones, 1990). Although the influence of a short experience may be quite limited and temporary, these studies show the great sensitivity that people have to this kind of information.

Given this, it is surprising to me how little research has been devoted to understanding how belief systems about the self and others arise and develop, starting in early life. Personality theorists have devoted much attention to this, but basic researchers, with a few exceptions (e.g., Lewis, 1990, 1992; Lewis & Brooks-Gunn, 1979; Main, Kaplan, & Cassidy, 1985; see Rochat, 1995), have not.

We know from research in other areas of developmental psychology that children develop an elaborate belief system about the physical world in their first few months, and about language in their early years. Knowledge of the self and the social world is certainly no less important to them. Children *must* be constructing a system of beliefs about themselves and their social world pretty much from the start. The greatest challenge in social development is to figure out what these beliefs are, what role they play in adaptive functioning, and how they may change with later experiences.

Although it is a daunting task, the rewards would be enormous. We could begin to understand more precisely the origins of important individual differences in personality, including the conditions under which different kinds of vulnerabilities arise. Viewed the other way, we could gain insight into the types of emerging beliefs that equip individuals to deal best with the challenges they face at each point in development, and we could tie these beliefs into the type of experiences that foster them.

☐ Implications for Mental Health

Cognitive Theories of Mental Health

In the past few decades, the field of mental health has witnessed the success of cognitive-oriented theories of mental health and psychotherapy. Both Aaron Beck's groundbreaking cognitive theory of depression and anxiety disorders (Beck, 1976; see also Beck, 1993, 1996) and Albert Ellis' highly influential rational-emotive therapy (Ellis, 1962, 1995) start with the assumption that people's erroneous beliefs can get them into trouble. Each has identified a series of beliefs that characterize individuals who are vulnerable to emotional distress. Attribution-based models that link depression to a pessimistic explanatory style are also cognitive models of vulnerability (e.g., Nolen-Hoeksema, et al., 1992; Peterson & Seligman, 1992; see also Dodge, 1993, for a cognitive-attributional model of vulnerability).

While not denying biological contributions to emotional disorders, research and therapy within this tradition is showing, more and more, that many people with depression or anxiety disorders are victims of their maladaptive beliefs and are helped greatly when these beliefs are altered (Beck, 1993, 1996; Chambless & Gillis, 1993; Hollon, DeRubeis, & Evans, 1996; Robins & Hays, 1993). Indeed, cognitive therapy adds significantly to the benefits of drug therapies (Hollon, DeRubeis, & Evans, 1996) and is often the form of psychotherapy that produces the greatest and most lasting changes (Chambless & Gillis, 1993; Robins & Hayes, 1993; see Beck, 1993).

Where does our work fit into this worthy tradition? Although it is premature to claim that our model sheds new light on depression, several of the studies I reviewed demonstrated a link between holding entity theories (Zhao, et al., 1998) or strong, generalized performance goals (Dykman, 1998) and exhibiting depression-like responses to failure (see Robins & Pals, 1998). One study also showed that holding entity theories predicted higher levels of depression and distress (Zhao et al., 1998, study 2).

These findings suggest that ideas about the self can create a meaning system that leads people to adopt goals and interpret events, sometimes in ways that make them vulnerable. Our model is consistent with previous cognitive approaches, but there are several differences. First, rather than identifying a series of separate beliefs that influence vulnerability, our model shows how many beliefs can be organized into a network that grows out of people's theories (see also Beck, 1996). For example, our work suggests that an entity-theory framework can lead people to overgeneralize from one experience, to categorize themselves in unflattering ways, to set self-worth contingencies, to exaggerate their failures relative to their successes, to lose faith in their ability to perform even simple actions, to underestimate the efficacy of effort—all things that have been implicated in depression.

Another difference between our model and past cognitive models is that our model (as Dykman, 1998, points out) introduces a motivational component. Vulnerable people don't just think and react in different ways from less vulnerable people. They also value different goals. That is, they often have different concerns and purposes. Compared with their less vulnerable peers, they are more concerned with validating themselves and less concerned with growth and self-development. As I argued earlier, this difference can lead us to understand ways in which vulnerable people differ even before they exhibit their vulnerability in their coping reactions.

These two differences—the network of beliefs and the motivational component—lead to another property of the model. The model may allow us to understand new things about personal conflict: what conflicts may most frequently arise within the different systems and how one system might generate more paralyzing conflicts among goals than the other. This would be important, because conflict is believed by many to be at the heart of much neurotic behavior (Shapiro, 1965).

What kinds of conflict might be most characteristic of each belief system? For purposes of this discussion, let us consider people who have generalized entity or incremental beliefs that cut across domains.

Within an incremental belief system, where personal attributes are seen as malleable and effort is seen as highly effective, we might predict that conflict would frequently arise about where to channel your efforts. More time spent building one set of skills means less time can be spent building another. If people have a very strong belief that they *should* be able to do everything and their self-worth is tied to doing it all, then problems are likely to arise. Otherwise, these are simply difficult choices and not the kind of conflict neurosis is usually built on.

Within the incremental system, conflicts may also frequently arise between the individual and society. To the extent that an incremental theory leads people to march to their own drummer, they may more often come up against skepticism, disapproval, or rejection for their unpopular ideas. This again can lead to extremely difficult and painful choices, and the costs and benefits of different courses of action have to be carefully evaluated.

However, an entity-theory framework may pose more irreconcilable internal conflicts, and ones that offer self-defeating solutions. For example, entity theorists tend to be highly concerned with validating their ability through performance-goal successes. However, they also tend to believe that high effort reveals low ability. This means that when faced with a difficult task, entity theorists are faced with a conflict. Should they try hard, thereby showing a lack of ability? Or should they not try hard, thereby increasing the chance of a failure (but leaving themselves a face-saving excuse for it)?

This is the stuff that self-defeating defensive behavior is made of. And indeed, as described earlier, Rhodewalt (1994) has shown that entity theories are more likely than incremental theorists to engage in self-handicapping behavior—the kind of behavior that risks failure but saves your view of your ability (like leaving a big term paper until the last minute or going out and then getting too little sleep the night before an exam). Moreover, Zuckerman, Kieffer, and Knee (1998) have recently found that habitual self-handicapping is indeed self-defeating. It erodes achievement and adjustment over time. This includes self-esteem, the very thing self-handicapping was designed to protect.

We have also seen that an entity theory sets up a conflict between learning and performance goals. Entity theorists will often sacrifice a chance to learn something important if the task is a difficult one that contains the risk of errors and confusion. I have discussed at length how this can be self-defeating. By choosing tasks and courses they are sure to do well at, and dropping ones that pose a challenge, entity theorists may limit their options and their accomplishments.

Finally, when entity theorists face a conflict about where to invest their time, it may be a more serious conflict than that faced by incremental theorists. For entity theorists, a failure, a lack of skill, or disapproval from others can reflect on a basic, permanent quality of the self. So a conflict between social and intellectual demands, professional and personal demands, or peers' and adults' demands may create greater anxiety for entity theorists because their estimation of themselves is at stake (see Dykman, 1998). In short, the conflicts that arise within an entity theory may promote more distress and maladaptive behavior.

Thus our model adds the idea that a core theory can create a network of coherent beliefs that in turn can generate maladaptive motivational patterns and neurotic conflicts.

Coping Theories of Mental Health

Another tradition in the mental-health field comes from the coping literature. Over the past few decades, several prominent researchers have defined mental health in terms of how people cope in important areas of their lives (Carver, et al., 1989; Lazarus & Folkman, 1984; Nolen-Hoeksema, 1998; Scheier, Weintraub, & Carver, 1986). Although most of these theorists view coping as a process and resist thinking in terms of traits or rigid coping styles, they have identified coping strategies that tend to be more mastery-oriented, active, and effective. And some people engage in these more than others.

Yet we have not really known very much about why different people might favor different coping strategies. Of course, we all do a mixture of things, but as we saw in the studies by Zhao et al. (1998), incremental theorists tend to take a more direct problem-solving approach, while entity theorists tend to get lost in negative feelings or turn away from the problem and try to make themselves feel better. Studies by Loeb and Dweck (1994) show a similar thing. When confronted with scenarios portraying them as victims, incremental theorists again reported that they would take a more active problem-solving stance, while entity theorists showed more passive acceptance but admitted they would harbor long-term hatred and wishes of revenge.

Thus, in part, coping preferences may grow out of meaning systems. Some beliefs and goals may help us to construct the lives we want and to maintain the flexibility to reconstruct them when things go wrong.

Development and Mental Health

What we are asked to cope with differs with age. And so does how best to cope. Successful coping in the younger years may involve learning about your parents, for example, figuring out how to get love and support without giving up too much freedom. My cousin recently reminded me of some words of wisdom I offered him when I was 6 years old and he was 5. He had just had a big fight with his mother over when he could eat his candy. As we then sat alone on the front steps, I shook my head with pity and scorn. "Don't you know," I told him, "grown-ups like to feel that they're in charge. Just tell them yes and then do what you want." That advice, he informed me, changed his young life.

Later, as we turn increasingly to our peers and romantic partners, and to school and then work, we must learn new ways to adapt and succeed. For example, with peers and romantic partners we must learn new forms of reciprocity.

This is good news and bad news. It means that at each point in development we get new chances to succeed. If we didn't do that well with our parents, maybe we can do better with our peers. But it also means that we get new chances to stumble. Maybe we did beautifully at getting our way with our parents, but the same strategies don't win friends.

An approach based on beliefs and goals is well-suited to understanding adjustment at different points in development. People must form new beliefs about themselves, others, and relationships in new spheres. They must adopt new goals, and they must learn new strategies for attaining their goals. Their successful adjustment depends on how well this is done.

Earlier I talked about the case of bright girls, which is an excellent example. They are extremely well suited to grade school. Things like wanting to be perfect don't yet get in the way. Wanting to please parents, teachers, and peers doesn't yet create great conflicts. However, when these girls hit junior high or high school, these same desires can cause problems. The work (especially the math) suddenly gets harder, and immediate mastery is often not possible. Peer relations may suddenly demand things that adults disapprove of. Good grades may jeopardize peer popularity. You can no longer be perfect to everyone. This is when we see a sharp increase in depression among females, especially among bright females (Nolen-Hoeksema, 1994; Ruble et al., 1993). Thus some of the luminaries of the earlier years can become the casualties of the later years.

Quite the reverse may happen for boys. They are often the misfits when it comes to fitting into the adult-structured world of the early years (Dweck et al., 1978; Dweck, Goetz, & Strauss, 1980). Sitting still for long periods of time to do things that bore them is not their forte. However, the greater challenges and the more peer-oriented culture that come later may allow boys to come into their own.

The idea of different issues and tasks coming to the fore at different points in development is a strong point of Erikson's theory of psychosocial development (Erikson, 1950). However, for him each stage posed one large issue (e.g., autonomy, initiative, industry) and the person emerged from that stage with one large outcome (a relatively strong or weak sense of autonomy, initiative, or industry). Our approach allows for a fuller and more specific analysis of changing demands and successful adjustment. It also allows a more precise understanding of how beliefs, goals, and strategies that are adaptive at one point can become maladaptive at another.

I have laid out an approach to personality, motivation, mental health, and development that is based on the belief systems people develop. These belief systems are relatively stable, but they are also dynamic and malleable. It is this fact—the fact that our personality is generally quite stable, but at the same time so responsive to situations and capable of change over time—that makes this field so exciting and so challenging. It is exciting to think of the potential that exists in people and to think of discovering the kinds of learning experiences that can help them realize this potential. Yet it is a formidable challenge for researchers to try to capture such dynamic processes in clear, precise, and parsimonious ways.

CHAPTER

Final Thoughts on Controversial Issues

Throughout this book, I have focused on the advantages of the incremental theory, learning goals, and a mastery-oriented pattern. But a number of tough questions remain that need to be examined further.

☐ Can't Effort Be Carried Too Far?

I have shown how, within an entity theory, effort is something to be avoided because it gives a negative message about ability. In contrast, within an incremental theory, effort is the key to achievement and self-esteem.

Yet we have all heard of parents who demand so much effort from their children from such an early age that they deprive these children of their childhood. Vastly enriched learning environments are created in the crib, tutors are employed during the preschool years, and teenagers are sleep-deprived because of all the studying they must do and all of the lessons they have to take.

I am not in favor of this kind of pressure and it is not in keeping with what I have presented as the incremental-theory framework.

First, within the incremental framework, effort is in the service of learning and growth. That is what is valued. For many of these parents and their children, learning and growth are secondary to getting the highest grades and getting into the best schools.

Second, within the incremental framework, self-esteem is experienced as you use your powers to the fullest. For many of these children, self-esteem stands and falls on pleasing their parents with their successes.

These parents have created a performance-oriented system, but they have demanded high effort in pursuit of achievement.

This is why I am hesitant to extol, without reservation, the practices in some Asian cultures. There is no doubt that we have many things to learn from them and

149

how they school their children. Their methods of classroom instruction are often impressive (Stigler, Lee, & Stevenson, 1987), as is the emphasis on malleable intelligence and effort (Stevenson et al., 1990). The achievement results are also enviable.

However, the emphasis on malleable intelligence and effort is often not accompanied by an emphasis on learning and the enjoyment of challenge. Instead, many students tend to experience great anxiety over their grades and test scores, great pressure not to shame their families, and depression or humiliation over poor performance. This is quite a burden for a student to carry and is not the incremental theory and learning goal framework I have described.

Now, this is not to say that there isn't an equal amount of anxiety, pressure, depression, and humiliation among our students (Crystal, Chen, Fu, et al., 1994). And we don't have the achievement to show for it! But why not try to take the best that other cultures have to teach us (the instructional methods, the emphasis on malleable intelligence and effort) and integrate this with a more learning-oriented framework? Why not try for achievement and a love of challenge and learning at the same time?

☐ Is Persistence Always Good?

I have portrayed persistence as a highly desirable tendency, but aren't there times when persistence is undesirable? What if a task is really beyond the students' current skills, and no amount of effort and strategizing will bear fruit? Would an incremental theory be a handicap here because it encourages persistence?

Not necessarily. An incremental theory does encourage persistence, but it doesn't compel persistence. There is nothing in an incremental theory that prevents students from deciding that they lack the skills a problem requires. In fact, it allows students to give up without shame or fear that they are revealing a deep and abiding deficiency.

In some of our studies entity theorists realized that the problems had become extremely difficult, but they still blamed their intelligence when they couldn't solve them. They couldn't give up without incriminating their intellect. An incremental theory, with its emphasis on learning over time, enables students to put something on hold until they have the skills and knowledge to tackle it successfully.

☐ Isn't Some Kind of Confidence Necessary Even In An Incremental Framework?

I have argued that confidence in intelligence is fragile within an entity framework and does not seem to be necessary within an incremental framework. But isn't *some* kind of confidence necessary in order for students to pursue learning challenges? Yes. But only the confidence that they can increase their skills and knowledge over time.

In the entity-theory framework, students need to feel confident that they have high intelligence, that they will do better than others, or that they are already good at the task, in order to willingly take on a task that appears challenging. And they need to keep feeling this way to stick with it.

It appalls me to think of how many times I have heard people say that they tried something once and they couldn't do it. Or that they tried something for a little while, but they weren't good at it and so gave it up. I have heard people say this about something as trivial as a popular exercise machine that seems to eject people when they first try it. And I have heard people say this about something that they dreamed would be their life's work.

It's not that students should fool themselves about what it takes to accomplish something or delude themselves about their current skill level. Absolutely not. It's just that becoming good at something most often requires effort over a period of time. In the incremental framework, confidence is simply the belief that effort will get you somewhere over that period of time.

☐ If an Entity Theory is Maladaptive, Why Do So Many People Hold It?

I have been stressing the vulnerability created by holding an entity theory, but we must ask: Why do so many people hold entity theories? Several things come to mind.

An entity theory may give people a sense of security in a complex world. For some personality theorists (Kelly, 1955), what people seek more than almost anything else is a sense that they can predict things, that they can anticipate future events. An entity theory certainly provides people with a sense that their social world is highly predictable (see Kruglanski, 1996; Kruglanski & Webster, 1996). It can be comforting to believe that you can know people—including yourself— easily and then know what to expect from them.

It could also be that so many people hold the entity view because it is so easy to transmit and learn. We saw how merely praising intelligence could transmit the view that intelligence is a fixed trait (Kamins & Dweck, in press; Mueller & Dweck, 1998).

Thus an entity theory can be simple and comfortable, but those benefits, as we have seen, come with some costs.

☐ Aren't Performance Goals Necessary in Our Society?

There are many times that students have to prove their ability, that they have to jump over ability hurdles to qualify for the next level. There are classroom tests, statewide tests, national achievement tests, the Scholastic Aptitude Test, and entrance examinations for certain schools. I have been extolling the virtues of learning goals, but aren't performance goals necessary?

Of course they are. One of the things I emphasized when I introduced the concepts of learning and performance goals was that both goals are entirely natural, desirable, and necessary. There are times when students need to master new tasks and acquire new skills, and there are times when they need to display and validate the skills they already have. Performance goals are indeed a critical part of achievement.

The problem with performance goals arises when proving ability becomes so important to students that it drives out learning goals. Problems also arise when the ability students are measuring is their fixed intelligence. Then performance-goal failures can catapult them into a helpless response.

These problems don't arise as readily within an incremental-theory framework. The ability that incremental students are proving when they pursue a performance goal is not their fixed intelligence, but rather the skills and knowledge they have at that time. If they do poorly on a test, this simply means that their present skills and knowledge need to be augmented, not that a permanent deficiency has been revealed. They are thus spurred to constructive effort and prompted to seek the learning opportunities they need to succeed the next time.

There is an irony here. An entity theory highlights the importance of performance goals for students, but it can hamper their achievement of them. It makes students vulnerable to a helpless reaction when they hit difficulty and it makes them reluctant to put forth effort when it is most needed.

In contrast, an incremental theory highlights the importance of learning goals, but it may also make students better able to attain their performance goals. Incremental theorists are more likely to have a mastery-oriented response to obstacles, and they are more willing to invest the necessary effort.

In short, performance goals play an important role in achievement. Ironically, students for whom performance goals are the basis of self-esteem—entity theorists—may be at a disadvantage in pursuing them successfully.

☐ Do Learning Goals Have Less Rigorous Standards?

Learning goals are sometimes misunderstood to be goals that coddle students: They do their best and whatever they come up with is fine. Although this may be true in some learning environments, it is certainly not an inherent part of learning goals.

In fact, learning goals allow teachers to set very rigorous standards. Within an incremental framework, critical feedback does not reflect on students' intelligence. It's merely information about what's wrong with their current work and how to improve it. So teachers can give candid, detailed feedback to students as they strive to meet high standards.

Another way to say it is that in an incremental framework students know that they are being taught, not evaluated as persons, and they can therefore welcome any and all feedback that will aid their learning.

☐ Does Everything Need To Be Enjoyable and Enriching?

I have talked at length about the importance of pursuing challenge and seeking learning. But aren't there a lot of things in life that are tedious and that we simply have to do? In my case, paperwork poses a particular horror—forms, reports, and so forth. Just writing these words fills me with dread. Don't people have to learn how to do these things, like it or not?

Yes. This doesn't mean that we can give students boring material and justify it in these terms. Everyone should try to make every task as interesting as possible for themselves and for others. For example, when I teach I not only try to make things interesting for the students, I try to pick topics that are fascinating to me and to approach them in a way that I find most rewarding. It is always useful to ask: Is there a more interesting way of doing this?

But sometimes the answer may be no. It is then that people need to learn how to apply themselves: when there is a painful process or nothing of interest to learn from the task. This is where "self-regulation" comes in. These are essential skills that we use to help ourselves when tasks are long, complex, or unpleasant. These skills can be taught, and students who have mastered them do far better than those who haven't, both in the short run and in the long run (see Mischel, 1974; Mischel, Shoda, & Rodriguez, 1989; see also Bandura, 1986; Schunk & Zimmerman, 1994).

☐ What's Wrong with Contingent Self-Worth?

Isn't a sense of contingent self-worth in some ways desirable? *Shouldn't* people feel bad about themselves if they've done something really awful? Interesting research by June Tangney (1995) has shown that those who feel like bad people after doing something wrong are *less* likely to repair their behavior or make it up to others than are people who simply feel as though they've done a bad thing. People who feel bad or worthless may just run away from the situation or even become angry at (and aggressive toward) the person they hurt in order to escape their feelings of self-contempt. In contrast, people who simply feel bad about what they've done still have the resources to contemplate why they behaved the way they did, what they will do to rectify the situations, and how they would ideally like to behave in the future.

This is true in achievement situations, too. We saw that those students who felt worthless after a setback were less likely to cope effectively compared with students who simply focused on what they had done wrong and what they needed to do now (Zhao et al., 1998; see also Dykman, 1998).

In short, feeling bad or worthless seems to promote antisocial and self-defeating behavior, rather than the kind of productive coping one would like to see.

☐ Isn't a Lot of Behavior Caused by Our Genes?

Aren't we all different genetically, and isn't that a lot of the reason we act differently? Doesn't this mean that we are who we are and that's that?

I discussed this issue in the previous chapter, but it is so important that I will more or less repeat what I wrote there: Yes, people come with different genes, and yes, genes can certainly influence our behavior and development. But if we care about how people lead their lives—whether they lead constructive lives, how effectively they can cope when it matters, whether they can attain their goals, how they treat others—genes don't give us the answers. If we care about whether people can sustain successful relationships, succeed in school, and hold meaningful jobs, then environment matters greatly. These depend on things we are taught. It may be that genes make it easier for some to learn adaptive skills, but under the right circumstances virtually everyone can. It is our responsibility to understand those circumstances.

In this book I have shown that the beliefs people hold are a large part of their personality and play an important role in their adaptive functioning. Our research has demonstrated that these beliefs can be taught.

☐ Isn't It Naive to Believe that Everyone Has the Potential to Change?

Although I have documented the many benefits of holding an incremental theory, is it really reasonable to think that everyone has the potential to grow or change in major ways? What about hardened criminals? What about slow learners? I have not tried to argue that anyone can become Albert Einstein or Mother Theresa, but I have tried to argue that we do not know what anyone's future potential is from their current behavior. We never know exactly what someone is capable of with the right support from the environment and with the right degree of personal motivation or commitment.

In addition, an incremental theory does not say that people *will* change. In many cases, it would be extremely foolish to believe that a person continuing in the same environment, without any psychological or educational help, will change. So an incremental theory does not predict that people left to themselves are likely to become better people over time. Not at all. It simply says that people are capable of change.

The danger of the entity theory is not so much that it argues for human limitation, but that it suggests we can know people's limitations so quickly and then grants them so little potential for growth. I believe that people and society gain a great deal when we search for ways to help people realize their potential instead of labeling or punishing them when they do not.

☐ A Lifetime of Performance Versus Learning Goals

We've all seen movies in which the protagonist has a life-transforming experience. He (for in these movies it usually is a he) suddenly realizes that the life of the ego he has been living is hollow and pointless, and that he has neglected the things that make life truly worthwhile. It is, of course, a cliché, but then many clichés have more than a grain of truth.

When I think of a person's life ruled by an entity theory and performance goals, I think of a life in which there is proof after proof of one's ability. What does it add up to? Thousands of proofs of ability, but, of course, never enough.

Or I think of a life in which time upon time there is a flight from risk, so as to protect an image of oneself. This adds up to an armed fortress containing all the things one could have been or done.

When I think of a life governed by an incremental theory and learning goals, I think of valued skills and knowledge accrued over time and put to use for oneself and others. Whether things have gone one's way or not, it adds up to a life of strong commitments and earnest effort.

Some years ago, as I reached one of the landmark ages, I asked myself what I would like to be able to say at the end of my life, and it was this: I want to be able to say that I kept my eyes open, faced my issues, and made wholehearted commitments to things I valued. I did not want to be haunted by a litany of regrets or left with a bundle of potentialities that were never realized.

As adults in this society our mission is to equip the next generations with the tools they need to live a life of growth and contribution. Can we make the commitment to help them become smarter than we were?

References

Abramson, L. Y., Garber, J., & Seligman, M. E. (1980). Learned helplessness in humans: An attributional analysis. In J. Garber & M. E. Seligman (Eds.), *Human helplessness* (pp. 3–37). New York: Academic Press.

Abramson, L. Y., Metalsky, G. I., & Alloy, L. B. (1989). Hopelessness depression: A theory-based subtype of depression. *Psychological Review, 96,* 358–372.

Abramson, L. Y., Seligman, M. E., & Teasdale, J. D. (1978). Learned helplessness in humans: Critique and reformulation. *Journal of Abnormal Psychology, 87,* 49–74.

Ames, C. (1984). Achievement attributions and self-instructions under competitive and individualistic goal structures. *Journal of Educational Psychology, 76,* 478–487.

Ames, C. (1992). Classrooms: Goals, structures, and student motivation. *Journal of Educational Psychology, 84,* 261–271.

Ames, C., & Archer, J. (1988) Achievement goals in the classroom: Students' learning strategies and motivational processes. *Journal of Educational Psychology, 80,* 260–267.

Andersen, S. (1997). The self in relation to others: Motivational and cognitive underpinnings. In J. G. Snodgrass & R. L. Thompson (Eds.), *The self across psychology: Self-recognition, self-awareness, and the self-concept* (pp. 233–275). New York: New York Academy of Sciences.

Andersen, S. M., Reznick, I., & Chen, S. (1997). The self in relation to others: Motivational and cognitive underpinnings. In J. G. Snodgrass (Ed). *The self across psychology: Self-recognition, self-awareness, and the self concept. Annals of the New York Academy of Sciences, Vol. 818* (pp. 233–275). New York: New York Academy of Sciences.

Anderson, C. (1983). Motivation and performance deficits in interpersonal settings: The effect of attributional style. *Journal of Personality and Social Psychology, 45,* 1136–1147.

Anderson, C., & Jennings, D. L. (1980). When experiences of failure promote expectations of success: The ineffective strategies. *Journal of Personality, 48,* 393–407.

Andrews, G. R., & Debus, R. L. (1978). Persistence and the causal perception of failure: Modifying cognitive attributions. *Journal of Educational Psychology, 70,* 154–166.

Aronson, J. (1998). *The effects of conceiving ability as fixed or improvable on responses to stereotype threat.* Unpublished manuscript.

Aronson, J., & Fried, C. (1998). *Reducing stereotype threat and boosting academic achievement of African Americans: The role of conceptions of intelligence.* Unpublished manuscript.

Aronson, J., Quinn, D., & Spencer, S. (1998). Stereotype threat and the academic underperformance of minority men and women. In J. Swim & C. Stangor (Eds.), *Stigma: The target's perspective*. New York: Academic Press.

Ashmore, R. D., & Jussim, L. J. (Eds.). (1997). *Self and identity: Fundamental issues*. New York: Oxford University Press.

Astin, H. (1974). Sex differences in scientific and mathematical precocity. In J. C. Stanley, D. P. Keating, & L. H. Fox (Eds.), *Mathematical talent: Discovery, description, and development*. Baltimore, MD: Johns Hopkins University Press.

Baillargeon, R. (1995). Physical reasoning in infancy. In M. S. Gazzaniga (Ed.), *The cognitive neurosciences* (pp. 181–204). Cambridge, MA: MIT Press.

Baillargeon, R., & DeVos, J. (1991). Object permanence in young infants: Further evidence. *Child Development, 62*, 1227–1246.

Baldwin, M. A., & Sinclair, L. (1996). Self-esteem and "if . . . then" contingencies of interpersonal acceptance. *Journal of Personality and Social Psychology, 71*, 1130–1141.

Bandura, A. (1986). *Social foundations of thought and action: A social cognitive theory*. Englewood Cliffs, NJ: Prentice-Hall.

Bandura, M., & Dweck, C. S. (1985). *The relationship of conceptions of intelligence and achievement goals to achievement-related cognition, affect, and behavior*. Unpublished manuscript, Harvard University.

Bargh, J. A. (1997). The automaticity of everyday life. In R. S. Wyer (Ed.), *Advances in social cognition*, (Vol. 10, pp. 1–61). Mahwah, NJ: Erlbaum.

Baron, J. B., & Sternberg, R. J. (Eds.). (1987). *Teaching thinking skills: Theory and practice*. New York: Freeman.

Baron, R. M., & Misovich, S. J. (1993). Dispositional knowing from an ecological perspective. *Personality and Social Psychology Bulletin, 19*, 541–552.

Baumeister, R. F. (1990). Suicide as an escape from self. *Psychological Review, 97*, 90–113.

Beck, A. T. (1976). *Cognitive therapy and the emotional disorders*. New York: International Universities Press.

Beck, A. T. (1993). Cognitive therapy: Past, present, and future. *Journal of Consulting and Clinical Psychology, 61*, 194–198.

Beck, A. T. (1996). Beyond beliefs: A theory of modes, personality, and psychopathology. In P. M. Salkovskis (Ed.), *Frontiers of cognitive therapy* (pp. 1–25). New York: Guilford.

Beck, A. T., Ward, C. H., Mendelson, M., Mock, J., & Erbaugh, J. (1961). An inventory for measuring depression. *Archives of General Psychiatry, 4*, 561–571.

Benenson, J., & Dweck, C. S. (1986). The development of trait explanations and self-evaluations in the academic and social domains. *Child Development, 57*, 1179–1189.

Bergen, R. (1992). *Beliefs about intelligence and achievment-related behaviors*. Unpublished doctoral dissertation, University of Illinois at Urbana-Champaign.

Bergen, R., & Dweck, C. S. (1989). The functions of a personality theory. In R. Wyer & T. Srull (Eds.), *Advances in social cognition* (Vol. II, pp. 81–92). Hillsdale, NJ: Erlbaum.

Berglas, S. (1990). Self-handicapping: Etiological and diagnostic considerations. In R. L. Higgins (Ed.), *Self-handicapping: The paradox that isn't* (pp. 151–186). New York: Plenum.

Berglas, S., & Jones, E. E. (1978). Drug choice as a self-handicapping strategy in response to noncontingent success. *Journal of Personality and Social Psychology, 36*, 405–417.

Berlyne, D. E. (1978). Curiosity and learning. *Motivation and Emotion, 2*, 97–175.

Binet, A. (1909/1973). *Les idees modernes sur les enfants* [Modern ideas on children]. Paris: Flamarion.

Blatt, S. J. (1995). The destructiveness of perfectionism: Implications for the treatment of depression. *American Psychologist, 50*, 1003–1020.

Block, J. (1995). A contrarian view of the five-factor approach to personality. *Psychological Bulletin, 117*, 187–215.

Bolger, N., Caspi, A., Downey, G., & Moorehouse, A. (Eds.). (1988). *Persons in context: Developmental processes.* New York: Cambridge University Press.

Breckler, S. J., & Greenwald, A. G. (1986). Motivational facets of the self. In R. M. Sorrentino & E. T. Higgins (Eds.), *Handbook of motivation and cognition* (pp. 145–164). New York: Guilford Press.

Bronfenbrenner, U., & Ceci, S. J. (1994). Nature-nurture concenceptualized in developmental perspective: A bioecological model. *Psychological Review, 101,* 568–586.

Brown, A. L. (1997). Transforming schools in to communities of thinking and learning about serious matters. *American Psychologist, 52,* 399–413.

Brown, A. L., & Campione, J. C. (1996). Psychological theory and the design of innovative learning environments: On procedures, principles, and systems. In L. Schauble & R. Glaser (Eds.), *Innovations in learning: New environments for education* (pp. 289–325). Mahwah, NJ: Erlbaum.

Brown, A. L., Palincsar, A. S., & Purcell, L. (1984). Poor readers: Teach don't label. In U. Neisser (Ed.), *The academic performance of minority children: A new perspective.* Hillsdale, NJ: Erlbaum.

Brown, J. D. (1998). *The self.* New York: McGraw Hill.

Burhans, K., and Dweck, C. S. (1995). Helplessness in early childhood: The role of contingent worth. *Child Development, 66,* 1719–1738.

Burgner, D., & Hewstone, M. (1993). Young children's causal attributions for success and failure: "Self-enhancing" boys and "self-derogating" girls. *British Journal of Developmental Psychology, 11,* 125–129.

Bushman, B. J., & Baumeister, R. F. (1998). Threatened egotism, narcissism, self-esteem, and direct and displaced aggression: Does self-love or self-hate lead to violence? *Journal of Personality and Social Psychology, 75,* 219–29.

Buss, A. (1989). Temperaments as personality traits. In G. A. Kohnstamm, J. E. Bates, & M. K. Rothbart (Eds.), *Temperament in childhood* (pp. 49–58). New York: Wiley.

Butler, R. (1987). Task-involving and ego-involving properties of evaluation: Effects of different feedback conditions on motivational perceptions, interest, and performance. *Journal of Educational Psychology, 79,* 474–482.

Butler, R. (1988) Enhancing and undermining intrinsic motivation: The effects of task-involving evaluation on interest and performance. *British Journal of Educational Psychology, 58,* 1–14.

Butler, R. (1992). What young people want to know when: Effects of mastery and ability goals on interest in different kinds of social comparison. *Journal of Personality and Social Psychology, 62,* 934–943.

Button, S. B., & Mathieu, J. E. (1996). Goal orientation in organizational research: A conceptual and empirical foundation. *Organizational Behavior and Human Decision Processes, 67,* 26–48.

Cain, K. M., & Dweck, C. S. (1995). The development of children's achievement motivation patterns and conceptions of intelligence. *Merrill-Palmer Quarterly, 41,* 25–52.

Cain, K. M., & Heyman, G. D. (1993, March). *Can Cinderella solve puzzles? Preschoolers' ability to make dispositional predictions within and across domains.* Paper presented at the Meeting of the Society for Research in Child Development, New Orleans, LA.

Cantor, N. (1990). From thought to behavior: "Having" and "doing" in the study of personality and cognition. *American Psychologist, 45,* 735–750.

Cantor, N., & Fleeson, W. (1994). Social intelligence and intelligent goal pursuit: A cognitive slice of motivation. In W. D. Spaulding (Ed.), *Nebraska symposium on motivation* (Vol. 41, pp. 125–179). Lincoln, NE: University of Nebraska Press.

Cantor, N., Markus, H. R., Niedenthal, P., & Nurius, P. (1986). On motivation and the self-concept. In R. M. Sorrentino & E. T. Higgins (Eds.), *Handbook of motivation and cognition* (pp. 96–121). New York: Guilford Press.

Cantor, N., & Zirkel, S. (1990). Personality, cognition, and purposive behavior. In L. Pervin (Ed.), *Handbook of personality: Theory and research* (pp. 135–164). New York: Guilford Press.

Carey, S. (1996). Cognitive domains as modes of thought. In D. R. Olson & N. Torrance (Eds.), *Modes of thought: Explorations in culture and cognition.* New York: Cambridge University Press.

Carugati, F. F. (1990). From social cognition to social representations in the study of intelligence. In G. Duveen & B. Loyd (Eds.), *Social representations and the development of knowledge.* Cambridge, UK: Cambridge University Press.

Carver, C. S., Scheier, M. F., & Weintraub, J. K. (1989). Assessing coping strategies: A theoretically based approach. *Journal of Personality and Social Psychology, 56,* 267–283.

Ceci, S. J. (1990). *On intelligence—more or less: A bio-ecological treatise on intellectual development.* Englewood Cliffs, NJ: Prentice Hall.

Ceci, S. J., & Williams, W. M. (1997). Schooling, intelligence, and income. *American Psychologist, 52,* 1051–1058.

Chambless, D. L., & Gillis, M. M. (1993). Cognitive therapy of anxiety disorders. *Journal of Consulting and Clinical Psychology, 61,* 248–260.

Chapin, M., & Dyck, D. G. (1976). Persistence in children's reading as a function of N length and attribution retraining. *Journal of Abnormal Psychology, 85,* 511–515.

Chiu, C., Dweck, C. S., Tong, J. Y., & Fu, J. H. (1997). Implicit theories and conceptions of morality. *Journal of Personality and Social Psychology, 73,* 923–940.

Chiu, C., Hong, Y., & Dweck, C. S. (1997). Lay dispositionism and implicit theories of personality. *Journal of Personality and Social Psychology, 73,* 19–30.

Cordova, D. I., & Lepper, M. R. (1996). Intrinsic motivation and the process of learning: Beneficial effects of contextualization, personalization, and choice. *Journal of Educational Psychology, 88,* 715–730.

Costa, P. T., & McCrae, R. R. (1994a). Depression as an enduring disposition. In L. Schneider, C. Reynolds, B. Lebowitz, & A. Friedhoff (Eds.), *Diagnosis and treatment of depression in late life: Results of the NIH consensus development conference.* Washington, DC: American Psychiatric Press.

Costa, P. T., & McCrae, R. R. (1994b). "Set like plaster?" Evidence for the stability of adult personality. In T. Heatherton & J. Weinberger (Eds.), *Can personality change?* Washington, DC: American Psychological Association.

Covington, M. V. (1992). *Making the grade: A self-worth perspective on motivation and school reform.* New York: Cambridge University Press.

Covington, M. V., & Omelich, C. L. (1979). Effort: The double-edged sword in school achievement. *Journal of Educational Psychology, 77,* 446–459.

Coyne, J. C., & Downey, G. (1991). Social factors and psychopathology: Stress, social support, and coping. In M. R. Rosenzweig & L. W. Porter (Eds.), *Annual Review of Psychology,* (Vol.42, pp. 401–425). Palo Alto, CA: Annual Reviews.

Cramer, J., & Oshima, T. C. (1992). Do gifted females attribute their math performance differently than other students? *Journal for the Education of the Gifted, 16,* 18–35.

Crandall, V. C., Katkovsky, W., & Crandall, V. J. (1965). Children's beliefs in their own control of reinforcement in intellectual-academic situations. *Child Development, 36,* 91–109.

Crystal, D. S., Chen, C., Fuligni, A. J., Stevenson, H. W., Hsu, C. C., Ko, H. J., Kitamura, S., & Kimura, S. (1994). Psychological maladjustment and academic achievement: A cross-cultural study of Japanese, Chinese and American high school students. *Child Development, 65,* 738–753.

Csikszentmihalyi, M. (1988). *Optimal experience: Psychological studies of flow in consciousness.* New York: Cambridge.

Damon, W. (1995). *Greater expectations: Overcoming the culture of indulgence in America's homes and schools*. New York: Free Press.

Damon, W. (1996). The lifelong transformation of moral goals through social influence. In P. B. Baltes & U. M. Staudinger (Eds.), *Interactive minds: Life-span perspectives on the social foundation of cognition* (pp. 198–220). New York: Cambridge University Press.

Deaux, K. (1993). Reconstructing social identity. *Personality and Social Psychology Bulletin, 19,* 4–12.

Deci, E. L., & Ryan, R. M. (1985). *Intrinsic motivation and self-determination in human behavior*. New York: Plenum.

Deci, E. L., & Ryan, R. M. (1991). A motivational approach to self: Integration in personality. In R. Dienstbier (Ed.), *Nebraska symposium on motivation* (pp. 237–288). Lincoln, NE: University of Nebraska Press.

Diener, C. I., & Dweck, C. S. (1978). An analysis of learned helplessness: Continuous changes in performance, strategy and achievement cognitions following failure. *Journal of Personality and Social Psychology, 36,* 451–462.

Diener, C. I., & Dweck, C. S. (1980). An analysis of learned helplessness: (II) The processing of success. *Journal of Personality and Social Psychology, 39,* 940–952.

Dodge, K. A. (1993). Social-cognitive mechanisms in the development of conduct disorders and depression. *Annual Review of Psychology, 44,* 559–584.

Dodge, K. A., Asher, S. R., & Parkhurst, J. T. (1989). Social life as a goal coordination task. In C. Ames & R. Ames (Eds.), *Research on motivation in education* (Vol. 3) (pp. 107–135). New York: Academic Press.

Downey, G., & Feldman, S. (1996). Implications of rejection sensitivity for intimate relationships. *Journal of Personality and Social Psychology, 70,* 1327–1343.

Downey, G., & Walker, E. (1992). Distinguishing family-level and child-level influences in the development of depression and aggression in children at risk. *Development and Psychopathology, 41,* 81–95.

Duda, J. L. (1992). Goal orientations and beliefs about the causes of sport success among elite skiers. *Sports Psychologist, 6,* 334–343.

Dweck, C. S. (1975). The role of expectations and attributions in the alleviation of learned helplessness. *Journal of Personality and Social Psychology, 31,* 674–685.

Dweck, C. S. (1986). Motivational processes affecting learning. *American Psychologist, 41,* 1040–1048.

Dweck, C. S. (1990). Motivation. In R. Glaser and A. Lesgold (Eds.), *Foundations for a cognitive psychology of education*. Hillsdale, NJ: Erlbaum.

Dweck, C. S. (1991). Self-theories and goals: Their role in motivation, personality, and development. In R. Dienstbier (Ed.), *Nebraska symposium on motivation* (pp. 199–235). Lincoln, NE: University of Nebraska Press.

Dweck, C. S. (1996a). Capturing the dynamic nature of personality. *Journal of Research in Personality, 30,* 348–362.

Dweck, C. S. (1996b). Implicit theories as organizers of goals and behavior. In P. Gollwitzer and J. Bargh (Eds.), *The psychology of action: Linking cognition and motivation to behavior* (pp. 69–90). New York: Guilford.

Dweck, C. S. (1996c). Social motivation: Goals and social-cognitive processes. In J. Juvonen and K. Wentzel (Eds.), *Social Motivation* (pp. 181–195). New York: Cambridge University Press.

Dweck, C. S. (1998). The development of early self-conceptions: Their relevance for motivational processes. In J. Heckhausen & C. S. Dweck (Eds.), *Motivation and self-regulation across the life span* (pp. 257–280). Cambridge: Cambridge University Press.

Dweck, C. S. (in press). Students' theories about their intelligence: Implications for talent and achievement. In R. Friedman (Ed.), *The development of the gifted child: The emotional price of excellence.* Washington, DC: American Psychological Association.

Dweck, C. S., & Bempechat, J. (1983). Children's theories of intelligence. In S. Paris, G. Olsen, & H. Stevenson (Eds.), *Learning and motivation in the classroom* (pp. 239–256). Hillsdale, NJ: Erlbaum.

Dweck, C. S., Chiu, C., & Hong, Y. (1995). Implicit theories and their role in judgments and reactions: A world from two perspectives. *Psychological Inquiry, 6,* 267–285.

Dweck, C. S., Davidson, W., Nelson, S., & Enna, B. (1978). Sex differences in learned helplessness: (II) The contingencies of evaluative feedback in the classroom and (III) An experimental analysis. *Developmental Psychology, 14,* 268–276.

Dweck, C. S., & Elliott, E. S. (1983). Achievement motivation. In P. Mussen and E. M. Hetherington (Eds.), *Handbook of child psychology* (pp. 643–692). New York: Wiley.

Dweck, C. S., Goetz, T. E., & Strauss, N. (1980). Sex differences in learned helplessness: (IV) An experimental and naturalistic study of failure generalization and its mediators. *Journal of Personality and Social Psychology, 38,* 441–452.

Dweck, C. S., & Leggett, E. L. (1988). A social-cognitive approach to motivation and personality. *Psychological Review, 95,* 256–273.

Dweck, C. S., & Reppucci, N. D. (1973). Learned helplessness and reinforcement responsibility in children. *Journal of Personality and Social Psychology, 25,* 109–116.

Dykman, B. M. (1998) Integrating cognitive and motivational factors in depression: Initial tests of a goal-orientation approach. *Journal of Personality and Social Psychology, 74,* 139–158.

Eccles, J. S. (1984). Sex differences in achievement patterns. *Nebraska Symposium on Motivation, 32,* 97–132.

Eccles, J., & Midgley, C. (1989). Stage-environment fit: Developmentally appropriate classrooms for young adolescents. In C. Ames & R. Ames (Eds.), *Research on motivation in education* (Vol. 3, pp. 139–186). New York: Academic Press.

Elliot, A. J. (1997). Integrating the "classic" and "contemporary" approaches to achievement motivation: A hierarchical model of approach and avoidance achievement motivation. In M. L. Maehr & P. R. Pintrich (Eds.), *Advances in motivation and achievement* (Vol. 10, pp. 143–179). Greenwich, CT: JAI Press.

Elliot, A. J., & Church, M. (1997). A hierarchical model of approach and avoidance achievement motivation. *Journal of Personality and Social Psychology, 72,* 218–232.

Elliot, A. J., & Harackiewicz, J. (1996). Approach and avoidance goals and intrinsic motivation: A mediational analysis. *Journal of Personality and Social Psychology, 70,* 461–475.

Elliott, E. S., & Dweck, C. S. (1988) Goals: An approach to motivation and achievement. *Journal of Personality and Social Psychology, 54,* 5–12.

Ellis, A. (1962). *Reason and emotion in psychotherapy.* Secaucus, NJ: Lyle Stuart.

Ellis, A. (1995). Rational-emotive therapy and beyond: Current status, recent revisions, and research questions. *Clinical Psychology Review, 15,* 169–185.

Emmons, R. A. (1986). Personal strivings: An approach to personality and subjective well-being. *Journal of Personality and Social Psychology, 51,* 1058–1068.

Emmons, R. A., & King, L. A. (1988). Conflict among personal strivings: Immediate and long-term implications for psychological and physical well-being. *Journal of Personality and Social Psychology, 54,* 1040–1048.

Epstein, S. (1990). Cognitive-experiential self-theory. In L. Pervin (Ed.), *Handbook of personality: Theory and research* (pp. 165–192). New York: Guilford.

Erdley, C. A. (1996). Motivational approaches to aggression within the context of peer relationships. In J. Juvonen and K. Wentzel (Eds.), *Social motivation* (pp. 98–125). New York: Cambridge University Press.

Erdley, C., Cain, K., Loomis, C., Dumas-Hines, F., & Dweck, C. S. (1997). The relations among children's social goals, implicit personality theories and response to social failure. *Developmental Psychology, 33*, 263–272.

Erdley, C. S., & Dweck, C. S. (1993). Children's implicit theories as predictors of their social judgments. *Child Development, 64*, 863–878.

Erikson, E. H. (1950). *Childhood and society.* New York: Norton.

Erikson, E. H. (1959). *Identity and the life cycle.* New York: International University Press.

Eysenck, H. J. (1982). *Personality, genetics and behavior.* New York: Praeger.

Faria, L. (1996). Personal conceptions of intelligence: A developmental study in Portugal. *Psychological Reports, 79*, 1299–1305.

Farrell, E. (1990). *Hanging in and dropping out: Voices of at-risk high school students.* New York: Teachers College Press.

Farrell, E., & Dweck, C. S. (1985). *The role of motivational processes in transfer of learning.* Unpublished manuscript.

Fowler, J. W., & Petersen, P. L. (1981). Increasing reading persistence and altering attributional styles of learned helpless children. *Journal of Educational Psychology, 73*, 251–260.

Fox, L. (1976). Sex differences in mathematical precocity: Bridging the gap. In D. P. Keating (Ed.), *Intellectual talent: Research and development.* Baltimore, MD: Johns Hopkins University Press.

Frese, M., & Sabini, J. (Eds.). (1985). *Goal-directed behavior: The concept of action in psychology.* Hillsdale, NJ: Erlbaum.

Freud, S. (1923/1960). *The ego and the id* (J. Riviere, Trans.). New York: Norton.

Freud, S. (1940/1949). *An outline of psychoanalysis* (J. Strachey, Trans.). New York: Norton.

Geen, R. G. (1995). *Human motivation: A social psychological approach.* Pacific Grove, CA: Brooks/Cole.

Gervey, B., Chiu, C., Hong, Y., & Dweck, C. S. (1999). Differential use of person information in decision-making about guilt vs. innocence: The role of implicit theories. *Personality and Social Psychology Bulletin, 25*, 17–27.

Goetz, T. E., & Dweck, C. S. (1980). Learned helplessness in social situations. *Journal of Personality and Social Psychology, 39*, 246–255.

Goldberg, L. R. (1990). An alternative "description" of personality: The big-five factor structure. *Journal of Personality and Social Psychology, 59*, 1216–1229.

Gollwitzer, P. M., & Wicklund, R. A. (1985). The pursuit of self-defining goals. In J. Kuhl & J. Beckmann (Eds.), *Action control: From cognition to behavior.* Heidelberg: Springer-Verlag.

Goodnow, J. J. (1980). Everyday concepts of intelligence and its development. In N. Warren (Ed.), *Studies in cross-cultural psychology* (Vol. 2, pp. 191–219). Oxford, UK: Pergamon Press.

Goodnow, J. J., & Collins, W. A. (1990). *Development according to parents: The nature, sources, and consequences of parents' ideas.* Hillsdale, NJ: Erlbaum.

Gould, S. J. (1981). *The mismeasure of man.* New York: Norton.

Graham, S., & Golon, S. (1991). Motivational influences on cognition: Task involvement, ego involvement, and depth of information processing. *Journal of Educational Psychology, 83*, 187–194.

Grant, H., & Dweck, C. S. (in press). A goal analysis of personality and personality coherence. In D. Cervone and U. Shoda (Eds.), *Social-cognitive approaches to personality coherence.* New York: Guilford Press.

Greenberg, L. S., & Pascuale-Leone, J. (1997). Emotion in the creation of personal meaning. In M. J. Power & C. R. Brewin (Eds.), *The transformation of meaning in psychological therapies: Integrating theory and practice* (pp. 157–173). Chichester, UK: Wiley.

Greenwald, A. G. (1992). New Look 3: Unconscious cognition reclaimed. *American Psychologists, 47*, 766–779.

Greenwald, A. G., & Banaji, M. R. (1995). Implicit social cognition: Attitudes, self-esteem, and stereotypes. *Psychological Review, 102*, 4–27.

Greenwald, A. G., & Pratkanis, A. R. (1984). The self. In R. Wyer & T. Srull (Eds.), *Handbook of social cognition* (Vol. 3, pp. 129–178). Hillsdale, NJ: Erlbaum.

Hamilton, D. L., & Sherman, S. J. (1996). Perceiving persons and groups. *Psychological Review, 103*, 336–355.

Harackiewicz, J. M., Barron, K. E., Carter, S. M., Lehto, A. T., & Elliot, A. J. (1997). Predictors and consequences of achievement goals in the college classroom: Maintaining interest and making the grade. *Journal of Personality and Social Psychology, 73*, 1284–1295.

Harter, S. (1975). Developmental differences in the manifestation of mastery motivation on problem-solving tasks. *Child Development, 46*, 370–378.

Harter, S. (1990). Causes, correlates, and the functional role of global self-worth: A life-span perspective. In R. Sternberg & J. Kolligian (Eds.), *Competence considered* (pp. 67–97). New Haven, CT: Yale University Press.

Hebert, C., & Dweck, C. S. (1985). *Mediators of persistence in preschoolers.* Unpublished manuscript.

Heckhausen, H. (1987). Emotional components of action: Their ontogeny as reflected in achievement behavior. In D. Gorlitz & J. F. Wohlwill (Eds.), *Curiosity, imagination, and play: On the development of spontaneous motivational processes* (pp. 326–348). Hillsdale, NJ: Erlbaum.

Heckhausen, J., & Dweck, C. S. (Eds.). (1998). *Motivation and self-regulation across the life span.* Cambridge: Cambridge University Press.

Heckhausen, J., & Schulz, R. (1995). A life-span theory of control. *Psychological Review, 102*, 284–304.

Heider, F. (1958). *The psychology of interpersonal relations.* New York: Wiley.

Henderson, V., & Dweck, C. S. (1990). Achievement and motivation in adolescence: A new model and data. In S. Feldman and G. Elliott (Eds.), *At the threshold: The developing adolescent.* Cambridge, MA: Harvard University Press.

Herrnstein, R. J., & Murray, C. (1994). *The bell curve: Intelligence and class structure in American life.* New York: Free Press.

Heyman, G. D., & Dweck, C. S. (1992). Achievement goals and intrinsic motivation: Their relation and their role in adaptive motivation. *Motivation and Emotion, 16*, 231–247.

Heyman, G. D., & Dweck, C. S. (1998). Children's thinking about traits: Implications for judgments of the self and others. *Child Development, 64*, 391–403.

Heyman, G. D., Dweck, C. S., & Cain, K. (1992) Young children's vulnerability to self-blame and helplessness. *Child Development, 63*, 401–415.

Heyman, G. D., & Gelman, S. A. (1997, April). Thinking about the origins of human dispositions. Paper presented at the biennial meeting of the Society for Research in Child Development, Washington, DC.

Higgins, E. T. (1987). Self-discrepancy: A theory relating self and affect. *Psychological Review, 94*, 319–340.

Higley, J., & Suomi, S. J. (1996). Effects of reactivity and social competence on individual responses to severe stress in children: Investigations using nonhuman primates. In C. R. Pfeffer (Ed.), *Severe stress and mental disturbance in children* (pp. 3–57). Washington, DC: American Psychiatric Press.

Hirschfeld, L. A. (1995). Do children have a theory of race? *Cognition, 54*, 209–252.

Hoffman, M. L. (1970). Conscience, personality, and socialization techniques. *Human Development, 13*, 90–126.

Hollon, S. D., DeRubeis, R. J., & Evans, M. D. (1996). Cognitive therapy in the treatment and prevention of depression. In P. M. Salkovskis (Ed.), *Frontiers of cognitive therapy* (pp. 293–317). New York: Guilford Press.

Hong, Y. (1994). Predicting trait versus process inferences: The role of implicit theories. Doctoral dissertation, Columbia University, New York.

Hong, Y. Y., Chiu, C., & Dweck, C. S. (1995). Implicit theories of intelligence: Reconsidering the role of confidence in achievement motivation. In M. Kernis (Ed.), *Efficacy, agency, and self-esteem*. New York: Plenum.

Hong, Y., Chiu, C., Dweck, C. S., & Lin, D. (1998). *A test of implicit theories and self-confidence as predictors of responses to achievement challenges*. Unpublished manuscript.

Hong, Y., Chiu, C., Sacks, R., & Dweck, C. S. (1997). Implicit theories and evaluative encoding of information. *Journal of Experimental Social Psychology, 33*, 296–323.

Horney, K. (1937). *Neurotic personality of our times*. New York: Norton.

Horney, K. (1945). *Our inner conflicts*. New York: Norton.

Horney, K. (1950). *Neurosis and human growth*. New York: Norton.

Howard, J. (1995). You can't get there from here: The need for a new logic in education reform. *Proceedings of the American Academy of Arts and Sciences, 124*, 85–92.

Hudley, C., & Graham, S. (1993). An attributional intervention to reduce peer-directed aggression among African-American boys. *Child Development, 64*, 124–138.

Hunt, J. McV. (1961). *Intelligence and experience*. New York: Ronald Press.

Hunt, J. McV. (1972). Heredity, environment, and class or ethnic differences. *Assessment in a pluralistic society*. Princeton, NJ: Educational Testing Service.

Hunt, J. McV. (1979). Psychological development: Early experience. In M. R. Rosenzweig & L. W. Porter (Eds.), *Annual Review of Psychology* (Vol. 30, pp. 103–143). Palo Alto, CA: Annual Reviews.

Janoff-Bulman, R. (1979). Characterological versus behavioral self-blame. *Journal of Personality and Social Psychology, 37*, 1798–1809.

Janoff-Bulman, R.(1992). *Shattered assumptions*. New York: Free Press.

Janoff-Bulman, R., & Brickman, P. (1981). Expectations and what people learn from failure. In N. T. Feather (Ed.), *Expectancy, incentive, and action* (pp. 207–237).

Jensen, A. R. (1969). How much can we boost IQ and scholastic achievement? *Harvard Educational Review, 39*, 1–123.

Jones, E. E. (1990). Constrained behavior and self-concept change. In J. M. Olson & M. P. Zanna (Eds.), *Self-inference processes: The Ontario symposium* (pp. 69–86). Hillsdale, NJ: Erlbaum.

Jones, E. E., & Berglas, S. (1978). Control of attributions about the self through self-handicapping strategies: The appeal of alcohol and the role of underachievement. *Personality and Social Psychology Bulletin, 4*, 200–206.

Jones, E. E., Kanouse, D. E., Kelley, H. H., Nisbett, R. E., Valins, S., & Weiner, B. (Eds.). (1972). *Attribution: Perceiving the causes of behavior*. Hillsdale, NJ: Erlbaum.

Jung, C. G. (1933). *Modern man in search of a soul*. New York: Harcourt, Brace & World.

Juvonen, J. (1995). Grade-level differences in the social value of effort: Implications for the self-presentational tactics of early adolescents. *Child Development, 66*, 1694–1705.

Jussim, L. (1989). Teacher expectations: Self-fulfilling prophecies, perceptual biases, and accuracy. *Journal of Personality and Social Psychology, 57*, 469–480.

Kagan, J., & Lamb, S. (Eds.). (1987). *The emergence of morality in young children*. Chicago: University of Chicago Press.

Kagan, J., & Snidman, N. (1991). Temperamental factors in human development. *American Psychologist, 46*, 856–862.

Kamins, M. L., & Dweck, C. S. (1998). *Contingent self-worth and its effects on young children's coping with setbacks*. Unpublished data.

Kamins, M., & Dweck, C. S. (in press). Person vs. process praise and criticism: Implications for contingent self-worth and coping. *Developmental Psychology*.

Kamins, M. L., Morris, S. M., & Dweck, C. S. (1996). Implicit theories as predictors of goals in dating relationships. Paper presented at the conference of the Eastern Psychological Association, Washington, DC.

Kelly, G. A. (1955). *The psychology of personal constructs*. New York: Norton.

Kihlstrom, J. F. (1987). The cognitive unconscious. *Science, 237,* 1445–1452.

Klinger, E. (1977). *Meaning and void: Inner experience and the incentives in people's lives*. Minneapolis: University of Minnesota Press.

Knee, C. R. (1998). Implicit theories of relationships: Assessment and prediction of romantic relationship initiation, coping, and longevity. *Journal of Personality and Social Psychology, 74,* 360–370.

Kohut, H. (1971). *The analysis of the self*. New York: International Universities Press.

Kohut, H. (1977). *The restoration of the self*. New York: International Universities Press.

Kruglanski, A. W. (1989). *Lay epistemics and human knowledge: Cognitive and motivational bases*. New York: Plenum.

Kruglanski, A. W. (1996). A motivated gatekeeper of our minds: Need-for-closure effects on interpersonal and group processes. In R. R. Sorrentino & E. T. Higgins (Eds.), *Handbook of motivation and cognitions* (Vol. 3) (pp. 465–496). New York: Guilford.

Kruglanski, A. W., & Webster, D. M. (1996). Motivated closing of the mind: "Seizing" and "freezing." *Psychological Review, 103,* 263–283.

Kunda, Z., & Nisbett, R. E. (1986). The psychometrics of everyday life. *Cognitive Psychology, 18,* 195–224.

Langer, E. L. (1989). *Mindfulness*. Reading, MA: Addison-Wesley.

Langer, S. K. (1967). *Mind: An essay on human feeling*. Baltimore, MD: Johns Hopkins Press.

Lazarus, R. S. (1991). *Emotion and adaptation*. New York: Oxford University Press.

Lazarus, R. S., & Folkman, S. (1984). *Stress, appraisal, and coping*. New York: Springer-Verlag.

Lee, S., Graham, T., & Stevenson, H. W. (1996). Teachers and teaching: Elementary school in Japan and the United States. In T. Rohlen & G. LeTendre (Eds.), *Teaching and learning in Japan* (pp. 157–189). New York: Cambridge University Press.

Leggett, E. L. (1985, March). Children's entity and incremental theories of intelligence: Relationships to achievement behavior. Paper presented at the annual meeting of the Eastern Psychological Association, Boston.

Leggett, E. L., & Dweck, C. S. (1986). *Individual differences in goals and inference rules: Sources of causal judgments*. Unpublished manuscript.

Lepper, M. R., Aspinwall, L. G., Mumme, D. L., & Chabay, R. W. (1990). Self-perception and social-perception processes in tutoring: Subtle social control strategies of experts. In J. M. Olson & M. P. Zanna (Eds.), *Self-inference processes: The Ontario symposium* (Vol. 6, pp. 217–237). Hillsdale, NJ: Erlbaum.

Lerner, M. J. (1980). *The belief in a just world: A fundamental delusion*. New York: Plenum Press.

Levy, S. R., (1998). *Children's static versus dynamic conceptions of people: Their impact on intergroup attitudes*. Doctoral dissertation, Columbia University, New York.

Levy, S. R., & Dweck, C. S. (1996, June). The relation between implicit person theories and beliefs in stereotypes. Paper presented at the Annual Convention of the American Psychological Society, San Francisco, CA.

Levy, S. R., & Dweck, C. S. (1998). Trait-focused and process-focused social judgment. *Social Cognition, 16,* 151–172.

Levy, S. R., & Dweck, C. S. (in press). Children's static vs. dynamic person conceptions as predictors of their stereotype formation. *Child Development*.

Levy, S. R., Freitas, A., & Dweck, C. S. (1998). *Acting on Stereotypes*. Unpublished manuscript.

Levy, S., Stroessner, S., and Dweck, C. S. (1998). Stereotype formation and endorsement: The role of implicit theories. *Journal of Personality and Social Psychology, 74*, 1421–1436.

Lewis, M. (1990). Self-knowledge and social development in early life. In L. A. Pervin (Ed.), *Handbook of personality: Theory and research* (pp. 277–300). New York: Guilford Press.

Lewis, M. (1992). *Shame, the exposed self.* New York: Free Press.

Lewis, M. (1997). *Altering fate: Why the past does not predict the future.* New York: Guilford Press.

Lewis, M., Alessandri, S. M., & Sullivan, M. W. (1992). Differences in shame and pride as a function of children's gender and task difficulty. *Child Development, 63*, 630–638.

Lewis, M., & Brooks-Gunn, J. (1979). *Social cognition and the acquisition of self.* New York: Plenum.

Lewis, M., & Feinman, S. (Eds.). (1991). *Social influences and socialization in infancy.* New York: Plenum.

Licht, B. G., & Dweck, C. S. (1984a). Determinants of academic achievement: The interaction of children's achievement orientations with skill area. *Developmental Psychology, 20*, 628–636.

Licht, B. G., & Dweck, C. S. (1984b). Sex differences in achievement orientations: Consequences for academic choices and attainments. In M. Marland (Ed.), *Sex differentiation and schooling.* London: Heinemann.

Licht, B. G., Linden, T. A., Brown, D. A., & Sexton, M. A. (1984, August). *Sex differences in achievement orientation: An "A" student phenomenon?* Paper presented at the meeting of the American Psychological Association, Toronto, Canada.

Licht, B. G., & Shapiro, S. H. (1982, August). *Sex differences in attributions among high achievers.* Paper presented at the meeting of the American Psychological Association, Washington, DC.

Little, B. R. (1989). Personal projects analysis: Trivial pursuits, magnificent obsessions, and the search for coherence. In D. Buss & N. Cantor (Eds.), *Personality psychology: Recent trends and emerging directions* (pp. 15–31). New York: Springer-Verlag.

Loeb, I. S., & Dweck, C. S. (1994, June). *Beliefs about human nature as predictors of reactions to victimization.* Paper presented at the Annual Convention of the American Psychological Society, Washington, DC.

Loehlin, J. C. (1992). Genes and environment in personality development. Newbury Park, CA: Sage.

Maccoby, E. E. (1992). The role of parents in the socialization of children: An historical overview. *Developmental Psychology, 28*, 1006–1017.

Maccoby, E. E. (1998). *The two sexes: Growing up apart, coming together.* Cambridge, MA: Belknap Press/Harvard.

Maehr, M. L., & Midgley, C. (1996). *Transforming school cultures.* Boulder, CO: Westview Press.

MacGyvers, V. L. (1993). Implicit beliefs about the self and real-world outcomes in children and adolescents. Doctoral dissertation, University of Illinois at Urbana-Champaign.

Main, M., Kaplan, N., & Cassidy, J. (1985). Security in infancy, childhood, and adulthood: A move to the level of representation. *Monographs of the Society for Research in Child Development, 50*, 66–104.

Mandler, J. M. (1996). Preverbal representation and language. In P. Bloom, L. Nadel, & M. F. Garrett (Eds.), *Language and space: Language, speech, and communication* (pp. 365–384). Cambridge, MA: MIT Press.

Markus, H. (1977). Self schemata and processing information about the self. *Journal of Personality and Social Psychology, 35*, 63–78.

Markus, H., & Cross, S. (1990). The interpersonal self. In L. A. Pervin (Ed.), *Handbook of personality: Theory and research* (pp. 576–608). New York: Guilford Press.

Markus, H., & Ruvolo, A. (1989). Possible selves: Personalized representations of goals. In L. Pervin (Ed.), *Goal concepts in personality and social psychology* (pp. 211–241). Hillsdale, NJ: Erlbaum.

Maslow, A. H. (1955). Deficiency motivation and growth motivation. In M. R. Jones (Ed.), *Nebraska symposium on motivation*. Lincoln, NE: University of Nebraska Press.

Maslow, A. H. (1962). *Toward a psychology of being*. Princeton, NJ: Van Nostrand.

McClelland, D. C. (1961). *The achieving society*. Princeton, NJ: Van Nostrand.

McClelland, D. C., Atkinson, J., Clark, R., & Lowell, E. (1953). *The achievement motive*. New York: Appleton, Century, Crofts.

McCrae, R. R., & John, O. P. (1992). An introduction to the five-factor and its applications. *Journal of Personality, 60*, 175–215.

Meyer, W. U. (1982). Indirect communications about perceived ability estimates. *Journal of Educational Psychology, 74*, 888–897.

Middleton, M. J., & Midgley, C. (1997). Avoiding a demonstration of lack of ability: An underexplored aspect of goal theory. *Journal of Educational Psychology, 89*, 710–718.

Midgley, C., Anderman, E., & Hicks, L. (1995). Differences between elementary and middle school teachers and students: A goal theory approach, *Journal of Early Adolescence, 15*, 90–113.

Midgley, C., Arunkumar, R., & Urdan, T. C. (1996). "If I don't do well tomorrow, there's a reason:" Predictors of adolescents' use of academic self-handicapping strategies. *Journal of Educational Psychology, 88*, 423–434.

Miller, A. T. (1985). A developmental study of the cognitive basis of performance impairment after failure. *Journal of Personality and Social Psychology, 49*, 529–538.

Mischel, W. (1973). Toward a cognitive social learning reconceptualization of personality. *Psychological Review, 80*, 252–283.

Mischel, W. (1974). Processes in delay of gratification. In L. Berkowitz (Ed.), *Advances in experimental social psychology* (Vol. 7). New York: Academic Press.

Mischel, W. (1990). Personality dispositions revisited and revised: A view after three decades. In L. Pervin (Ed.), *Handbook of personality: Theory and research* (pp. 111–134). New York: Guilford.

Mischel, W., & Shoda, Y. (1995). A cognitive-affective systems theory of personality: Reconceptualizing the invariances in personality and the role of situations. *Psychological Review, 102*, 246–268.

Mischel, W., Shoda, U., & Rodriguez, M. L. (1989). Delay of gratification in children. *Science, 244*, 933–938.

Molden, D., & Dweck, C. S. (in press). Meaning and motivation. In C. Sansone & J. Harackiewicz (Eds.), *Intrinsic motivation*. New York: Academic Press.

Mueller, C. M., & Dweck, C. S. (1996). Implicit theories of intelligence: Relation of parental beliefs to children's expectations. Paper presented at the Third National Research Convention of Head Start, Washington, DC.

Mueller, C. M., & Dweck, C. S. (1997). *Implicit theories of intelligence: Malleability beliefs, definitions, and judgments of intelligence*. Unpublished data.

Mueller, C. M., & Dweck, C. S. (1998). Intelligence praise can undermine motivation and performance. *Journal of Personality and Social Psychology, 75*, 33–52.

Murphy, G. L., & Medin, D. L. (1985). The role of theories in conceptual coherence. *Psychological Review, 92*, 289–316.

Murray, H. A. (1938). *Explorations in personality*. New York: Oxford University Press.

Nelson, K. (1996). *Language in cognitive development: Emergence of the mediated mind*. New York: Cambridge University Press.

Nicholls, J. (1984). Achievement motivation: Conceptions of ability, subjective experience, task choice, and performance. *Psychological Review, 91*, 328–346.

Nickerson, R. S., Perkins. D. N., & Smith, E. E. (1985). *Teaching thinking.* Hillsdale, NJ: Erlbaum.

Nisbett, R. E., & Wilson, T. D. (1977). Telling more than we can know: Verbal reports on mental processes. *Psychological Review, 84*, 231–259.

Nolen-Hoeksema, S. (1994). An interactive model for the emergence of gender differences in depression in adolescence. *Journal of Research on Adolescence, 4*, 519–534.

Nolen-Hoeksema, S. (1998). Ruminative coping with depression. In J. Heckhausen & C. S. Dweck (Eds.), *Motivation and self-regulation across the life-span* (pp. 237–256). New York: Cambridge University Press.

Nolen-Hoeksema, S., Girgus, J. S., & Seligman, M. E. (1992). Predictors and consequences of childhood depressive symptoms: A 5-year longitudinal study. *Journal of Abnormal Psychology, 101*, 405–422.

Ogbu, J. (1991). Minority coping and school experience. *Journal of Psychohistory, 84*, 433–456.

Overton, W. F. (1990). Competence and procedures: Constraints on the development of logical reasoning. In W. F. Overton (Ed.), *Reasoning, necessity and logic: Developmental perspectives* (pp. 1–32). Hillsdale, NJ: Erlbaum.

Paley, V. G. (1988). *Bad guys don't have birthdays: Fantasy play at four.* Chicago: University of Chicago Press.

Parsons, J. E., & Ruble, D. N. (1977). The development of achievement-related expectancies. *Child Development, 48*, 1075–1079.

Paulhus, D. L., (1984). Two-component models of socially desirable responding. *Journal of Personality and Social Psychology, 46*, 598–609.

Pepper, S. C. (1942). *World hypotheses.* Berkeley, CA: University of California Press.

Pervin, L. A. (1983). The stasis and flow of behavior: Toward a theory of goals. In M. M. Page (Ed.), *Personality: Current theory and research* (pp. 1–53). Lincoln, NE: University of Nebraska Press.

Pervin, L. A. (Ed.) (1989). *Goal concepts in personality and social psychology.* Hillsdale NJ: Erlbaum.

Pervin, L. A. (1994a). A critical analysis of current trait theory. *Psychological Inquiry, 5*, 103–113.

Pervin, L. A. (1994b). Personality stability, personal change, and the question of process. In T. Heatherton & J. Weinberger (Eds.), *Can personality change?* Washington, DC: American Psychological Association.

Peterson, C., & Seligman, M. E. P. (1984). Causal explanations as a risk factor for depression: Theory and evidence. *Psychological Review, 91*, 347–374.

Piaget, J., Garcia, R., Davidson, P., & Easley, J. (1991). *Toward a logic of meanings.* Hillsdale, NJ: Erlbaum.

Piaget, J., Garcia, R., and Feider, H. (1989). *Psychogenesis and the history of science.* New York: Columbia University Press.

Pintrich, P. R., & Garcia, T. (1991). Student goal orientation and self-regulation in the college classroom. In M. L. Maehr & P. R. Pintrich (Eds.), *Advances in motivation and achievement* (Vol. 7, pp. 371–402). Greenwich, CT: JAI Press.

Pintrich, P. R., & Garcia, T. (1994). Self-regulated learning in college students: Knowledge, strategies, and motivation. In P. R. Pintrich, D. R. Brown, C. E. Weinstein (Eds.), *Students' motivation, cognition, and learning: Essays in honor of Wilbert J. McKeachie.* Hillsdale, NJ: Erlbaum.

Pintrich, P. R., McKeachie, W. J., & Lin, Y. (1987). Teaching a course in learning to learn. *Teaching of Psychology, 14*, 81–86.

Plaks, J., & Dweck, C. S. (1997, May). Implicit person theories and attention to counter-expectant social information. Paper presented at the Annual Convention of the American Psychological Society, Washington, DC.

Pomerantz, E. M., & Ruble, D. N. (1997). Distinguishing multiple dimensions of conceptions of ability: Implications for self-evaluation. *Child Development, 68*, 1165–1180.

Pomerantz, E. M., & Ruble, D. N. (1998). The multidimensional nature of control: Implications for the development of sex differences in self-evaluation. In J. Heckhausen & C. S. Dweck (Eds.), *Motivation and self-regulation across the life span* (pp. 159–184). New York: Cambridge University Press.

Rabiner, D. L., & Gordon, L. V. (1992) The coordination of conflicting social goals: Differences between rejected and nonrejected boys. *Child Development, 63*, 1344–1350.

Read, S. J., & Miller, L. C. (1989). Inter-personalism: Toward a goal-based theory of persons in relationships. In L. A. Pervin (Ed.), *Goal concepts in personality and social psychology* (pp. 413–472). Hillsdale, NJ: Erlbaum.

Renshaw, P. D., & Asher, S. R. (1983). Children's goals and strategies for social interaction. *Merrill-Palmer Quarterly, 29*, 553–574.

Resnick, L. B. (1983). Mathematics and science learning: A new conception. *Science*, 477–478.

Rhodewalt, F. (1994). Conceptions of ability, achievement goals, and individual differences in self-handicapping behavior: On the application of implicit theories. *Journal of Personality, 62*, 67–85.

Roberts, T. (1991). Gender and the influence of evaluations on self-assessments in achievement settings. *Psychological Bulletin, 109*, 297–308.

Roberts, T., & Nolen-Hoeksema, S. (1994). Gender comparisons in responsiveness to others' evaluations in achievement situations. *Psychology of Women Quarterly, 18*, 221–240.

Robins, C. J., & Hayes, A. M. (1993). An appraisal of cognitive therapy. *Journal of Consulting and Clinical Psychology, 61*, 205–214.

Robins, R. W., & Pals, J. (1998). *Implicit self-theories of ability in the academic domain: A test of Dweck's model.* Unpublished manuscript.

Rochat, P. (1995). *The self in infancy: Theory and research.* Amsterdam: North-Holland/Elsevier.

Roeser, R. W., Midgley, C., & Urdan, T. C. (1996). Perceptions of the school psychological environment and early adolescents' psychological and behavioral functioning in school: The mediating role of goals and belonging. *Journal of Educational Psychology, 88*, 408–422.

Rogers, C. R. (1961). *On becoming a person.* Boston: Houghton Mifflin.

Rosenthal, R., & Jacobson, L. (1968). *Pygmalion in the classroom: Teacher expectation and pupils' intellectual development.* New York: Holt, Rinehart, Winston.

Ross, L., & Nisbett, R. E. (1991). *The person and the situation.* New York: McGraw-Hill.

Rothbaum, F., Weisz, J. R., & Snyder, S. S. (1982). Changing the world and changing the self: A two-process model of perceived control. *Journal of Personality and Social Psychology, 42*, 5–37.

Rotter, J. B. (1954). *Social learning and clinical psychology.* New York: Prentice-Hall.

Rotter, J. B. (1966). Generalized expectancies for internal versus external control of reinforcement. *Psychological Monographs, 80*, 609.

Ruble, D. N., & Dweck, C. S. (1995). The development of self-conceptions and person conceptions. In N. Eisenberg (Ed.), *Review of personality and social psychology* (Vol. 15) (pp. 109–139). Thousand Oaks, CA: Sage.

Ruble, D. N., Greulich, F., Pomerantz, E. M., & Gochberg, B. (1993). The role of gender-related processes in the development of self-evaluation and depression. *Journal of Affective Disorders, 29*, 97–128.

Saarni, C. (1993). Socialization of emotions. In M. Lewis & J. M. Haviland (Eds.), *Handbook of emotions*. New York: Guilford Press.

Scheier, M. F., & Carver, C. S. (1987). Dispositional optimism and physical well-being: The influence of generalized expectancies on health. *Journal of Personality, 55,* 169–210.

Scheier, M. F., Weintraub, J. K., & Carver, C. S. (1986). Coping with stress: Divergent strategies of optimists and pessimists. *Journal of Personality and Social Psychology, 51,* 1257–1264.

Schunk, D. H. (1982). Effects of effort attributional feedback on children's perceived self-efficacy and achievement. *Journal of Educational Psychology, 74,* 548–556.

Schunk, D. H., & Zimmerman, B. J. (1994). *Self-regulation of learning and performance.* Hillsdale, NJ: Erlbaum.

Seegers, G., & Boekaerts, M. (1996). Gender-related differences in self-referenced cognitions in relation to mathematics. *Journal for Research in Mathematics Education, 27,* 215–240.

Seligman, M. E., Kamen, L. P., & Nolen-Hoeksema. S. (1988). Explanatory styles across the life span: Achievement and health. In E. M. Hetherington, R. M. Lerner, & M. Perlmutter (Eds.), *Child Development in life-span perspective* (pp. 91–114). Hillsdale, NJ: Erlbaum.

Seligman, M. E., & Maier, S. F. (1967). Failure to escape traumatic shock. *Journal of Experimental Psychology, 74,* 1–9.

Seligman, M. E., & Nolen-Hoeksema, S. (1987). Explanatory style and depression. In D. Magnusson & A. Ohman (Eds.), *Psychopathology: An interactional perspective* (pp. 125–139). Orlando, FL: Academic Press.

Seligman, M. E., Reivich, K., Jaycox, L., & Gilham, J. (1995). *The optimistic child.* Boston: Houghton Mifflin.

Semin, G. R., & Gergen, K. J. (Eds.). (1990). *Everyday understanding.* London: Sage Publications.

Shapiro, D. (1965). *Neurotic styles.* New York: Basic Books.

Shoda, Y., Mischel, W., & Wright, J. C. (1994). Intraindividual stability in the organization and patterning of behavior: Incorporating psychological situations into the idiographic analysis of behavior. *Journal of Personality and Social Psychology, 667,* 674–687.

Shweder, R. A. (1993). The cultural meaning of emotions. In M. Lewis & J. M. Haviland (Eds.), *Handbook of emotions* (pp. 417–431). New York: Guilford Press.

Shweder, R. A., & LeVine, R. A. (Eds.). (1984). *Culture theory: Essays on mind, self, and emotion.* New York: Cambridge University Press.

Skinner, E. A. (1995). *Perceived control, motivation, and coping.* Thousand Oaks, CA: Sage.

Skinner, E. A., & Wellborn, J. G. (1994). Coping during childhood: A motivational perspective. In D. L. Featherman, R. M. Lerner, & M. Perlmutter (Eds.), *Life-span development and behavior* (Vol. 12, pp. 91–130). Hillsdale, NJ: Erlbaum.

Smiley, P. A., & Dweck, C. S. (1994). Individual differences in achievement goals among young children. *Child Development, 65,* 1723–1743.

Sorich, L., & Dweck, C. S. (1996). *Implicit theories and beliefs about the accuracy of rapid trait judgments.* Unpublished data.

Sorich, L., & Dweck, C. S. (in press). Mastery-oriented thinking. In C. R. Snyder (Ed.), *Coping.* New York: Oxford University Press.

Steele, C. M. (1997a). Race and the schooling of Black Americans. In L. A. Peplau & S. E. Taylor (Eds.), *Sociocultural perspectives in social psychology* (pp. 359–371). Upper Saddle River, NJ: Prentice Hall.

Steele, C. M. (1997b). A threat in the air: How stereotypes shape intellectual identity and performance. *American Psychologist, 52,* 613–629.

Steele, C. M., & Aronson, J. (1995). Stereotype threat and the intellectual test performance of African-Americans. *Journal of Personality and Social Psychology, 68,* 797–811.

Stern, R. (Ed.). (1987). *Theories of the unconscious and theories of the self.* Hillsdale, NJ: Erlbaum.

Sternberg, R. J. (1985). *Beyond IQ.* New York: Cambridge University Press.

Sternberg, R. J. (1990). *Metaphors of mind: Conceptions of the nature of intelligence.* New York: Cambridge University Press.

Sternberg, R. J. (1997). Intelligence and lifelong learning: What's new and how can we use it? *American Psychologist, 52,* 1134–1139.

Sternberg, R. J., Conway, B., Ketron, J., & Bernstein, M. (1981). People's conceptions of intelligence. *Journal of Personality and Social Psychology, 41,* 37–55.

Sternberg, R. J., & Jensen, A. R. (1992). Can intelligence be increased? In B. Slife & J. Rubenstein (Eds.), *Taking sides: Clashing views on controversial psychological issues* (pp.144–165). Guilford, CT: Dushkin Publishing Group.

Stevenson, H. W., Lee, S., Chen, C., & Stigler, J., Hsu, C. C., & Kitamura, S. (1990). Contexts of achievement: A study of American, Chinese, and Japanese children. *Monographs of the Society for Research in Child Development, 55,* (1–2).

Stigler, J. W., Lee, S., & Stevenson, H. W. (1987). Mathematics classrooms in Japan, Taiwan, and the United States. *Child Development, 58,* 1272–1285.

Stipek, D. J. (1984). Young children's performance expectations: Logical analysis or wishful thinking? In J. G. Nicholls (Ed.), *Advances in motivation and achievement* (Vol. 3). Greenwich, CT: JAI Press.

Stipek, D. J. (1995). The development of pride and shame in toddlers. In J. P. Tangney & K. W. Fischer (Eds.), *Self-conscious emotions: The psychology of shame, guilt, embarrassment, and pride* (pp. 237–252). New York: Guilford Press.

Stipek, D. J. (1996). Motivation and instruction. In D. C. Berliner & R. C. Calfee (Eds.), *Handbook of educational psychology* (pp. 85–113). New York: Macmillan.

Stipek, D. J., & Gralinski, H. (1991). Gender differences in children's achievement-related beliefs and emotional responses to success and failure in mathematics. *Journal of Educational Psychology, 83,* 361–371.

Stipek, D. J., & Gralinski, H. (1996). Children's beliefs about intelligence and school performance. *Journal of Educational Psychology, 88,* 397–407.

Stipek, D. J., & Hoffman, J. (1980). Development of children's performance-related judgments. *Child Development, 51,* 912–914.

Stipek, D. J., & Kowalski, P. S. (1989). Learned helplessness in task-orienting versus performance-orienting testing conditions. *Journal of Educational Psychology, 81,* 384–391.

Stipek, D. J., Recchia, S., & McClintic, S. (1992). Self-evaluation in young children. *Monographs of the Society for Research in Child Development, 57* (226).

Stone, J. (1998). *Theories of intelligence and the meaning of achievement goals.* Doctoral dissertation, New York University.

Suomi, S. J. (1977). Early determinants of behaviour: Evidence from primate studies. *British Medical Bulletin, 53,* 170–184.

Surber, C. (1984) Inferences of ability and effort: Evidence for two different processes. *Journal of Personality and Social Psychology, 46,* 249–268.

Tangney, J. P. (1995). Shame and guilt in interpersonal relationships. In J. P. Tangney & K. W. Fischer (Eds.), *Self-conscious emotions: The psychology of shame, guilt, embarrassment, and pride* (pp. 114–139). New York: Guilford.

Uleman, J. S., & Bargh, J. A. (1989). *Unintended thought.* New York: Guilford.

Wagner, R. K., & Sternberg, R. J. (1984). Alternative conceptions of intelligence and their implications for education. *Review of Educational Research, 54,* 179–223.

Wechsler, D. (1974). *Manual for the Wechsler Intelligence Scale for Children.* New York: Psychological Corporation.

Wegner, D. M., & Vallacher, R. R. (1977). *Implicit psychology: An introduction to social cognition.* New York: Oxford University Press.

Weiner, B. (1984). An attribution theory of achievement motivation and emotion. *Psychological Review, 92,* 548–573.

Weiner, B. (1990). Attribution theory in personality psychology. In L. Pervin (Ed.), *Handbook of personality: Theory and research* (pp. 465–485). New York: Guilford.

Weiner, B., Heckhausen, H., & Meyer, W. (1972). Causal ascriptions and achievement behavior: A conceptual analysis of effort and a reanalysis of locus of control. *Journal of Personality and Social Psychology, 21,* 239–248.

Weiner, B., & Kukla, A. (1970). An attributional analysis of achievement motivation. *Journal of Personality and Social Psychology, 15,* 1–20.

Weinstein, C. E., & Mayer, R. (1986). The teaching of learning strategies. In M. Wittrock (Ed.), *Handbook or research on teaching and learning* (pp. 315–327). New York: Macmillan.

Weisz, J. R., & Weiss, B. (1989). Cognitive mediators of the outcome of psychotherapy with children. In B. B. Lahey & A. E. Kazdin (Eds.), *Advances in clinical child psychology* (Vol. 12, pp. 227–51). New York: Plenum.

Wellman, H. M., & Gelman, S. A. (1992). Cognitive development: Foundational theories of core domains. *Annual Review of Psychology, 43,* 337–375.

Wentzel, K. (1996). Social goals and social relationships as motivators of school adjustment. In J. Juvonen & K. Wentzel (Eds.), *Social motivation* (pp. 226–247). New York: Cambridge University Press.

White, R. W. (1959). Motivation reconsidered: The concept of competence. *Psychological Review, 66,* 297–333.

Whitehead, A. N. (1929). *Process and reality.* New York: Free Press.

Whitehead, A. N. (1938). *Modes of thought.* New York: Free Press.

Whiting, B. B., & Whiting, J. M. (1975). *Children of six cultures: A psycho-cultural analysis.* Cambridge, MA: Harvard University Press.

Wood, R. E., & Bandura, A. (1989). Impact of conceptions of ability on self-regulatory mechanisms and complex decision-making. *Journal of Personality and Social Psychology, 56,* 407–415.

Yussen, S., & Kane, P. (1985). Children's conceptions of intelligence. In S. R. Yussen (Ed.), *The growth of reflection in children* (pp. 207–241). New York: Academic Press.

Zhao, W., Dweck, C. S., & Mueller, C. (1998). *Implicit theories and depression-like responses to failure.* Unpublished manuscript.

Zuckerman, M. Kieffer, S. C., & Knee, C. R. (1998). Consequences of self-handicapping effects on coping, academic performance, and adjustment. *Journal of Personality and Social Psychology, 74,* 1619–28.

Appendix:

Measures of Implicit Theories, Confidence, and Goals

☐ Implicit Theory Measures

Before presenting the implicit theory measures, it is important to highlight a few points.

Self-theories vs. Other-theories

In deciding which form of an implicit theory measure to use, it is important to distinguish between the "self" form of each scale and the "other" form. The "self" form asks people to report their theories about their own intelligence or personality ("You have a certain amount of intelligence. . . ."), and it is used to predict the person's own self-goals, self-judgments, and helpless vs. mastery-oriented reactions. The "other" form asks them their theory about people in general ("Everyone has a certain amount of intelligence . . ."), and is used to predict the judgments people make of others and their reactions to the behavior and outcomes of others.

Domain-specific vs. Domain-general Implicit Theories

Some of our implicit theory measures are domain-specific in that they refer to one specific attribute, such as intelligence, personality, or moral character. One of our measures is domain-general (the "kind of person" theory) in that it refers to the person as a whole. The domain-specific measures are preferable when the study focuses on one particular domain—for example, intellectual judgments and behavior or moral judgments and behavior.

The domain-general measure is used when the study focuses on judgments and behavior that cut across the social and intellectual domains (such as certain stereotypes). However, this measure is used only with adults, since children have trouble understanding what is meant by "kind of person." For studies of stereotyping with children (Levy, 1998; Levy & Dweck, in press), we have used the implicit theory of personality measure (and, indeed, most of the stereotypes we have studied in children have to do with social attributes).

The Entity and the Incremental Theory Items

Originally we used scales that included only entity theory items. This was because the incremental theory items we originally formulated were too appealing and drew excessively high rates of agreement. More recently, we have been able to design incremental items that are not as appealing and that show a very high negative correlation with the entity theory items.

Both scales (the ones that contain just the entity theory items and the ones that contain both entity and incremental theory items) are valid.

The entity-only scale is still preferable in certain circumstances. First, if one is doing a longitudinal study that involves a number of repeated administrations of the measure, there is still the risk that participants will drift toward the incremental items over time. Thus in the case of a longitudinal study, it might be advisable to administer the entity-only form of the scale. Second, grade-school children (or children with lower reading proficiency) can sometimes become confused by the mixture of entity and incremental items. We have dealt with this by putting the incremental items on a second, separate page after the entity items, or by using only the entity theory items.

References for Reliability and Validity Data

Detailed reliability and validity data for the various implicit theory scales can be found in the following articles: Dweck, Chiu, & Hong, 1995; Levy, Stroessner, & Dweck, 1998; Levy & Dweck, in press; see also Erdley & Dweck, 1993; Erdley et al., 1997.

In general, the implicit theory scales are not correlated with other scales (see Dweck, Chiu, & Hong, 1995; Levy, Stroessner, & Dweck, 1998). For example, they are not correlated with measures of self-esteem or measures of self-presentation concerns; they are not correlated with measures of optimism; they are not correlated with general measures of political ideology, religious preference, or religiosity; and they are not typically correlated with measures of cognitive or motivational styles or needs. Also important is the fact that they are not correlated with measures of cognitive abilities. Thus implicit theories represent assumptions about the self that have cognitive, motivational, emotional, and behavioral consequences, but they are distinct from other cognitive and motivational constructs.

☐ Implicit Theories of Intelligence Scale for Children—Self Form

(For Children Age 10 and Older)

Read each sentence below and then circle the *one* number that shows how much you agree with it. There are no right or wrong answers.

*1. You have a certain amount of intelligence, and you really can't do much to change it.

1	2	3	4	5	6
Strongly Agree	Agree	Mostly Agree	Mostly Disagree	Disagree	Strongly Disagree

*2. Your intelligence is something about you that you can't change very much.

1	2	3	4	5	6
Strongly Agree	Agree	Mostly Agree	Mostly Disagree	Disagree	Strongly Disagree

*3. You can learn new things, but you can't really change your basic intelligence.

1	2	3	4	5	6
Strongly Agree	Agree	Mostly Agree	Mostly Disagree	Disagree	Strongly Disagree

4. No matter who you are, you can change your intelligence a lot.

1	2	3	4	5	6
Strongly Agree	Agree	Mostly Agree	Mostly Disagree	Disagree	Strongly Disagree

5. You can always greatly change how intelligent you are.

1	2	3	4	5	6
Strongly Agree	Agree	Mostly Agree	Mostly Disagree	Disagree	Strongly Disagree

6. No matter how much intelligence you have, you can always change it quite a bit.

1	2	3	4	5	6
Strongly Agree	Agree	Mostly Agree	Mostly Disagree	Disagree	Strongly Disagree

*These three items can be used alone.

☐ Theories of Intelligence Scale—Self Form For Adults

This questionnaire has been designed to investigate ideas about intelligence. There are no right or wrong answers. We are interested in your ideas.

Using the scale below, please indicate the extent to which you agree or disagree with each of the following statements by writing the number that corresponds to your opinion in the space next to each statement.

1	2	3	4	5	6
Strongly Agree	Agree	Mostly Agree	Mostly Disagree	Disagree	Strongly Disagree

*_____ 1. You have a certain amount of intelligence, and you can't really do much to change it.

*_____ 2. Your intelligence is something about you that you can't change very much.

_____ 3. No matter who you are, you can significantly change your intelligence level.

*_____ 4. To be honest, you can't really change how intelligent you are.

_____ 5. You can always substantially change how intelligent you are.

*_____ 6. You can learn new things, but you can't really change your basic intelligence.

_____ 7. No matter how much intelligence you have, you can always change it quite a bit.

_____ 8. You can change even your basic intelligence level considerably.

*These items can be used alone.

Note: For studies of how people's theories of intelligence affect how they judge and treat others, use the "Others" form of the theories of intelligence scales. The "Others" form is constructed by replacing the word "you" with the words "people," "someone," or "everyone" (as in the "kind of person" scale below).

☐ Implicit Theories of Personality—"Others" Form

(For Children Age 9 and Older)

Read each sentence below and then circle the *one* number that shows how much you agree with it. There are no right or wrong answers.

*1. People can't really change what kind of personality they have. Some people have a good personality and some don't and they can't change much.

1	2	3	4	5	6
Strongly Agree	Agree	Mostly Agree	Mostly Disagree	Disagree	Strongly Disagree

*2. Someone's personality is a part of them that they can't change very much.

1	2	3	4	5	6
Strongly Agree	Agree	Mostly Agree	Mostly Disagree	Disagree	Strongly Disagree

*3. A person can do things to get people to like them, but they can't change their real personality.

1	2	3	4	5	6
Strongly Agree	Agree	Mostly Agree	Mostly Disagree	Disagree	Strongly Disagree

4. No matter who somebody is and how they act, they can always change their ways.

1	2	3	4	5	6
Strongly Agree	Agree	Mostly Agree	Mostly Disagree	Disagree	Strongly Disagree

5. Anybody can change their personality a lot.

1	2	3	4	5	6
Strongly Agree	Agree	Mostly Agree	Mostly Disagree	Disagree	Strongly Disagree

6. People can always change their personality.

1	2	3	4	5	6
Strongly Agree	Agree	Mostly Agree	Mostly Disagree	Disagree	Strongly Disagree

Note: For studies of how children's implicit theories of personality affect their self-judgments and reactions in social situations, use the "self" form of this scale. The "self" form in constructed by substituting "you" and "your" for "someone," "people," "anybody," "a person," and "they."

☐ "Kind of Person" Implicit Theory—"Others" Form For Adults

Using the scale below, please indicate the extent to which you agree or disagree with each of the following statements by writing the number that corresponds to your opinion in the space next to each statement.

1	2	3	4	5	6
Strongly Agree	Agree	Mostly Agree	Mostly Disagree	Disagree	Strongly Disagree

*_____ 1. The kind of person someone is, is something very basic about them and it can't be changed very much.

*_____ 2. People can do things differently, but the important parts of who they are can't really be changed.

_____ 3. Everyone, no matter who they are, can significantly change their basic characteristics.

*_____ 4. As much as I hate to admit it, you can't teach an old dog new tricks. People can't really change their deepest attributes.

_____ 5. People can always substantially change the kind of person they are.

*_____ 6. Everyone is a certain kind of person, and there is not much that can be done to really change that.

_____ 7. No matter what kind of person someone is, they can always change very much.

_____ 8. All people can change even their most basic qualities.

*These items can be used alone.

Note: The "Self" form of this scale can be constructed by substituting "you" for "people," "everyone," and "someone" (with, of course, any appropriate change in the verb), as in the Theories of Intelligence Scale above.

☐ Implicit Theories of Others' Morality (for Adults)

1. A person's moral character is something basic about them and they can't change it much.

1	2	3	4	5	6
Strongly Agree	Agree	Mostly Agree	Mostly Disagree	Disagree	Strongly Disagree

2. Whether a person is responsible and sincere or not is deeply ingrained in their personality. It cannot be changed very much.

1	2	3	4	5	6
Strongly Agree	Agree	Mostly Agree	Mostly Disagree	Disagree	Strongly Disagree

3. There is not much that can be done to change a person's moral traits (e.g., conscientiousness, uprightness, and honesty).

1	2	3	4	5	6
Strongly Agree	Agree	Mostly Agree	Mostly Disagree	Disagree	Strongly Disagree

Note: Substitute "you" and "your" to form the "self" form of this scale.

☐ Implicit Theory of the World (for Adults)

Note: Although I have not discussed it in this book, in some of our work, we have examined whether people see the world they live in as fixed or malleable (i.e., a fixed "given" or something that can be shaped by people) (see, for example, Chiu, Dweck, Tong, & Fu, 1997). These beliefs predict how people think of justice, and they also show interesting cross-cultural differences (Chiu et al., 1997).

1. Though we can change some phenomena, it is unlikely that we can alter the core dispositions of our world.

1	2	3	4	5	6
Strongly Agree	Agree	Mostly Agree	Mostly Disagree	Disagree	Strongly Disagree

2. Our world has basic or ingrained dispositions, and you really can't do much to change them.

1	2	3	4	5	6
Strongly Agree	Agree	Mostly Agree	Mostly Disagree	Disagree	Strongly Disagree

3. Some societal trends may dominate for a while, but the fundamental nature of our world is something that cannot be changed much.

1	2	3	4	5	6
Strongly Agree	Agree	Mostly Agree	Mostly Disagree	Disagree	Strongly Disagree

☐ Confidence Measures

These are measures we have administered in conjunction with the implicit theory measures. For example, the confidence in intelligence measure has been given with the implicit theory of intelligence measure ("self" form); the confidence in personality has been given with the implicit theory of personality ("self" form); the confidence in people's morality has been given with the implicit theory of morality ("others" form).

The confidence measures are typically used to show that entity and incremental theorists do not differ in how confident they are about their own attributes or how positive or optimistic they are about others' attributes (before they encounter personal setbacks or before they observe other people's behavior). We have also used these measures to examine the role of confidence in relation to implicit theories, often finding that in the face of setbacks or negative events, implicit theories are stronger predictors of judgments and actions than are people's feelings of confidence when they entered the situation (see, e.g., Henderson & Dweck, 1990; Hong, Chiu, Dweck, & Lin, 1998; see also Hong, Chiu, & Dweck, 1995).

☐ Confidence in One's Intelligence

1. Check the sentence that is most true for you.
_____I usually think I'm intelligent.
_____I wonder if I'm intelligent.

Now, show how true the statement you chose is for you.

very true for me	true for me	sort of true for me

2. Check the sentence that is most true for you.
_____When I get new work in school, I'm usually sure I will be able to learn it.
_____When I get new work in school, I often think I may not be able to learn it.

Now, show how true the statement you chose is for you.

very true for me	true for me	sort of true for me

3. Check the sentence that is most true for you.
_____I'm not very confident about my intellectual ability.
_____I feel pretty confident about my intellectual ability.

Now, show how true the statement you chose is for you.

very true for me	true for me	sort of true for me

SCORING: This is scored as a 6-point scale from "very true for me" on the low confidence option to "sort of true for me" on the high confidence option.

☐ Confidence in One's Personality

Note: See above Confidence in Intelligence Scale for scoring of this scale.

1. Check the sentence that is most true for you:
_____When I meet new people, I am not sure if they will like me.
_____When I meet new people, I am sure that they will like me.

Now, show how true the statement you chose is for you.

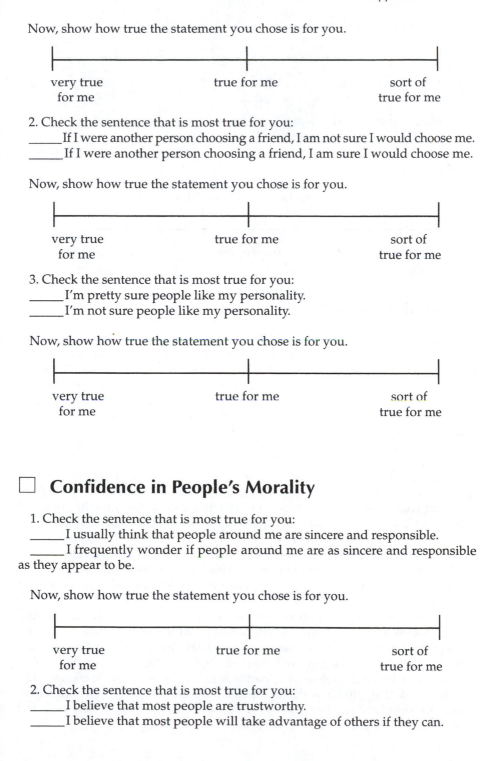

very true for me true for me sort of true for me

2. Check the sentence that is most true for you:
_____If I were another person choosing a friend, I am not sure I would choose me.
_____If I were another person choosing a friend, I am sure I would choose me.

Now, show how true the statement you chose is for you.

very true for me true for me sort of true for me

3. Check the sentence that is most true for you:
_____I'm pretty sure people like my personality.
_____I'm not sure people like my personality.

Now, show how true the statement you chose is for you.

very true for me true for me sort of true for me

☐ Confidence in People's Morality

1. Check the sentence that is most true for you:
_____I usually think that people around me are sincere and responsible.
_____I frequently wonder if people around me are as sincere and responsible as they appear to be.

Now, show how true the statement you chose is for you.

very true for me true for me sort of true for me

2. Check the sentence that is most true for you:
_____I believe that most people are trustworthy.
_____I believe that most people will take advantage of others if they can.

Now, show how true the statement you chose is for you.

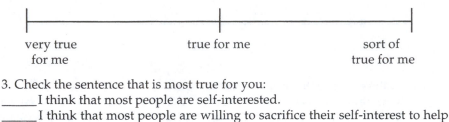

very true   true for me   sort of
for me   true for me

3. Check the sentence that is most true for you:

_____I think that most people are self-interested.

_____I think that most people are willing to sacrifice their self-interest to help other people.

Now, show how true the statement you chose is for you.

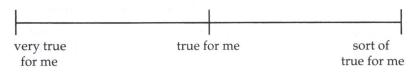

very true   true for me   sort of
for me   true for me

☐ Goal Measures

There are now a number of scales in the field that measure learning and performance goals. On these scales, learning and performance goals are assessed independently, so that students can indicate the value they place on learning goals and performance goals separately. We have used some of these scales in our own work, and when we do, we often find no difference between entity and incremental theorists. Both entity and incremental theorists value learning and performance goals when they are measured separately. Both say they are interested in demonstrating their ability or doing well, and both say that they are interested in learning new things.

However, when we use measures that *pit* learning goals against performance goals—asking which is more important to the students (looking smart vs. attempting challenging learning tasks), then we find a clear relation with students' theories of intelligence (Dweck & Leggett, 1988; Stone, 1998; see also Mueller & Dweck, 1998; cf. Elliott & Dweck, 1988). Entity theorists prefer the tasks that will allow them to demonstrate their high ability (or allow them to avoid demonstrating low ability) and incremental theorists prefer the tasks that will allow them to meet a challenge and learn new things, even at the risk of making mistakes and revealing ignorance.

The two sets of goal questions presented below are ones that pit learning against performance goals. The first is a choice that we offer to students during an experiment. It asks them to choose among tasks that embody different goals. Choices 1 and 3 offer a task that will allow them to avoid looking dumb (a performance goal with no challenge; or a "performance-avoidance" goal); choice 4 represents a task that will allow them to look smart (a performance goal with challenge); and choice 2 is a task that will allow them to learn something new and important, but holds the risk of looking dumb (a learning goal).

Notice that the learning goal requires the student to overcome performance concerns for the sake of learning. It is important for students to believe that if they choose a challenging learning task, they will actually receive it (if not immediately then at least later in the session). This prevents them from choosing that task because they might think it is a socially desirable choice. In addition, we present three performance goal choices and one learning goal choice to further offset the potential social desirability of the learning goal choice.

The second goal measure is a series of questions we have used with students as part of a battery of measures. It asks them which concern is most important to them in their courses—performance concerns or challenge-oriented learning concerns.

☐ Task-choice Goal Measure

(Suitable for Age 10 and Older)

(Sample instruction: We may have more time later. If we do, which kind of task would you like to work on most? Mark only one answer!)

(Alternative instruction: We have different kinds of problems here for you to choose from. There is no right answer—different students make different choices. Just put a check in front of your choice.)

I would like to work on:
_____Problems that aren't too hard, so I don't get many wrong.
_____Problems that I'll learn a lot from, even if I won't look so smart.
_____Problems that are pretty easy, so I'll do well.
_____Problems that I'm pretty good at, so I can show that I'm smart.

☐ Questionnaire Goal Choice Items

(Suitable for Age 12 and Older)

1. If I knew I wasn't going to do well at a task, I probably wouldn't do it even if I might learn a lot from it.

1	2	3	4	5	6
Strongly Agree	Agree	Mostly Agree	Mostly Disagree	Disagree	Strongly Disagree

2. Although I hate to admit it, I sometimes would rather do well in a class than learn a lot.

1	2	3	4	5	6
Strongly Agree	Agree	Mostly Agree	Mostly Disagree	Disagree	Strongly Disagree

3. It's much more important for me to learn things in my classes than it is to get the best grades.

1	2	3	4	5	6
Strongly Agree	Agree	Mostly Agree	Mostly Disagree	Disagree	Strongly Disagree

4. If I *had* to choose between getting a good grade and being challenged in class, I would choose . . . (Circle one)

"good grade"   "being challenged"

Index